The Battlecruiser
HOOD

Hood leaving Portsmouth in October 1936 on completion of a refit in which the searchlight platform was removed from the foremast and an air defence position fitted above the fore bridge. Note also the fitting of a steel screen to the platforms abreast the compass platform – formerly guardrails with a canvas screen.
Wright and Logan

ANATOMY OF THE SHIP

The Battlecruiser
HOOD

CONWAY
MARITIME PRESS

JOHN ROBERTS

© John Roberts 1982
Revised edition © John Roberts 2001
First published in Great Britain in 1982 by
Conway Maritime Press.

Reprinted 1983 and 1989
This revised edition published in 2001 by
Conway Maritime Press,
a division of Chrysalis Books Plc.
9 Blenheim Court,
Brewery Road
London N7 9NY

www.conwaymaritime.com

A member of the Chrysalis Group plc

ISBN 0 85177 900 X

Printed and bound in Spain by bookprint, S.L., Barcelona

CONTENTS

ACKNOWLEDGEMENTS

My thanks are due to Mr D K Brown, RCNC, Mr J Campbell and Mr D Lyon for their help with information, and to Mr R A Burt for invaluable assistance with photographs.

Between the two World Wars the Royal Navy operated against a background of financial restrictions, a strong campaign for naval disarmament and a widely held belief that the battleship had been made obsolete by aircraft and submarines. This led the Admiralty to court public support by promoting its belief in the battlefleet, and emphasising the quality of its ships, men and equipment. Of these ships *Hood*, more than any other, lent herself to a public relations exercise. Apart from the endless lists of amazing facts which could always be produced for a battle unit, she was the largest, fastest and one of the most handsome capital ships in the world. Early in her career, being the newest and most prestigious ship of the fleet, she was employed on several international assignments as a representative of the British Empire, culminating in 'showing the flag' on a grand scale in the world cruise of 1923-24, and for most of her life she enjoyed the glamorous status of flagship of the battlecruiser force. Thus she became one of the major symbols of the Royal Navy, a position she would no doubt have occupied without Admiralty help, and was held in high regard by both the British public and the men of the Fleet to whom she was affectionately known as "the mighty 'ood". Little wonder that the news of her destruction in action with the German battleship *Bismarck* in May 1941 was received with shocked disbelief throughout the country.

To the comparative few who knew the details of *Hood*'s design – the senior officers of the Admiralty and the Director of Naval Construction's (DNC) department – *Hood*'s loss, although no less of a shock, was easier to understand. She had been unfortunate in being designed during the First World War at a time when the lessons of that war, principally those learnt at the Battle of Jutland in 1916, had not been fully evaluated. Many changes *were* applied as the design and construction of the ship progressed but it was not until 1919-20, when *Hood* was completing, that some of the more important conclusions regarding the lessons of the war were reached. Principal among these was the need for future capital ships to have horizontal protection of armour plate, instead of the built-up layers of protective plating previously employed, an alteration which could not be applied to *Hood*, without enormous expense and delay, because of the advanced state of her construction.

Before the ship completed it was known that her protection was not up to modern standards and at several times in the following twenty years proposals were made for modernisations which were to include improved protection. However, other, older, ships were in greater need and, with finance limited, *Hood* was placed well down the list for improvement. She was eventually booked for a full reconstruction, to begin in 1942, but the outbreak of war ensured that it was never to take place and so she served her entire 21 years without major improvement despite her known defects; defects which, unlike her attributes, were not made public. It must be said however, that *Hood*'s faults were not the result of poor design but of unfortunate circumstance, lack of money and the inability to take advantage of improvements unthought of when she was designed. In fact the very inclusion of improvements after completion of the original design created several problems – principally a substantial loss in freeboard. By the standards of 1915-17 she was an advanced ship and, as the postwar designs which would have made her obsolete were never built, she could claim considerable advantages over the majority of existing capital ships for many years after her completion.

DESIGN

In 1914-15 the operations of the Grand Fleet under war conditions revealed a number of defects in the quality of its capital ships. Foremost among these was wetness caused by low freeboard, a situation made worse in the newer vessels by the cutting back of the ships' sides above the upper deck to form embrasures for the secondary armament. The latter weapons also proved difficult to operate in heavy, or even moderate, weather due to their close proximity to the waterline, and as the gunports could not be made completely water-tight, they effectively reduced the ship's reserve of buoyancy. Ships were also going to sea more heavily loaded than was normal in peacetime, which not only exacerbated all the above mentioned problems but added substantially to the ships' draughts. This last was also regarded as serious because, in the event of damage to a ship's hull well below water, the force of water entering the ship, and hence the rapidity of flooding, would be that much greater.

From reports of these conditions it was decided that what was required was a ship with a high, uninterrupted freeboard, a shallow draught and a secondary armament mounted well above the waterline. To take advantage of these conclusions, the Admiralty asked and obtained Cabinet and Treasury sanction for the construction of an experimental battleship, and in October 1915 the Director of Naval

Construction (DNC), Sir Eustace Tennyson-d'Eyncourt, was asked to investigate the design of a battleship based on the *Queen Elizabeth* class but including the latest ideas in underwater protection and with the draught reduced about 50 per cent.

However, the reduction in draught required a corresponding increase in length and beam which involved problems with hull strength and docking and it soon became clear that the 50 per cent asked for was impractical. In the designs subsequently produced the best that could be achieved was 20 per cent.

Between November 1915 and February 1916 five battleship designs were submitted to the Board (see Table 1). Design 'A' had the same armament and machinery as *Queen Elizabeth*, but owing to the altered hull form was slightly faster and had reduced protection (presumably due to the greater area to be armoured). Design 'B' was a modified version of 'A' in which to ease the docking problem the beam was reduced to that of *Queen Elizabeth* by reducing the engine power and accepting a slightly deeper draught. However, experiments in December 1915 revealed that the greater beam was necessary to provide adequate underwater protection and in design 'C1' length was reduced instead of beam by a further reduction in speed to the standard 22kts of the battlefleet. 'C2' was a variation on this design with the best bulge and draught possible on the same length as *Queen Elizabeth*. Finally 'D' was a modified 'A' with length reduced by accepting a lower speed.

These designs were sent for comment to Admiral Sir John Jellicoe, C-in-C of the Grand Fleet, who stated that he was comparatively strong in battleships and that there was a much greater need for battlecruisers capable of countering the 15in gunned, 30kt ships believed to be under construction by the Germans. Consequently, design effort was shifted to vessels of 30kts, or greater speed, with reduced armour, but otherwise similar to the earlier battleship designs. This entailed still further increases in dimensions in order to accommodate the machinery but in all but one of the six designs (see Table 2) produced in February 1916 the DNC was able to save space and weight by specifying small-tube boilers. This was an innovation he had long advocated but which had previously been resisted because of the greater maintenance required (more frequent cleaning etc, and hence more time out of service) compared with the standard large-tube boiler.* The effect can be seen by comparing designs 1 and 2 (Table 1) the latter giving a 3500 ton saving in weight and a small increase in speed. In design 3 the saving was utilised to provide a 30 per cent increase in power, to give a further 2kts speed, and even then it was 2500 tons lighter than design 1, and it was this design, despite the increased length, which the Board decided on for working out in detail.

---

*This only applied to large ships, whose numbers were limited. Smaller vessels and the battlecruisers *Courageous*, *Glorious* and *Furious* (but only because they were classified as large light cruisers) were fitted with small-tube boilers. The Germans had been taking advantage of the savings possible with small-tube boilers in their large ships for several years.

In the detailed design it was found possible to achieve the required speed with only 144,000shp but, apart from a reduction in the belt armour, the design followed closely the original outline particulars. Two versions were submitted to the Board on 27 March 1916, one with a secondary armament of twelve 5.5in guns and another with sixteen 5.5in guns but otherwise similar. The latter version was approved on 7 April (see Table 4) and on the same day three ships were ordered to this design – the *Hood*, from John Brown, the *Howe* from Cammell Laird and the *Rodney* from Fairfield. A fourth ship, *Anson*, was ordered from Armstrongs in July 1916.

The *Hood* was laid down on 31 May 1916 but was almost immediately suspended pending investigations into the lessons of the Battle of Jutland, which took place in the North Sea on the same day. As a result of these deliberations the design was modified to include improved protection which, with other additions, increased the displacement by 1200 tons (see Table 4). However, while these changes were being made the DNC put forward more extensive proposals which would effectively convert the design from one for a battlecruiser into one for a fast battleship. These proposals involved an average increase of 50 per cent in the principal thickness of armour (but not deck plating) and 4000 tons in displacement, but resulted in a loss of speed of only 1kt. The draught of course, was also increased but would still be 2ft less than in *Queen Elizabeth*. The basic particulars of this design (together with others requested by the First Sea Lord and the Controller incorporating triple 15in mountings) were submitted to the Board in July 1916 (see Table 3). Design 'A', the DNC's original submission, was approved by the Board in August and *Hood* was laid down, to this new design, for the second time on 1 September 1916. However the design continued to be the subject of alterations for some time as the evaluation of the lessons of Jutland was continued, both by the Admiralty and by various committees within the Grand Fleet. The principal modifications made were again directed towards further improving protection, particularly on the decks, for which the main impetus came from the Grand Fleet. Consequently the final design legend for *Hood* was not approved until 30 August 1917 (see Table 4).

In this final design displacement had increased to 41,200 tons, almost 5000 tons above the original figure. Consequently, the original requirements for shallow draught and high freeboard were almost completely lost. However, this weight was not simply loaded onto the original design; the hull strength was increased and the resultant 3ft loss in freeboard compensated for by adding 1ft to the hull depth and 2ft to the sheer aft, so the loss in freeboard in the legend condition was 3ft forward, 2ft amidships and *none* aft. Besides the improvements in protection, the addition of four dynamos (making a total of eight) and eight above-water torpedo tubes was approved during 1916-17, and shortly after approval of the final legend, a further 55 tons was added to allow for additions to the gunhouse armour, 80 tons for dredger hoists for the 5.5in guns and 45 tons for lagging the crowns and walls of the 15in magazines. These latter weights were taken from the Board margin which was consequently reduced to 20 tons.

CONSTRUCTION

Hood's protection continued to be a source of debate and concern throughout her period of construction and as a result still further additions were made to her decks. In August 1918 it was approved to double the thickness of magazine crowns to 2in by fitting additional 1in protective plates; weight compensation being provided by omitting the 1in and 2in splinter protection to the funnel uptakes above the forecastle deck. In May 1919 it was approved to increase the thickness of the flats above the slopes of the main deck to 3in in the vicinity of the magazines; compensation for the additional 100 tons being provided by omitting the four aftermost 5.5in guns (two on shelter deck, two on forecastle deck) together with their dredger hoists.

Finally in July 1919 approval was given to increase the thickness of the main deck over the magazines to 6in aft and 5in forward but this work was never carried out. However, compensation was provided for the additional 440 tons by omitting the four forward, above-water tubes and reducing the thickness of the walls of the after torpedo conning tower from 6in to 1½in. Despite all these efforts to save weight the inclining of *Hood*, at Rosyth on 21 February 1920, showed her to have a load displacement of 42,670 tons, 1470 tons above her legend displacement of 1917. This increased the mean draught and reduced the freeboard amidships by 1ft but as the trim by the stern was greater than that specified in the legend the freeboard forward remained at 29ft while the stern was 17ft from the waterline, 2ft lower than designed. At deep displacement she trimmed more forward lowering the freeboard to 25ft 6in at the stem and to 15ft aft. Oddly enough these figures are close to those of earlier British ships but nevertheless this low freeboard caused much greater problems of wetness, particularly aft where her quarterdeck was often awash – this deck at the break of the forecastle being about 6ft lower than the extreme stern. It seems likely that this may have been due to her great length, combined perhaps with her steadiness, causing her to cut through waves rather than ride over them as her shorter contemporaries might have done. Also, when running at speed, her stern tended to dig in, like that of a destroyer, thus increasing the chances of taking on green water aft. This situation was to worsen for, while many older ships gained in freeboard when they were bulged, and were thus able to cope with substantial additional weights in later refits, the *Hood* steadily increased in displacement and reduced in freeboard as her career progressed.

The *Hood* ran her steam trials in March 1920 (see Table 5) and on her measured mile full power trial achieved 32.07kts with 151,280shp, 5 per cent above her designed maximum power. However, in one of her 3-hour full power trials she made just over her designed speed with just over her designed maximum power. These and her gunnery and torpedo trials proved highly satisfactory and after a final fitting out and inspection at Rosyth Dockyard she was accepted into RN service on 15 May 1920. *Hood* entered service as a battlecruiser not a fast battleship, perhaps reflecting the realisation that her protection was not sufficient to justify this classification. However, the Admiralty do appear to have adopted a policy of defining the difference between the types by speed since the 'G3' battlecruisers, designed in 1921 but never built, were far better protected than any existing battleship (the contemporary 'N3' battleship design was better protected but was armoured against 18in rather than 16in shells) and when the early designs for the *King George V* class were under consideration in the 1930s the faster versions were initially classified as battlecruisers.

Very little work was done on *Hood*'s three sisters before, under the pressure of work in the shipyards, they were suspended on 9 March 1917. Being less far advanced than *Hood* various additional modifications were proposed for these ships including armoured decks. However, with the end of the war and the consequent reduction in naval expenditure, plus the realisation that more advanced designs were possible, they were cancelled in October 1918.

SERVICE HISTORY

1 September 1916: Laid down
22 August 1918: Launched
January 1920: Transferred to Rosyth for completion and trials
14 May 1920: Inspected at Rosyth
15 May 1920: Accepted from builders and commissioned
15 May 1920 – November 1923: Flagship, Battlecruiser Squadron, Atlantic Fleet
27 November 1923 – 29 September 1924: Flagship of Special Service Squadron (*Repulse* and First Light Cruiser Squadron) for world cruise – travelled 40,000 miles and was visited by over 700,000 people
January 1925 – January 1928: Flagship of Battlecruiser Squadron, Atlantic Fleet
January 1928 – May 1929: Battlecruiser Squadron, Atlantic Fleet
17 May 1929 – 12 May 1931: Major refit at Portsmouth
12 May 1931 – September 1936: Flagship of Battlecruiser Squadron, Home Fleet
8 September 1936 – January 1939: Mediterranean Fleet (flagship of Vice Admiral Sir G Blake)
February – August 1939: Refit at Portsmouth
13 August 1939 – March 1940: Flagship of Battlecruiser Squadron, Home Fleet
March – May 1940: Refit at Devonport
June – August 1940: Flagship, Force 'H', based at Gibraltar
August 1940 – May 1941: Flagship of Battlecruiser Squadron, Home Fleet
24 May 1941: Sunk in action with *Bismarck*

THE LOSS OF HOOD

On 23 May 1941 the *Hood*, flying the flag of Admiral Holland, and *Prince of Wales* were patrolling south west of Iceland when, at 1939, a signal was intercepted from the cruiser *Suffolk* reporting the German battleship *Bismarck* and the cruiser *Prinz Eugen* in the Denmark Strait. Fifteen minutes later Admiral Holland ordered his ships onto an interception course and speed was increased to 27kts. At 0400 the next morning they were steering a course of 240° at 28kts with the intention of engaging the enemy shortly after dawn, the crews being brought to full action stations at 0510. Twenty five minutes later *Prince of Wales* reported the enemy in sight at a range of 17 miles and course was altered 40° to starboard in order to close the range. Admiral Holland's intention was to close as quickly as possible and he adopted an end on approach, with *Prince of Wales* in open order 1000yds off *Hood*'s starboard quarter. This approach did, however, mean that the British ships would only be able to bring their forward turrets to bear in the initial stages of the action.

At 0550 the two British ships altered course a further 20° to starboard and two minutes later *Hood* opened fire with 'A' and 'B' turrets at a range of 26,500yds. *Prince of Wales* opened fire shortly afterwards at the enemy at 0555. *Hood* fired on the leading enemy ship, the *Prinz Eugen*, which had been mistaken for *Bismarck*, while *Prince of Wales* concentrated on the correct target. Both enemy ships concentrated on the British flagship.

As *Bismarck* fired her first salvo, course was again altered 20° to port, possibly to avoid the enemy fall of shot but more likely to compensate for the enemy crossing the bows from starboard to port. The first salvo landed ahead of *Hood*, the second astern but the third straddled the ship and produced a hit on the port side of the shelter deck in the area of the mainmast (this may have been an 8in shell from *Prinz Eugen*). This hit caused a fire among the ready-use lockers for the UP and 4in ammunition which spread fore and aft but died down after a few minutes. *Bismarck*'s fourth salvo was a close short but her fifth, at a range of about 16,500yds, straddled *Hood* as she was turning 20° to port to open her 'A' arcs and bring her full broadside to bear. One or two hits were produced and a sheet of flame shot up from the vicinity of *Hood*'s mainmast followed by an enormous cloud of smoke which almost enveloped the ship. She broke in two and the after part, which had little buoyancy, rolled over and sank almost immediately while the forward section reared up at an angle of about 40°, slid back into the sea and disappeared in three minutes. One midshipman and two ratings survived from her crew of 1419.

The subsequent Board of Enquiry into the loss of *Hood* concluded that a shell or shells had detonated *Hood*'s after 15in magazines either directly or via the after 4in magazines. However, there are areas of doubt due principally to the appearance of the sheet of flame so far forward of the after magazines. The only reasonable alternative explanation came from the DNC, Sir Stanley Goodall (who, with A L Attwood, had been in charge of *Hood*'s design when he was a constructor) who conjectured that a shell detonated the torpedo warheads in one of the pairs of above-water torpedo tubes. This would have caused serious damage to the hull structure in this area (already weakened by the previous hit and resultant fire) and a combination of the loss of strength in the upper section of the hull girder and the pressure of water entering the damaged side may have been sufficient to cause the ship to break her back. On balance the detonation of the magazines seems more likely but some doubt must always exist unless at some time in the future somebody finds a means of investigating the wreck which lies in position 63°20′N, 31°50′W at a depth of over 5000ft.

GENERAL ARRANGEMENT AND HULL STRUCTURE (see drawing sections A and B)

In the distribution of her compartments *Hood* followed standard practice except that her senior officers were accommodated at the after end of the forecastle deck instead of at the after end of the main deck. Her hull was subdivided into 25 principal water-tight compartments by transverse bulkheads, although these were further subdivided both longitudinally and transversely. Below the main deck the principal bulkheads were unpierced except where absolutely necessary, for such items as hydraulic pipes and electric cables, and all access was vertical. Outside the main machinery spaces those compartments which would be occupied in action, such as the steering compartment and the generator rooms, were provided with trunked access direct to main or upper decks. These were intended to prevent the spread of flooding either from that compartment to the deck above or vice versa, and to allow men to escape from the compartments in either case. Above the main deck the accommodation spaces and workshops made fore and aft communication essential to efficient working and all the principal bulkheads were fitted with water-tight doors. However, most of these would have been closed in action except those in the fore and aft ammunition passages, which had to be open to allow transfer of the 5.5in ammunition.

Like all British battlecruisers *Hood* had one less deck than contemporary battleships, partially due to the origin of the type in the armoured cruiser, but principally to the different proportions required to accommodate a greater length of machinery and to provide for high speed. The battleship *Queen Elizabeth* for example was 53ft 6in deep and 600ft long while *Hood* was 51ft 6in deep and 850ft long, ratios respectively of 11.2:1 and 16.5:1. This meant that *Hood*'s hull structure had to be relatively stronger to cope with the greater hogging and sagging stresses on the hull. In detail she followed the well established methods of construction but in other respects she varied from previous practice. The double bottom, instead of extending round the bilge and up to the level of the protective deck, terminated at the base of the torpedo bulkhead and was virtually flat. The torpedo bulkhead and the skin plating behind the armour formed a single longitudinal boundary to the hull proper, the bulge structure, although an integral part of the hull, being exterior to this. The forecastle and upper decks provided the principal upper strength members of what was virtually a giant box girder with outward sloping sides. Longitudinal rigidity was also assisted by the wing bulkheads of the boiler rooms which continued forward as far as the double bottom, and aft through the engine rooms as deep girders.

The details of the principal structural features and their variations from standard practice are noted below:

Keel: Of box construction (first introduced into the RN in *Renown* Class battlecruisers) over the length of double bottom and of standard form, with single vertical keel, beyond. Docking keels employing the base of the wing bulkheads as vertical members were fitted on each side.

Longitudinal frames: Longitudinal strength being of prime importance in large ships these were continuous over the length of the double bottom and spaced about 8ft apart. As the hull narrowed fore and aft some were terminated against bulkhead frames but those continued beyond the double bottom, where longitudinal strength was less important, were tapered down to form flanged stringers. These were fitted intercostally between the transverse frames but had continuous angle bars on their inner edges. Similarly constructed stringers were fitted over the length of the bulge compartments and between decks fore and aft.

Transverse frames: In the double bottom these were fitted intercostally between the longitudinals at 4ft intervals and were of three basic types (see drawing B3): 1) Bracket frame – the standard and most common type; 2) Water-tight and oil-tight – to form the boundaries of oil tanks and water compartments and for fitting below water-tight bulkheads; 3) Lightened plate frames – formed of solid plates except for an access hole – fitted in areas under heavy weights (boilers, barbettes etc). Fore and aft, beyond the double bottom, the transverse frames were continuous, constructed of zed bar and joined to the keel by floor plate frames. Under heavy weights, and other stressed areas, the zed bars were strengthened by deep web frames. At the sides, the frames consisted of deep channel bars whose prime purpose was to support the armour and the torpedo bulkhead, both structurally and against impact. The frame spacing, normally about 4ft, was reduced to 2ft in these areas, by the fitting of intermediate frames. In the bulge the frames consisted of channel bars and web frames.

Beams: The transverse beams were constructed of angle bulb, with some exceptions under heavy structures, such as the conning tower, where channel bar was employed. Normally these were continuous, except where broken by the funnel hatches but in *Hood* the need for great longitudinal strength in the strength decks led to their being omitted from under the forecastle amidships in favour of 12in longitudinal 'I' girders, six each side amidships, transverse beams being fitted only at widely spaced intervals and between the innermost longitudinal girders along the middle line. Forward of the funnels the normal arrangement of beams was employed, some of the longitudinal girders being terminated as the ship's beam narrowed. These continuous girders were solid 'I' girders but forward of the funnel and under the upper deck, where it formed the after section of the strength deck, 'I' girders were of standard configuration being 'built up' from angles and plates and fitted intercostally between the beams. Vertical support was normally provided by the bulkheads but in large open spaces, under heavy weights and in areas subject to the blast of the main armament steel pillars were fitted under the beams.

Decks: All the principal decks were of continuous construction running unbroken through the length of the ship. In the case of the forecastle and upper decks this was for strength purposes, but in the case of the main deck, and the lower deck fore and aft of the machinery, it was to maintain the continuity of the deck protection. Below the protective decks the water-tight bulkheads were continuous and the

---

TABLE 1: **SHALLOW DRAUGHT BATTLESHIP DESIGNS 1915-16**

	A	B	C1	C2	D
Date	29.11.1915	1.1.1916	18.1.1916	18.1.1916	1.2.1916
Length oa/pp (ft)	810/760	800/750	707/660	657/610	757/710
Beam (ft)	104	90	104	100	104
Draught fwd/aft (ft)	23/24	25.25/26.25	23/24	24.25/25.25	23/24
Displacement (tons)	31,000	29,500	27,600	25,250	29,850
Shp	75,000	60,000	40,000	40,000	65,000
Speed (kts)	26.5 – 27	25	22	22	25.5

Note: All were armed with 8–15in (4×2), 12–5in (12×1) and 1–3in HA except 'C1' and 'C2' which had ten 5in and 'A' which had 2–3in HA. The alternative 'B' design of 1.1.1916 was similar to 'B' but had the same machinery as *Queen Elizabeth* (75,000shp) giving a speed of 27kts and increasing the displacement to 30,350 tons. All were weakly protected for battleships with a 10in belt, average 1⅛in decks and 11in–9in gun positions.

TABLE 2: **BATTLECRUISER DESIGNS 1916**

	1	2	3	4	5	6
Date	1.2.1916	1.2.1916	17.2.1916	17.2.1916	17.2.1916	17.2.1916
Length oa/pp (ft)	885/835	840/790	860/810	757/710	830/780	880/830
Beam (ft)	104	104	104	104	104	104
Mean draught (ft)	26	25	26	25	25	26
Displacement (tons)	39,000	35,500	36,500	32,500	35,500	39,500
Shp	120,000	120,000	160,000	120,000	120,000	120,000
Speed (kts)	30	30.5	32	30	30.5	30
Armament	8–15in	8–15in	8–15in	4–18in	6–18in	8–18in

Note: All carried a secondary armament of 12–5.5in guns and two torpedo tubes and were protected by an 8in belt and 9in barbette (except '3' with a 10in belt). Design '1' had large-tube boilers, the remainder small-tube.

TABLE 3: **DNC'S PROPOSED FAST BATTLESHIP DESIGNS, JULY 1916**

	A	B	C	D
Draught fwd/aft (ft)	27.75/28.75	29.5/30.5	28.5/29.5	28/29
Displacement (tons)	40,600	43,100	41,700	40,900
Speed (kts)	31	30.5	30.5 – 30.75	30.75
Armament	8–15in (4×2)	12–15in (4×3)	10–15in (2×3 + 2×2)	9–15in (3×3)

Note: Other particulars for all designs were: length 860ft oa, 810ft pp; beam 104ft; shp 144,000; secondary armament 16–5.5in, 4–4in HA, 4 torpedo tubes; armour 12in belt and barbettes, 15/12in gunhouses, decks 1in–2in.

TABLE 4: **LEGENDS FOR HOOD 1916-17**

	As approved on 7.4.1916	**As approved on 4.8.1916**	**As approved on 30.8.1917**
Length oa/pp	860/810	860/810	860/810
Beam (ft)	104	104	104
Draught fwd/aft (ft)	25/26	25.75/26.75	28/29
Displacement (tons)	36,300	37,500	41,200
Deep draught (ft)	29	29.5	31.5
Shp	144,000	144,000	144,000
Speed (kts)	32	31.75–32	31
Oil fuel capacity (tons)	4000	4000	4000
Armament	8–15in	8–15in	8–15in
	16–5.5in	16–5.5in	16–5.5in
	2–3in AA	2–3in AA	4–4in AA
	2-torpedo tubes	2-torpedo tubes	10-torpedo tubes
Armour (ins):			
Belt	8/5/3	8/3	12/7/5
Belt fore and aft	5/4	5/4/3	6/5
Bulkheads	4/3	4/3	5/4
Barbettes	9	9	12
Gunhouses	11/10/4¼	15/11/5	15/12/11/5
CT	10	10	11
Torp bulkheads	1½/¾	1½/¾	1½/¾
Decks	¾-2½	¾-2½	¾-3
Weights (tons):			
General equipment	750	750	800
Armament	4800	4950	5200
Armour & protective plating	10100	10600	13550
Oil fuel	1200	1200	1200
Hull	14070	14520	14950
Machinery	5200	5300	5300
Board margin	180	180	200
Total	36300	37500	41200

flats of the platform deck and hold were fitted between them. The principal strength deck, the forecastle, was constructed nominally of 1¾in plating but to compensate for the large openings this was increased to 2in around the funnel hatches and 1½in around the barbettes, the former also having deep coamings. Here as in all decks, the principal strength members were the stringer plates, at the deck edges, which ran unbroken along the entire boundary. The upper deck was the principal strength deck over the after section being of 2in thickness at the break of the forecastle, gradually reducing to ¾in forward and aft, except abreast the funnels and forward barbettes where the stringer plates (and the boundary plates to the funnel hatch) were 1in thick. The strength and protection areas of deck were constructed of HT (high tensile) steel and the remainder of comparatively thin (usually 3/8in) mild steel. The shelter deck did not contribute to the strength and was fitted with two expansion joints, one between the funnels and one across the forward end of the boat deck. The forecastle and upper decks, where they were open to the atmosphere, and the shelter deck abaft the second expansion joint were planked with teak. The superstructure platforms, living spaces, lobbies, passages and store rooms were covered with corticene (a type of linoleum), glued to the deck and held down by brass edge strips. Other areas including the forward end of the shelter deck were plain steel although the flats below the upper deck were usually of chequered plating.

Skin plating: The construction of the outer bottom followed normal practice for thickness and form but the inner bottom was slightly thicker than normal. However, the skin plating behind the armour was 2in thick, compared with the ¾in thickness more usual in capital ships. The principal strength member of this plating was the sheer strake, the uppermost length of plating which ajoined the forecastle deck and aft the upper deck. The plates of the torpedo bulkhead below the armour were worked vertically and did not contribute materially to longitudinal strength (drawing B18). The plating of the flat bottom was 1in thick reducing to 5/8in on the turn of the bilge and ½in on the top strake of the bulge. Fore and aft the skin plating reduced to about 3/8in (1in at waterline forward for protective purposes).

Protection: In the distribution of her armour and protective plating *Hood* generally followed pre-1914 practice. However, the sloping of the armour belt, at 12° to the vertical, was a recent innovation partly resulting from the need to keep the belt inside the bulge structure to allow torpedo hits to vent upwards to the atmosphere. The angled belt had the advantage of increasing its relative thickness as any hits on the belt would be at a relatively greater angle of impact than on an equivalent vertical belt. The only disadvantage was a reduction in the relative height of the belt increasing the chances of shells going under or over it.

Some idea of how far advanced *Hood* was on prewar designs can be gained from the fact that her protection was better than that of the *Queen Elizabeth* class battleships, the 13in belt of these ships being compensated for by the sloping of the belt in *Hood*. It is worth noting that percentages are of little use for comparison in this respect, except with ships of the same displacement, because in two ships of different size, but identical thicknesses and proportional areas of armour, the smaller ship will show a higher percentage of displacement as protection weight.

The system of underwater protection represented the final development of a series of experiments begun before the war and *Hood* was the first ship to have such an arrangement included from the design stage (earlier ships had only torpedo bulkheads, except *Renown* and *Repulse* which had been designed with an intermediate form of bulge, but no previous system was as comprehensive as that in *Hood*). The bulge consisted of an outer air space, an inner buoyancy space and the 1½in thick protective bulkhead. The buoyancy space was filled with crushing tubes – sealed steel tubes intended to both absorb the force of an underwater explosion and distribute it over as large an area of the protective bulkhead as possible. The official drawings for *Hood* also show crushing tubes in the triangular space at the top of the bulge and these have been shown in the drawings in this book but the exact purpose of this is not apparent and it is possible that this is an error (rare in Admiralty drawings). Inboard the wing compartments prevented the spread of flooding should the protective bulkhead be ruptured, although only narrow wing compartments could be fitted abreast the engine rooms owing to the great width required by the turbines.

Two types of steel protection were fitted (see Table 7) – 'armour' and 'protective plating'. The former consisted of thick cemented plates: that is, steel with a carbon enriched case hardened face but a comparatively soft back, which were fixed to the hull barbettes and so on by means of large bolts screwed into the backs of the plates through the skin plating. It was employed only on vertical surfaces except for the turret and CT roofs, etc (the turret roof plates were bolted from the outside to allow for removal of the guns). Protective plating which was employed for protective decks and bulkheads, was HT steel of uniform but tough consistency and was riveted in place as part of the ship's structure – thus the HT steel of the strength decks also contributed to protection although not primarily fitted for this purpose.

MACHINERY (see drawing section C)
Boilers: Steam for the turbines and the considerable amount of auxiliaries was generated by 24 Yarrow 3-drum small-tube boilers each with a heating surface of 7290 sq ft and a working pressure of 235lbs per sq in (see drawings C2-C3). The two principal features of the Yarrow boiler were its large furnace and its straight water-tubes; the latter unlike the curved tubes fitted in other types of water-tube boiler, making cleaning easier. The boilers required cleaning after about 500 hours steaming but more frequent removal of the soot (which collected on top of the water drums) was required and soot doors were fitted in the casing to allow this to be done when the boiler was in operation. Six Weir feed pumps, for supplying water to the boilers, were fitted in each boiler room, four as main pumps and two as auxiliaries to allow for maintenance and repair. These drew water, via a feed water heater, from the four main 30 ton feed tanks in the engine rooms and were also used to top up the main tanks from the 109.8 ton reserve feed tanks under each boiler room.

Each boiler had eight oil fuel sprayers, supplied by the four oil fuel pumps in each boiler room. Oil fuel was taken only from the tanks adjacent to each boiler room, in the wings and double bottoms, fuel being transferred to these from the tanks forward and aft when they required topping up or refilling. Two of the oil fuel pumps in 'A' boiler room were of double capacity (ie 24 tons), so they could be used to transfer oil from the forward tanks. The after tanks were served by four oil fuel tank pumps, one in the forward and middle engine rooms and two in the after engine room. Six oil fuel heaters (one for each boiler) were fitted in each boiler room to pre-heat the fuel before it entered the sprayers.

The steam from the boilers was transferred to the turbines by 19in diameter pipes run along each side of the boiler rooms and connected, via shut-off valves, to a single athwartship pipe in the forward engine room from which two additional 19in pipes were run to the middle and after engine rooms.

Turbines: These were fitted in four sets, two for the wing shafts in the forward engine room, one for the port inner shaft in the middle engine room and one for the starboard inner shaft in the after engine room. Their design originated from the US Curtis turbine, modified by its UK licencee, John Browns, to become the Brown Curtis turbine. It differed from the Parsons turbine, which was more widely used in British service, in being an impulse turbine rather than a reaction turbine, although it did use reaction stages, known as velocity compound wheels (oddly enough the Parsons turbine used an initial impulse stage). Each set consisted of one HP (high pressure) and one LP (low pressure) turbine driving the propeller shaft through a single reduction gear. In addition each LP turbine casing contained a reverse turbine at its forward end, while the two sets in the forward engine room also had a cruising turbine (for economy at low powers) clutched to the forward end of the HP turbine. Steam could be admitted, by means of valves on the control platforms of the engine rooms, to either the HP turbine for normal working, the cruising turbine or the astern turbine. The cruising turbine exhausted into the HP turbine, the HP into the LP and thence to the condenser, while the astern turbine exhausted directly into the condenser. The amount of steam supplied could also be controlled by the nozzle control valves on the turbines themselves.

Hood was the first British capital ship (excluding the *Courageous* type) to be fitted with geared turbines, these giving much improved efficiency over the direct drive arrangement because turbines are most efficient at high speeds whereas propellers are most efficient at low

TABLE 5: **PARTICULARS OF TRIALS**

Date	Shp	Speed	Rpm	Displacement
March 1920	9103	13.5	80	42090
(trials at load	14630	15.6	93	41700
displacement)	20050	17.2	103	41700
	29080	20.4	124	41600
	58020	25.2	154	41850
	89010	27.8	176	42100
	116150	29.7	191	42150
	151280	32.1	207	42200
8 March 1920	150473	31.8	205	–
(3-hour full	144984	31.4	202	–
power)				
22–23 March 1920	8735	13.2	81	45000
(trials at deep	14020	15.8	96	45000
displacement)	24720	19.1	116	45000
	40780	22	136	44600
	69010	25.7	161	44600
	112480	28.4	185	44600
	150220	31.9	204	44600

speeds. The gearing reduced the 1500rpm of the HP turbine and 1100rpm of the LP turbine to a shaft speed of 210rpm at maximum designed power.

Condensers: Each turbine set was provided with a Weir Uniflex condenser which was bolted to the underside of the LP turbine and weighed, when full, 70 tons. They had a cooling surface of 24,400 sq ft provided by 12,144 tubes and were designed to give a vacuum of 28in, with a sea temperature of 55°F and a barometric pressure of 30in. The vacuum increased the efficiency of the engines by increasing the pressure difference between the input and output and, as this was directly effected by the temperature of the cooling water, the machinery was more efficient when the sea temperature was low and less efficient when it was high. Water was circulated through the cooling pipes by two 31½in centrifugal pumps driven by steam reciprocating engines. The condensate, vapour and any air drawn into the turbine through the glands or leaky joints was pumped out of each condenser by two Weir dual air pumps which discharged via a feedwater filter (or grease extractor) into the main feed water tanks in the engine room. Each of these tanks, had its own feed water pump in the engine room which could either transfer water to or from the reserve feed tanks or, in the event of too much water being produced, into the overflow feed tanks, one of which was fitted in the double bottom under each engine room.

The middle and after engine rooms also contained an auxiliary condenser, with a cooling surface of 5330 sq ft and 5390 tubes, to deal with the exhaust steam from the auxiliary machinery. Each was provided with its own auxiliary air pumps, circulating pump and grease extractors the water again being discharged into the main feed water tanks.

Evaporators: The evaporators were used to boil sea water with exhaust steam, the resultant vapour being condensed to produce make-up feed water (distilled water was necessary for the boilers to avoid the formation of scale). Three evaporators, each with a capacity of 80 tons per day, were fitted in both the middle and after engine rooms. In each case, two were arranged as a compound set which could be worked singly for maximum output or with one discharging its generated steam into the heating coils of the next for maximum economy. These sets were completed by a distiller condenser and a combined fresh water, brine and air pump. They were used to supply fresh water for washing and drinking as well as boiler feed. The third evaporator was supplied with sea water by a small fire and bilge pump and was used solely for feed water as it discharged directly into the auxiliary condenser.

Forced lubrication system: Each set of turbines had two forced lubrication pumps and two oil coolers (one set for use and one as a stand-by), and a water service pump to circulate water through the oil cooler. In addition there was a third forced lubricating pump, with its own oil cooler and auxiliary (water) pump, in the after engine room to supply oil to the plummer blocks (or shaft bearings) in the shaft passages.

Electricity generating machinery: The main generating plant consisted of eight 200kW dynamos, all of the same design but driven by different means, four being provided with 2-cylinder steam reciprocating engines, two with steam turbines, and two with diesel engines. These supplied current at 220 volts DC into a common ring main from which branches were taken within each water-tight compartment thus ensuring that only the ring main pierced the principal water-tight bulkheads. Fore and aft water-tight cable passages for both the electric and hydraulic power ring mains were provided abreast the boiler rooms. All the dynamos, and the connections to and from the ring main, were controlled from a main switchboard on the lower deck, forward. The dynamos could also supply 135 volts AC which was passed through a transformer in the dynamo room and used to supply the ship's 100 ton and 350 tons salvage pumps at 220 volts AC. *Hood* was the first RN ship to have an AC supply although the system employed was not repeated in later ships. Besides the main generating system there were large numbers of small motor generators (ie dynamos driven by mains electric motors) providing low power supplies for the gun firing, fire-control, searchlight and telephone circuits.

Hydraulic system: Four steam driven hydraulic pumping engines were fitted for supplying power to operate the main armament and torpedo gear. Normally each supplied a single turret but all were interconnected to allow any engine to supply any turret, or turrets. The hydraulic medium was water, stowage being provided for 31.4 tons in the forward tanks and 48.8 tons in the after tanks. Power was transferred to the 15in turrets via 'walking' pipes under the working chamber – a scissor like arrangement which opened out as the turret trained, thus allowing transfer from the fixed to the moving structure.

Compressors: A low pressure general service compressor was fitted in the middle engine room to supply air at 120lbs per sq in for testing condensers, emptying the boilers to the sea, cleaning boilers, testing water-tight compartments, operating pneumatic tools and the pneumatic transmission of messages. This last was a system of tubes through which cylindrical containers holding written messages were propelled by air pressure – it was used mainly for transferring signals between the bridge and wireless offices. In addition there were four high pressure compressors, one in each hydraulic engine room, capable of supplying air up to a pressure of 4000lbs per sq in. These were used for charging air bottles for torpedo launching, pneumatic run-out and air blast for the 15in guns and starting the diesel engines, and for charging the air vessels of the torpedoes.

Pumping and Flooding system: For normal ship services ten steam driven 75 ton fire and bilge pumps, two in each engine room and one in each boiler room, and ten electrically driven 50 ton centrifugal hull and fire pumps fitted outside the machinery spaces, were provided. They were all arranged to draw water from the sea (for flooding compartments or charging the fire main) or from the bilges for discharge overboard. The 50 ton pumps were also arranged to draw from

TABLE 6: **PARTICULARS OF DIMENSIONS, DISPLACEMENT AND STABILITY**

Length 860ft 7in (oa), 810ft 6in (pp), beam 104ft 2in

Date	Condition	Displment (tons)	Draught (ft–in)			Freeboard (ft–in)			GM (ft)	Angle of max stability	Range
			Fwd	Mean	Aft	Fwd	Amidships at side	Aft			
21.2.20	Light	41125		28–3			22		3.2	36°	64°
21.2.20	Load	42670	27–1	29–3	30–7	29	21	17	3.25	36°	66°
21.2.20	Deep	46680	31–4	31–11	32–6	25–6	18–4	15	4.2	37°	73°
14.3.31	Light	42037	27–6½	28–10½	30–2½	29–2½	20–6½	17–6	3.1	35°	64°
14.3.31	Standard	42600	28	29–3	30–6	28–9	20–2	17–2½	3.1		
14.3.31	Half oil	45693	31–6	31–5	31–4	25–3	18–10	16–4½	2.9	35°	65°
14.3.31	Deep	48000	33–9½	33	32–2½	23	17–5	15–6	3.13	35°	68°
1.39	Light	42752		29–3½			21		2.85		
1.39	Deep	48650	33–11	33–4¾	32–10½	22–10½	17–0¼	14–10	3.23		
5.40	Light	42462		29–5			20–10		2.99		
5.40	Deep	48360	33–3¼	33–1¾	33–0¼	23–6¼	17–3¼	14–8¼	3.25		

TABLE 7: **PARTICULARS OF PROTECTION**

ARMOUR:
Main belt: 12in (562ft × 9ft 6in) reducing to 6in and 5in forward and 6in aft
Middle belt: 7in reducing to 5in forward
Upper belt: 5in
Lower belt: 3in (abreast boiler rooms only)
Bulkheads: 5in and 4in
Barbettes: 12in (max)
Gunhouses: 15in face, 12in and 11in sides, 11in back, 5in roof
Conning tower: 11in (max)
Communication tube: 3in
Director hood: 6in front, 2in sides, 3in roof
Torpedo control tower: 3in roof, 1½in sides, ¾in communication tube, 3in–4in rangefinder hood

PROTECTIVE PLATING (HORIZONTAL)
Forecastle deck: 1¾in–2in
Upper deck: ¾in – 2in
Main deck: 1in – 3in (2in on slope)
Lower deck: 1in – 3in
Conning tower floors: 2in

PROTECTIVE PLATING (VERTICAL)
Torpedo bulkheads: 1½in – 1¾in
Lower belt: ¾in abreast magazines and engine rooms
Longitudinal bulkheads abreast funnels and ammunition passages: 1in
Bulkheads to 5.5in working spaces, TS etc: 1in – 2in

the double bottom and other compartments, and were fitted as independent units within each principal water-tight compartment to avoid piercing the main water-tight bulkheads. Hose connections were provided for pumping out compartments not directly connected to the system. The fire main ran fore and aft below protection with branches to hose connections on all decks for fire fighting and wash deck purposes. Branches were also taken to gravity sanitary tanks in the superstructure for supplying water to the heads, WCs, etc. For dealing with flooding after damage, nine electrically driven 350 ton submersible salvage pumps were fitted in the main compartments outside the machinery spaces and one electrically driven 100 ton submersible salvage pump in each 15in shell room. In the engine rooms large quantities of water could be pumped overboard by the main circulating pumps, which had bilge suctions for this purpose. Each boiler room was provided with a 1000 ton turbo bilge pump while each auxiliary engine room and submerged torpedo room had a 300 ton steam ejector.

Fresh water service: Two (three after 1929-31 refit) main fresh water tanks were fitted, one forward and one aft, these being filled or topped up as necessary from the evaporator plant, a shore connection or a water boat. Each tank supplied a 10 ton fresh water pump operated by a float switch in a gravity tank in the superstructure. The gravity tank provided a suitable 'head' of water in the fore and aft fresh water main which supplied branches for drinking and washing purposes etc.

Steering gear: Main steering positions were fitted in the conning tower, lower conning tower and after engine room connected by telemotor pipes to control valves on the two 3-cylinder steam steering engines in the after engine rooms. Only one engine was required to operate the rudder, the second serving as a stand-by to allow for maintenance and in case of breakdown. The rudder was too heavy to be operated by hand so auxiliary steering was provided by a Williams Janney electro-hydraulic variable speed motor. This latter type of motor was also employed for the main boat hoist machinery, the after capstan and the variable speed winches.

Ventilation: Particular care was exercised in the arrangement of *Hood*'s ventilation system and it was regarded as a substantial advance on previous practice. The accommodation and working spaces had fan supplies and natural exhausts except in those compartments where the rapid extraction of air was essential, such as the heads, WCs, paint stores, galleys etc, where the fans were on the exhaust side. Each of the auxiliary machinery compartments had two 17½in exhaust fans and a natural supply, via the access and escape trunks, while the engine rooms had both supply and exhaust fans. The boiler rooms had closed stokeholds as the boilers operated under forced draught provided by six 90in supply fans, exhaust being via the boilers which had adjustable air doors to control the flow of air into the furnace. All fans were driven by electric motors except the boiler room fans which were propelled by steam piston engines.

Cooling machinery: Three cooling or refrigeration plants were provided, two for cooling the air circulated through the magazines and one for the meat and vegetable store rooms. Each plant consisted of a CO_2 compressor, a condenser, an evaporator and a motor brine pump.

General: All the pumps in the machinery spaces, with the exception of the dual air pumps, turbo pumps and main circulating pumps, were of the same basic design with a single cylinder steam piston driving, in most cases, two pumping cylinders. Typical examples of this type of pump are shown in the drawings of the fire and bilge pumps (C12/1) and the feed water pump (C8/5).

ARMAMENT (see drawing section G)

Main armament: The *Hood* was originally to have carried the twin 15in Mk I mountings fitted in all British capital ships since the *Queen Elizabeth* class but after Jutland the mounting was redesigned to meet demands for action at longer ranges and to accommodate improvements suggested by service experience since the mounting first went to sea in 1915. The new mountings, which only *Hood* carried, were manufactured by Vickers and designated Mk II. They differed from the Mk I mounting as follows:

1) Elevation increased from 20° to 30° which required a longer elevating cylinder, a deeper gun well and an increase in the height of the gunhouse roof at the forward end. The original mounting was designed for all-angle loading but as the basic mechanism remained unchanged *Hood*'s guns could not be loaded beyond 20° elevation.
2) 15ft rangefinders in gunhouse roof replaced by 30ft to improve accuracy at long range.
3) Improved flash-tightness.
4) Sighting hoods in gunhouse roof, which proved a source of weakness in protection, replaced by sighting ports in the turret face.
5) Officer's cabinet armoured.
6) Hydraulic run-out for guns replaced by pneumatic run-out.

Secondary armament: The 5.5in gun was introduced to British service in the cruisers *Birkenhead* and *Chester*, building for Greece in 1914

and taken over by the RN on the outbreak of war. It was subsequently mounted in the light battlecruiser *Furious*, the carrier *Hermes*, the submarine *K17* and the *Hood*. It was chosen because its 82lb shell was easier to load than the 100lb shell of the more usual 6in gun. Nevertheless, due to the high elevation provided difficulties *were* experienced in loading the gun at low angles.

TABLE 8: SUMMARY OF ARMAMENT

Main armament:	8—15in Mk I, four twin Mk II mountings
Secondary armament:	12—5.5in Mk I, twelve single CPII mountings (2 removed 1938-39, all removed 1940)
Saluting guns:	4—3 pdr Hotchkiss (removed 1939)
Torpedo tubes:	2 submerged (removed 1937), 2 above-water Mk V

AA armament

	4in	4in	4in	UP	2pdr	2pdr	0.5in	0.5in
Gun Mk	V	V	XVI	–	VIII	VIII	III	III
Mounting Mk	III	IV	XIX	–	V	VI	I	III
Type of mounting	Single	Single	Twin	20-barrel	8-barrel	8-barrel	Quad	Quad
1920	4	–	–	–	–	–	–	–
1931	4	–	–	–	2	–	–	–
1933	4	–	–	–	2	–	2	–
1937	4	2	–	–	2	1	2	2
1938	4	4	–	–	2	1	2	2
1939 (June)	4	2	4	–	2	1	2	2
1939 (August)	–	–	4	–	2	1	2	2
1940	–	–	7	5	2	1	2	2

TABLE 9: PARTICULARS OF GUNS

15in BL Mk I

Calibre:	15in
Length of bore:	42 cal (630in)
Length of gun:	650.4in
Dimensions of chamber	20in dia × 107.68in long; 30,650 cu in
Weight of gun excluding breech mechanism:	97 tons 3cwt
Weight of breech mechanism:	2 tons 17cwt
Rifling:	Polygroove plain section Mk I, 76 grooves
Length of rifling:	516.33in
Twist of rifling:	Uniform right hand, 1 turn in 30 calibres
Charge:	Cordite MD45, full charge 428lbs, reduced charge 321lbs, practice charge 214lbs
Chamber pressure:	19.5 tons per sq in
Weight of shell:	1920lbs (4crh)
Weight of burster:	129lbs 5ozs (CPC shell), 48lbs 8ozs (APC shell)
Muzzle velocity (new gun):	2462fs
Muzzle energy (new gun):	82,370ft-tons
Maximum range:	30,180yds at 30° elevation (new gun)
Penetration:	15in KC plate at 14,300yds (theoretical at normal inclination using APC shell)
Mounting:	Twin Mk II, hydraulically operated, revolving weight 890 tons (average), maximum elevation 30°, maximum depression 5°, training speed 2° per sec, elevating speed 5° per sec
Shell stowage:	As built – 289 CPC, 672 APC, 30 shrapnel (forward turrets only), 82 practice. After 1929-31 refit – 160 CPC (TNT burster), 640 APC (Shellite burster), 48 shrapnel, 96 practice

Note: as built, ammunition was not evenly distributed but after 1931 all the types were divided equally between the four shell rooms

5.5in BL Mk I

Calibre:	5.5in
Length of bore:	50 cal (275in)
Length of gun:	284.728in
Dimensions of chamber:	7.6in dia × 36.3in long, 1500 cu in
Weight of gun and breech mechanism	6 tons 4 cwt 2qtrs 18lbs
Rifling:	Polygroove plain section Mk I 40, grooves
Length of rifling:	235.92in
Twist of rifling:	Uniform right hand, 1 turn in 30 calibres
Charge:	Cordite MD19, full charge 22lbs 4oz, reduced charge 14lbs 13oz
Chamber pressure:	18 tons per sq in
Weight of shell:	82lbs (4crh)
Weight of burster:	5lbs 4oz
Muzzle velocity:	2790fs (2025fs with reduced charge)
Muzzle energy:	4425ft-tons
Maximum range:	18,500yds at 30° elevation
Mounting:	Single CPII, hand operated, maximum elevation 30°, maximum depression 5°
Shell stowage:	As built – 1728 Lyddite, 582 common, 96 shrapnel, 464 practice. After 1929-31 refit – 1368 HE, 624 Shellite, 360 HENT, 50 starshell (forward shell room only), 449 practice

4in QF Mk V

Calibre:	4in
Length of bore:	45 cal (180in)
Length of gun:	187.8in
Weight of gun:	2 tons 1cwt 1qtr 10lbs
Weight of breech mechanism:	1cwt 2qtrs 8lbs
Rifling:	Polygroove plain section Mk I, 32 grooves
Length of rifling:	149.725in
Twist of rifling:	Uniform right hand, 1 turn in 30 calibres
Charge:	MD16 cordite, 7lbs 11oz
Total weight shell, charge and case:	54lbs
Chamber pressure:	18.5 tons per sq in
Weight of HE shell:	31.43lbs
Weight of bursters:	1lb 13ozs (HE shell)
Muzzle velocity:	2643fs
Muzzle energy:	1567ft-tons
Maximum range:	16,300yds at 45° elevation, 28,750ft ceiling at 80° elevation
Mounting:	HA Mk III and Mk IV, hand operated, maximum elevation 85°, maximum depression 5°. Weight (excluding gun) 4 tons 13cwt 5qtrs 22lbs (Mk III)
Shell stowage:	600 HE, 200 starshell

4in QF Mk XVI

Calibre:	4in
Length of bore:	45 cal (180in)
Length of gun:	190.5in
Weight of gun:	2 tons 1cwt 11lbs (including breech mechanism and counter-balance weight)
Rifling:	32 grooves
Twist of rifling:	Uniform right hand, 1 turn in 30 calibres
Charge:	SC cordite 9lbs
Total weight of shell charge and case:	63lbs 8ozs
Weight of HE shell:	35lbs 14ozs
Muzzle velocity:	2650fs
Muzzle energy:	1934ft-tons
Maximum range:	21,300yds at 45°; 40,000ft ceiling at 80°
Mounting:	Twin HA/LA Mk XIX, hand operated, maximum elevation 80°, maximum depression 10°. Weight (including guns) 16 tons 11cwt
Ammunition stowage:	1939–2000 HE, 250 starshell. 1940–4600

2pdr QF Mk VIII pom-pom

Calibre:	40mm (1.575in)
Length of bore:	40 cal (62in)
Length of gun:	102.6in
Weight of gun:	850lbs
Rifling:	12 grooves
Length of rifling:	54.84in
Twist of rifling:	Uniform right hand, 1 turn in 30 calibres
Charge:	3.4ozs
Total weight shell, charge and case:	2lbs 15ozs
Weight of shell:	2lbs
Muzzle velocity:	1920fs
Maximum range:	3800yds
Mountings:	Mk V and Mk VI, power operated. Weight (Mk V) 11 tons 16 cwt 44lbs, (Mk VI) 15 tons 14cwt, maximum elevation 80°, maximum depression 10°
Ammunition stowage:	720 rounds per barrel

0.5in MG Mk III

Calibre:	0.5in
Length of bore:	62 cal (31.11in)
Length of gun:	52in
Weight of gun	56lbs (62lbs with cooling water)
Charge:	0.24ozs
Total weight of bullet, charge and case:	2.9ozs
Weight of bullet:	1.32ozs
Muzzle velocity:	2520fs
Mountings:	Mk I and Mk III hand operated. Weight excluding guns (Mk I) 12 cwt, (Mk III) 1 ton 1cwt 79lbs. Maximum elevation 80°, maximum depression 10°
Ammunition stowage:	2500 rounds per barrel

Long range AA: The 4in Mk V gun was originally a low angle weapon but was chosen for use as an AA gun late in the First World War. Until the late 1930s it was the fleet's main long range AA weapon being fitted in the majority of capital ships and cruisers. It was superseded by an even more popular weapon, the twin 4in Mk XIX mounting designed for low angle as well as high angle fire which proved useful when *Hood*'s secondary armament was removed in 1940.

Torpedo armament: The *Hood* was equipped with 21in Mk IV and IV* torpedoes, which weighed 3357lbs, carried a 515lbs TNT warhead and had a range of 13,500yds at 25kts or 5000yds at 40kts. The two submerged tubes were side loading and were fired by compressed air, supplied from air reservoirs in the mining and torpedo gunners' stores. The reservoirs were refilled after launching from air bottles in the same compartments. Hydraulic power was used for torpedo loading and traversing, for the torpedo lifts and operating the sluice valve doors. This was normally taken from the main hydraulic system but a secondary hydraulic pump, fitted in the illuminating gear store below the torpedo rooms, could be used for these purposes if necessary. The two torpedo head magazines originally stowed 14 Mk IV warheads and

2 Mk V collision (practice) heads. The collision heads were later replaced by warheads giving a total of 32 but it is not known if sufficient torpedo bodies were carried for all these heads. the four above-water Mk V torpedo tubes were also side loading but launched their Mk IV torpedoes by a cordite charge. Four torpedoes were kept in the tubes and four reloads were slung from rails immediately over the tubes. The warheads of both the tube and reload torpedoes were within an armoured box (provided in design but not fitted – reinstated during 1929-31 refit).

CONTROL SYSTEMS (see drawing section H)

Main armament: Primary control was from either of the directors and secondary control from the local director sight (LDS) in 'B' turret. Divided control was achieved with one DCT, or 'B' turret, controlling the forward guns and 'X' turret controlling the after guns. In addition all turrets could be controlled separately by their own LDS. Additional fire-control instruments were fitted in the CT, fore bridge and spotting top to provide target indication, to supplement the information available from the primary control positions and as back-up controls.

Secondary armament: In primary control the guns on each side were controlled from the 5.5in directors on the bridge. Quarters firing was provided by either the 5.5in directors controlling the forward groups and the midships officer of quarters' positions the after groups or by all positions controlled from the four officer of quarters' positions (this last was not possible after 1931 as the forward positions were removed). In addition, the guns could, of course, be controlled individually by their own crews.

Torpedo control: This was simpler than that for the guns as no elevation data was required. Target bearing and deflection (aim off) was provided by the torpedo deflection sights and range data by the torpedo rangefinders. This information was originally resolved via a Dreyer table in the Torpedo TS but this gear was removed in 1929-31, the necessary calculations being carried out thereafter in the torpedo control position on the bridge.

Searchlight control: These were laid on target by bearing indicators on the bridge or in the night defence position aft, and were controlled

TABLE 10: **SUMMARY OF FIRE CONTROL GEAR**

Main Armament

Tripod type director:	One in each 15in DCT
Open director sights:	One in each 15in gunhouse
Dreyer fire control table Mk V:	One in 15in TS
Evershed bearing transmitter:	One in 15in spotting top, two on fore bridge, two in 15in CT
Rangefinders:	Five 30ft, one in each turret and one in armoured DCT. One 15ft in aloft DCT (removed 1940)
Range clocks:	One in 15in spotting top, two in 15in CT

Secondary Armament

Pedestal type sights:	One in each 5.5in director tower
Fire control clocks Type F:	Two in 5.5in TS
Dumaresq	Two in 5.5in spotting tops, two in 5.5in CTs
Evershed bearing indicators:	Two in 5.5in spotting tops, two in 5.5in CTs, two on fore bridge
Rangefinders:	Two 9ft (12ft after 1924)
Range clocks:	Two in 5.5in spotting tops
Starshell eversheds:	Two on fore bridge

HA Armament

HACS:	One Mk I (1931-38), three Mk III (1939)
Rangefinders:	One 2m (1920), one 15ft (1926), one 12ft (in HACS director, 1931), three 15ft (in HACS directors, 1939)
Air lookouts:	Fitted on bridge (1936)

Torpedo Armament

Torpedo deflection sights Mk III:	Four on fore bridge, two in conning tower, two in after torpedo control tower
Dreyer table:	One in torpedo TS (removed during 1929-31 refit)
Rangefinders:	Three 15ft, one in revolving hood on aft CT (removed 1937, and two in midship rangefinder towers (removed 1940). After 1940 refit the former 5.5in, 12ft rangefinders on the single platform were used to control the above-water tubes.

Searchlights

Evershed bearing indicators:	Two on fore bridge, four in night defence position aft

remotely from positions below (above for foremast searchlights after 1927) the searchlights.

Concentrating positions: To enable ships in company to concentrate on one target, concentrating positions were fitted fore and aft to allow visual information, displayed on concentration dials (usually referred

TABLE 11: **PARTICULARS OF SHIP'S BOATS**

Steam Boats

Type	Length	Beam (excluding rubbers)	Rig	Oars	Armament	Weight (including 2 men and all gear)	Life Saving Capacity	Remarks
50ft steam pinnace	50ft	9ft 9in	11kts	–	1–3pdr QF	320cwt	70	Two fitted until 1940
45ft Admiral's barge	45ft	9ft 6in	10¾kts	–	–	320cwt	55	Overall length 50ft due to counter stern. One fitted until 1940
45ft steam pinnace	45ft	9ft 7½in	10¾kts	–	1–3pdr QF	260cwt	60	Fitted 1940, removed 1941

Sailing boats

Type	Construction	Length	Beam (excluding rubbers)	Rig	Oars	Armament	Weight (including 2 men and all gear)	Life Saving Capacity	Remarks
42ft launch	Double diagonal	42ft	11ft 6in	Single mast. De Horsey	14 × 17ft 4 × 16ft	Twin Lewis MG (originally one Maxim MG)	198cwt	130	*Hood* carried one with an auxiliary motor (7kts) throughout her life and one with sail power only during 1923–29
36ft sailing pinnace	Double diagonal	36ft	9ft 9½in	Single mast. De Horsey	12 × 17ft 4 × 16ft	Twin Lewis MG (originally one Maxim MG)	110cwt	86	Replaced by 35ft motor boat by 1923
32ft cutter	Clinker	32ft	8ft 6½in	Single mast. De Horsey or lug sloop	8 × 15ft 4 × 14ft	Twin Lewis MG (originally one Maxim MG)	52cwt	59	Four carried until 1940, two thereafter. Two employed as seaboats on davits with quick release gear, for transferring at sea, life saving, mooring etc
30ft gig	Double skin carvel	30ft	5ft 10½in	Two mast. Dipping lug	4 × 17ft 2 × 16ft	–	28cwt	26	Two carried (sometimes three) until 1940 when reduced to one. One was captain's and one Admiral's personal boat
27ft whaler	Clinker	27ft	6ft	Two mast. Montagu	4 × 17ft 1 × 16ft	–	26cwt	27	Two carried throughout
16ft dinghy	Clinker	16ft	5ft 6in	Single mast. Gunter	2 × 14ft 2 × 10ft	–	14cwt	14	Two carried until 1939 when one replaced by motor dinghy

Motor boats

Type	Length	Beam (excluding rubbers)	Speed	BHP	Armament	Weight (including 2 men and all gear)	Life Saving Capacity	Remarks
45ft motor launch	45ft	11ft 6in	8kts	36	Twin Lewis MG	250cwt	200	Carried from 1931. Fitted with auxiliary sails
35ft motor boat	35ft	7ft 8in	8kts	33	Twin Lewis MG	106cwt	46	One fitted from completion, second added by 1923 and third in 1931. One replaced by 30ft FMB 1934, remainder removed 1939. Fitted with various designs of canvas covers and cabins

Fast Motor Boats

Type	Length	Beam (excluding rubbers)	Speed	BHP	Armament	Weight including 2 men and all gear	Life Saving capacity	Remarks
35ft fast motor boat	35ft	8ft 6in	16–18kts	130	–	100cwt	50	One fitted 1940 as Admiral's barge, two more replaced steam boats in 1941
30ft fast motor boat	30ft	7ft 9in	13–16kts	95	–	70cwt	35	One fitted 1934, removed c1939
25ft fast motor boat	25ft	6ft 9in	12–14kts	65	–	50cwt	21	Two fitted 1939–40
16ft motor dinghy	16ft	5ft 6in	17–21kts	50	–	25cwt	7	Fast type, one fitted

NOTE: Motor boats had round bilge double diagonal hulls, fast motor boats were of hard chine construction.

to as range clocks) to be passed to or received from ships ahead or astern. Range information was displayed on the dials and enemy bearing indicated by scales painted on the turrets (wartime only). The system enabled ships to fire on targets they could not see themselves and provided for maximum rate of fire on targets which might only be visible for short periods. To avoid confusion in spotting, ships in company fired alternately at predetermined time intervals. In the late 1920s the visual system was superseded by short range W/T and radio telephone communication and the range dials were removed.

Communication: Internal communications were provided by voice pipes, telephones, loudspeakers and pneumatic transmission (for signals). The main 'flat roof' W/T aerials rigged between the W/T yards provided for long range communication and the auxiliary W/T from the second W/T office for medium range. The other wireless gear and the radio telephones served as short range systems for fleet intercommunication, etc. The other signalling systems were the standard flags, semaphores, signalling searchlights and signalling lamps.

GROUND TACKLE (see drawing section J)
Bower anchor: Two 192½cwt Wasteney-Smith stockless anchors were employed for normal anchoring and mooring. They were let go by releasing the slips holding the cable, the cable holders running free. For weighing the cable holders were clutched to the main steam capstan engine.

Sheet anchor: One 191½cwt Wasteney-Smith stockless anchor served for emergency use as a spare bower. Its cable holder was not connected to the capstan engine and could be used for letting go only, under the control, if required, of a friction brake. For weighing the sheet anchor cable had to be transferred to the capstan or the starboard bower cable holder.

Stream anchor: One 61cwt Wasteney-Smith was originally provided but this seems to have been replaced by a 60cwt Byers shortly after completion. It was used as a stern anchor and operated via a steel cable rather than a chain and was weighed by the after, electrically driven, capstan.

Kedge anchor: *Hood* carried one 16cwt and one 12cwt Admiralty pattern anchors for kedging, warping and hauling out the launch for laying the bower or sheet anchor at a distance from the ship. They were stowed amidships on the forecastle deck.

Boat anchors: Each boat carried an Admiralty pattern anchor ranging from 20lbs for the 16ft dinghies to 120lbs for the launches and steam boats.

Anchor cables: *Hood*'s bower and sheet anchor cables were constructed from links of 3⅜in diameter steel. Each cable was 41 shackles in length made up in 35 full shackles and 12 half shackles. Each shackle was 12½ fathoms long (75ft) making the total length 3075ft.

AIRCRAFT (see drawing section L)
Like most capital ships in the 1920s *Hood* carried aircraft flying-off platforms on 'B' and 'X' turrets but these do not seem to have seen much service, although there is at least one photograph of her with a Fairey Flycatcher on 'B' turret. The flying-off ramps for fitting over the muzzles of the guns were usually folded up and stowed on top of the main platform on the turret roof. The after platform was removed during her 1929-31 refit and that forward a few years later.

During her 1929-31 refit an FIVH (Folding Mk IV Heavy) catapult was fitted on her quarterdeck, together with a crane for use with a FIIIF seaplane. Two aircraft were allotted to Hood although only one could be carried, stowed on the catapult itself. The catapult was manufactured at the RAE, Farnborough, and differed from other types in use in the RN in that the launching mechanism consisted of a series of telescopic rams actuated by compressed air. This mechanism also allowed for the stowage arrangement which consisted of folding the forward half of the structure back against the main section.

The arrangement proved very difficult to operate in anything but calm weather and the aircraft was vulnerable to damage in handling, from bad weather and from the blast of the after 15in guns. Consequently it was removed after only 10 months service. Thereafter *Hood* was one of the few capital ships in the Navy without aircraft.

MODIFICATIONS 1920–1941

January 1920: On leaving John Brown's yard *Hood* had no director fitted on her fore top. This and the aircraft platforms on 'B' and 'X' turret were added during her final fitting out at Rosyth.

Refits of 20–25 May and 7 September – 8 October 1920 (Rosyth): After concentrating position added under overhang of after searchlight platform. Compass platform raised 5ft, original windows blocked off (partial roof removed making platform completely open) and chart table added on port side. Captain's and signalman's shelters on fore bridge converted to W/T office. Flagpole added to foretopmast.

Refits of 6 December 1920 – 6 January 1921, June – July 1921 (Devonport) and Autumn 1921 (Rosyth): Roof and windows added to compass platform (this was carried out before any of the following alterations). Gyro repeater on roof of fore bridge cabins replaced by 8ft navigation rangefinder. Two forward 36in searchlights on platform between funnels removed. Davits fitted at sides abreast mainmast to provide harbour positions for 30ft gigs. Torpedo rangefinder fitted on extension to foremast searchlight platform. Shelter deck above fore foremost 5.5in guns cut away to allow full elevation at extreme angles of training.

1922–1923: During this period the *Hood* carried a small lattice tower on the after searchlight platform. It was surmounted by a piece of equipment very similar in appearance to the Type 71 W/T aerial gear which came into general use later in the 1920s, so this may have been a prototype set under sea trials.

MODIFICATIONS 1920–1941 – contd

Refit of August – November 1923 (Devonport, preparatory to world cruise): Two foremost 36in searchlights between funnels replaced.

Refit of October – December 1924 (Devonport, on return from world cruise): 9ft rangefinders, for 5.5in armament, on fore top replaced by 12ft rangefinders in enclosed towers. Two foremost 36in searchlights between funnels again removed (never replaced). Main topgallant mast replaced by flagpole. (Note that the topgallant mast was housed down in home waters and raised, to increase wireless range, on foreign service – as in the world cruise – it was not removed during the 1920-24 period.)

Refit on November 1925 – January 1926 (Rosyth): 2 metre HA rangefinder on after searchlight platform replaced by 15ft HA rangefinder and, to accommodate this change, 36in searchlights repositioned athwartships at forward end of platform. Petrol lockers for motor boats repositioned on boat deck and increased in number. Gaff added to mainmast.

Refit of November – December 1927 (Devonport): Foremost 24in signalling searchlights on Admiral's bridge moved down to CT platform. Stowage for stream anchor provided on shelter deck. Torpedo rangefinder and platform on forward edge of foremost searchlight platform removed. Concentration dials on foremast removed and positions converted for searchlight control. Searchlight control position above fore bridge converted to torpedo control position and 8ft rangefinder removed. 9ft rangefinder for navigation added on roof of compass platform. Teak platforms added abreast torpedo control position/compass platform.

Note: Date of alterations not known but by 1928 the third W/T office (on the upper deck at the base of the CT) had been expanded into the auxiliary coding office, to port, and the intelligence office, on the deck above, and accommodated W/T Types 81, 43 and 45.

Major refit of 3 June 1929 – 28 May 1931 (Portsmouth): High Angle Control System (HACS) Mk I fitted, with director on after searchlight platform in place of HA rangefinder and High Angle Control Position (HACP) fitted in former searchlight control position under the platform. Night defence position in after superstructure converted to sailmaker's shop. Platforms for loading 4in guns at low angles removed from 4in mountings (this may have been done earlier). Two Mk V pom-pom mountings fitted abreast fore funnel displacing 32ft cutters (seaboats) which were refitted amidships; these in turn displaced the amidships accommodation ladder which was refitted further aft. Engineers' stores to port and starboard of 'B' 15in magazine on platform deck converted to 2pdr magazines. 2pdr ready-use magazines fitted on forecastle deck below pom-poms – officer of quarters' positions in these areas removed. Positions for pom-pom directors fitted abaft fore top but only starboard position fitted with director. FIVH aircraft catapult fitted on quarterdeck together with crane and 300 gallon jettisonable aviation spirit tank. Aircraft platform removed from 'X' turret. Gun cotton magazine on platform deck aft converted to bomb room and new gun cotton magazine built into corner of spirit room. Marines' store converted to fireworks magazine and new marines' store built just forward of original. 15in transmitting station (TS) made gas-tight. Torpedo TS converted to lower plotting room. Upper plotting position fitted at rear of Admiral's bridge. W/T office and Admiral's plotting position on fore bridge converted to remote control office and navigating officer's sea cabin. Signalmen's shelters fitted at fore end of signal deck. Harbour position for 30ft gigs moved 20ft further aft and 300 gallon jettisonable petrol tanks fitted in original position to port and starboard of mainmast (original petrol stowage arrangements for boats removed). Wireless rig modernised, the original multi-wire aerials being replaced by single wire aerials. Fitted with short range WT sets Types 31 (with office in 15in TS) and 71. 24in signalling searchlights on CT platform moved to signal platform. New paravane derricks and derrick posts fitted, with new position abreast 'A' turret (former locations retained as alternate positions but deck fittings needed modification as old derrick post had no stays). Water-tight compartments in hold forward (stations 21–23) converted to additional fresh water tank. Oil fuel stowage increased from 3895 to 4615 tons by converting double bottom compartments between forward end of 'A' boiler room and forward end of 'A' shell room, and water-tight compartments abreast middle and after engine rooms, to oil fuel tanks. Box protection fitted to above-water torpedo tubes.

Refit of 21 March – 20 June 1932 (Portsmouth): Aircraft gear removed from quarterdeck. 12ft rangefinder towers removed from fore top.

Refit 31 March – 10 May 1933 (Portsmouth): Raised platform for two quadruple 0.5in MG mountings fitted at fore end of signal deck.

Refit of September – December 1933 (Portsmouth): Two 0.5in MG Mk I mountings fitted. Aircraft platform removed from 'B' turret.

Refit of 1 August – 5 September 1934 (Portsmouth): 12ft rangefinder towers, for 5.5in guns, refitted on signal deck. Pom-pom director positions moved to positions formerly occupied by 5.5in rangefinders on fore top.

1 April – 13 May 1935 (probably at Gibraltar): Second pom-pom director fitted on fore top.

Refit of 26 June – 10 October 1936 (Portsmouth): Pom-pom directors moved to positions at rear corners of fore bridge. 36in searchlight platform removed from foremast. Air defence positions fitted above compass platform and on roof of torpedo control position. Type 31 W/T set replaced by Type 75 VHF set with aerials on fore top roof and mainmast starfish.

Refit of 8 November – 16 December 1937 (Malta): After torpedo control tower removed and replaced by pom-pom ready-use magazine (mounted off-centre to starboard), with bandstand and 2pdr pom-pom Mk VI mounting on its roof. Aerial trunk from second W/T office moved aft to clear pom-poms' arc of fire. Two quadruple 0.5in MG Mk III mountings fitted on raised platforms abreast after superstructure. Two single 4in HA Mk IV mountings fitted on shelter deck amidships. Submerged torpedo tubes removed and compartments sub-divided for later conversion into HACP (work not completed until 1938 refit).

Refit of 16 May – 22 June 1938 (Malta): Pom-pom director Mk II fitted on after superstructure. Two 5.5in mountings at fore end of shelter deck replaced by two 4in HA Mk IV mountings. W/T gear modernised.

Refit February – June 1939 (Portsmouth): Four twin 4in HA/LA Mk XIX mountings fitted on shelter deck, two midships 4in Mk IV mountings removed. Two HACS Mk III directors fitted on signal deck. Signal deck extended aft, new flag lockers fitted at after end and 24in signalling searchlight replaced by modern 20in model. Four 44in searchlights fitted on raised platforms abreast after funnel and after superstructure. Harbour positions for 30ft gigs modified to permanent positions for 27ft whalers. FH3 HF/DF office fitted on mainmast starfish with aerial at head of mainmast flagpole.

Refit of July – August 1939 (Portsmouth): This represents the second half of the previous refit, the ship having gone to sea in June for trials. All single 4in HA removed and forward 5.5in guns on shelter deck replaced. After HACS Mk I replaced by HACS Mk III with new director and table. 36in searchlights removed, the two on the after superstructure being replaced by 44in searchlights (making a total of 6). Searchlight towers removed from around MF/DF office amidships and DF booms replaced by fixed metal frame aerial spreaders. Platform fitted around front of Admiral's bridge. HACP fitted in former submerged torpedo rooms (previously sub-divided at Malta). Water-tight sub-divisions of main deck aft improved.

Refit of 29 March – 27 May 1940 (Devonport): All 5.5in guns, directors, fire control gear and ammunition arrangements including dredger hoists removed. Former 5.5in rangefinder towers on shelter deck modified for use as torpedo rangefinders and original torpedo rangefinders amidships removed. Three twin 4in HA/LA Mk XIX mountings and four UP mountings fitted on shelter deck and one UP mounting on 'B' turret. Old 4in ready-use lockers replaced by new 'light-type' and UP ready-use lockers added. 15ft rangefinder removed from aloft director tower. Forward and after 5.5in magazines and shell rooms and after SA magazine converted to 4in HA magazines. Splinter screens fitted around 4in, 2pdr and UP mountings and forward openings for 5.5in guns plated over. 5.5in spotting tops converted to 4in control positions as a back up to the HACS. Low angle fire-control system fitted for 4in guns with LA fire-control table in each HACP. Sheet anchor and associated gear removed. Degaussing coil fitted around exterior of hull. Navigation rangefinder above compass platform removed.

Refit of 16 January – 15 March 1941 (Rosyth): Type 284 gunnery radar fitted with aerials on aloft director tower. Transmitting aerial for Type 279 air warning radar fitted on main topmast but no receiving aerial fitted (this would have been fitted on a pole mast abaft the fore top) – it is not known if the set itself was fitted but it would in any case have been non-operational without the second aerial. HF/DF office and aerial removed from mainmast. Torpedo lookout removed from foremast. Fore topmast removed (aerial yard re-fitted on bracket at rear of starfish). 50ft steam pinnaces replaced by 35ft fast motor boats.

After her 1929–31 refit *Hood's* deep displacement was found to have increased by 1320 tons in the deep condition but a large part of this increase resulted from the addition, during this refit, of 720 tons to the oil fuel stowage and 130 tons to the fresh water stowage. Removing this 850 tons leaves only 470 tons added to the ship and its equipment since completion. As the majority of the additional liquid was accommodated in the fore part of the ship she trimmed by the bow at deep load which reduced the freeboard forward to 23ft, 2ft 6in lower than when completed, but owing to the altered trim, the stern was actually 6in higher. In the half oil condition, which approximated to an average condition, the trim was almost level and at her standard displacement of 42,600 tons she had much the same trim and freeboard as in her legend condition when completed. The additional oil fuel increased *Hood's* endurance by about 1000nm but, as ships are ideally designed to trim by the stern to produce the best speed performance, her new condition would have lowered slightly her maximum speed and endurance in the half oil to deep condition. It also, of course, increased her wetness forward.

Her refits of 1937–39 were part of a programme to improve the ship's AA defences and in the middle of this period, in January 1939, it was estimated that her deep displacement had risen a further 650 tons although much of this must have been added aft because her trim had improved slightly. Consequently the freeboard at the stern had reduced to 14ft 10in making the freeboard at the break of the forecastle only 9ft. No displacement figures are available for her condition after the 1939 refit but, considering the additions made, it seems likely that she was even deeper at this time. Her 1940 refit was intended to reduce her overloaded condition, largely by removing her secondary armament, and it was estimated in May 1940 that her deep displacement had been lowered to 48,360 tons while the trim was substantially improved although she was still slightly down by the head when deep.

THE PHOTOGRAPHS

1. *Hood* in the final stages of fitting-out at John Brown's yard, Clydebank on 9 January 1920. The wood stowed under the shelter deck is deck planking for the after part of the forecastle deck. The boat stowage is almost complete, only the 45ft Admiral's barge and 35ft motor boat are missing. The position of the inner 50ft steam pinnace and the 45ft barge were exchanged shortly after completion. Note the carley rafts awaiting stowage, the loading platform on the rear of the 4in mounting, the night lifebuoy on the deck edge in the foreground, and the Admiralty pattern kedge anchor stowed against the bulkhead forward of the 5.5in guns.

John Brown

2. *Hood*'s forward superstructure on 20 January 1920.
John Brown

3. *Hood* on 9 January 1920, showing clearly the layout amidships. Workmen are unshipping the midships platform of the accommodation ladder, which is laying on the forecastle deck behind them. Just inboard of that is the tower of the midships officer of quarters' hood, the forward hood being at the shelter deck edge under the 32ft cutter. The armoured doors of the above-water torpedo tubes can be seen abreast the mainmast, and the blanked doors for the pair which were removed during construction, below the accommodation ladder platform. The ship's balsa rafts, which were used when painting the ship's side, are stowed on the boiler room vents abreast the after funnel. Note the two signal lockers inboard of the 5.5in gun on the shelter deck; these were moved to the signal deck before or shortly after completion.
John Brown

4. *Hood* shortly after completion in 1920, with the after concentrating position added under the after searchlight platform and the main topgallant mast housed down.
Abrahams

5. *Hood* in 1921 with a roof added to her raised compass platform and the main topgallant mast raised.
Gieves

2

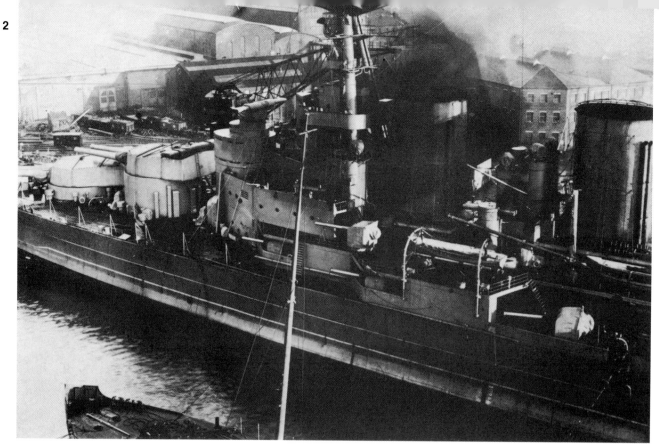

3

6

9

7

8

6. The port side of the shelter deck, looking forward from abaft the mainmast, prior to the world cruise of 1923. On the extreme right is a 4in ready-use locker and above that one of the sighting ports of the night defence position. The pipe running up the mainmast strut is the diesel exhaust from the after diesel dynamo room. Note the DF boom projecting outward from between the funnels, the 4in Mk III mounting on the left and the ladderway to the forecastle deck. *Cribb*

7. The forecastle prior to 1923. In the immediate foreground is the roof of the armoured director hood, showing two periscopes (one circular, one rectangular) and beyond that the 30ft rangefinder and aircraft platforms on the roof of 'B' turret. Note the paravane derrick and ammunition boom prepared for use on the port side and the paravane houses behind the breakwater. *Cribb*

8. *Hood*'s bridge structure and forward turrets viewed from the forecastle between 1921 and 1924. Note the ship's badge on the tompions of the 15in guns and the starboard bower and sheet anchor cable holders in the foreground.
Courtesy R A Burt

9. *Hood* in May 1929 shortly before her first major refit. The aircraft platform on 'B' turret is rigged for flying – the runways, normally stowed on the turret roof, being attached to the 15in gun barrels.
Wright & Logan

10. *Hood* viewed from astern in July 1931. One of her 50ft steam pinnaces is alongside together with a supply vessel.
R Perkins

11. The *Hood*'s quarterdeck in July 1931 showing the aircraft arrangements fitted during her 1929-31 refit. The catapult is folded, the nearest section being the forward end folded back towards the stern, and the aircraft is a Fairey IIIF floatplane. Note the aviation fuel tank, mounted on ramps for jettisoning overboard when going into action, and the stern light and fog lamp on the ensign staff stanchion.
R Perkins

12. The ward room – a large, well furnished but hardly palatial compartment. Note the stove, and its funnel, on the left and the arched opening to the ward room ante room aft. This and the following internal views of *Hood* were taken on 18 July 1932.
Wright & Logan

13. Messes 18, 20, 22, 24 and 26 on the port side of the upper deck amidships immediately abreast the aftermost funnel hatch. This view is taken from inboard looking toward the port forward corner of the seamen's mess. Each table was regarded as a separate mess, two men being assigned in strict daily rotation to collect the food from the galleys (in the containers shown on the tables) and to clean up. As with most armoured ships there was no natural light for the men (except that from hatches when open) as the side armour could not be pierced. The electric lights for two of the messes can be seen adjacent to their numbers against the ship's side, which is almost invisible behind a wall of mess racks and wooden ditty boxes (containing each sailor's personal possessions). In the distance against the athwartship bulkhead can be seen a six compartment kit locker, and hanging from the deckhead, ventilation trunks (with rectangular grills), hooks for stowing the mess tables, and bars for slinging hammocks. Note also the fore and aft longitudinal girders – which in *Hood* supplanted the more usual transverse beams under the midships section of the forecastle deck – and two of their supporting pillars.
Wright and Logan

14

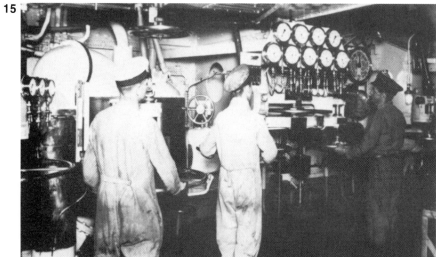

15

16

14. The foremost Mk V above-water torpedo tube on the starboard side with the reload torpedo suspended from the overhead rails above it. Both the end of the tube and the head of the reload project into the protective armoured box against the ship's side. Beyond, another torpedo has been split for servicing, the tail on the left, and the body on the right.
Wright and Logan

15. The control platform of the forward engine room, an obviously posed shot as all the pressure gauges are at zero. The cylindrical object in front of the nearest man is one of the feed water heaters.
Wright and Logan

16. The control platform of the forward engine room looking from port to starboard and showing the main steam and manoeuvring valve control wheels. In the distance the ladder leads to a platform over the forward end of starboard wing low pressure turbine, the spindles for its steam nozzles being just visible. When installed, the turbines were fitted with insulating jackets giving them a smooth cylindrical appearance.
Wright and Logan

17. *Hood* in July 1934 with 0.5in MG mountings added abreast the conning tower, the 5.5in rangefinders removed and the pom-pom director positions at the after end of the foremast starfish. Note the new paravane derrick rigged abreast 'A' turret and the swinging booms for the boats.
R Perkins

18. The *Hood* in Grand Harbour, Malta in June 1937.
Courtesy R A Burt

19. A close up of *Hood*'s superstructure as she leaves Portsmouth on completion of her last prewar refit in August 1939.
Wright and Logan

20 The sick bay looking from amidships into the starboard forward corner, with open doors to the surgeon's examining room, on the extreme left, and to the operating room. Oil lamps as well as electric lights (which are 'on' in this view) are hung from the deckhead as well as the usual ventilation trunks and hammock bars; the pipe is a salt water main. The two pillars support one of the longitudinal girders under the forecastle deck.
Wright and Logan

21. Looking aft from the fore top in 1940, showing all six of the 44in searchlights fitted in 1939, and four of her seven twin 4in mountings.
Courtesy R A Burt

21

22. *Hood*'s bridge structure and forward turrets in April 1941 with the aerials of her Type 284 gunnery radar set fitted to the aloft DCT. Note the UP mounting (covered with canvas) on 'B' turret, the absence of the sheet anchor cable holder, the hydrant for washing down the anchors, with hoses connected (just abaft the bollard in the foreground) and the portable roller just to the right of the canvas cover over the forecastle hatch.
Courtesy R A Burt

23. The *Hood* at Scapa Flow shortly before her loss. The aerial of the partially fitted Type 279 radar is just visible at the head of the mainmast in the original photograph.
Courtesy R A Burt

THE DRAWINGS

A NOTE ON THE DRAWINGS

The ship drawings are based on Admiralty official draughts held by the National Maritime Museum, Greenwich. The general arrangements are drawn to a scale of 1/600 (50ft = 1in), with the details drawn to multiples of that scale wherever possible (ie 1/300, 1/150, 1/75, etc). Scales are included in the headings to the keys where applicable.

A General arrangements

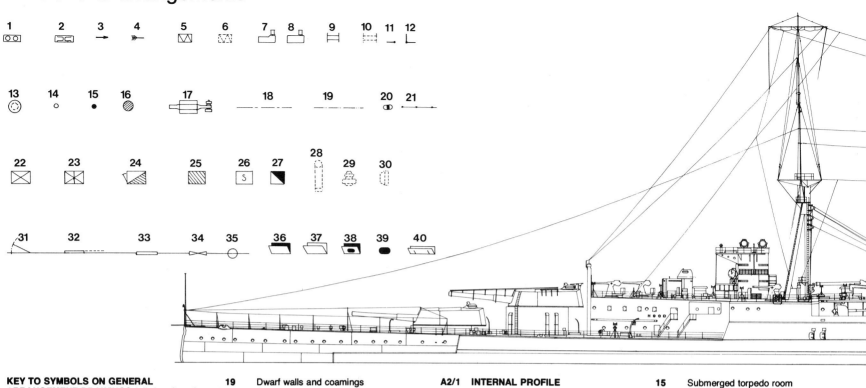

KEY TO SYMBOLS ON GENERAL
ARRANGEMENT DRAWINGS (all drawings in
this section are 1/600 scale)

1	Bollard
2	Fairlead
3	Ladder (up)
4	Ladder (down)
5	Water tank
6	Water tank (over)
7	Variable speed winch
8	Electric winch
9	Hawser reel
10	Hawser reel (over)
11	Awning stanchion
12	Awning stanchion
13	Mushroom top vent
14	Vent (below upper deck only)
15	Pillar
16	Masts, mast struts and derrick posts
17	Magazine cooling machinery
18	Overhead rail

19	Dwarf walls and coamings
20	Scupper
21	Guardrails
22	5.5in ammunition dredger hoist
23	4in ammunition hoist
24	Escape and access trunks
25	Electric lift
26	Air lock
27	Ventilation trunk
28	Ventilation trunk (over)
29	Ventilation fan
30	Ventilation heater
31	Door
32	Sliding door
33	Arched opening
34	Opening (windows, hand-throughs, etc)
35	Side scuttle
36	Hatch
37	Skylight
38	Hatch with escape manhole
39	Manholes, and manhole type hatches
40	Wash deck locker

A2/1 INTERNAL PROFILE

1	Water-tight compartment
2	Fresh water compartment
3	Torpedo head magazine
4	15in shell room
5	Shell bin
6	5.5in magazine
7	5.5in handing room
8	Boiler room
9	Fan compartment
10	5.5in shell room
11	15in transmitting station
12	15in magazine
13	15in handing room
14	Pump room

15	Submerged torpedo room
16	Capstan engine room
17	Boatswain's store
18	Inflammable liquid store
19	Paint store
20	Canvas room
21	Carpenter's store
22	Cable locker
23	Torpedo lift
24	Refridgerating machinery compartment
25	Vegetable room
26	Flour store
27	Motor generator compartment
28	Medical distributing station
29	Main switchboard room
30	Fan room

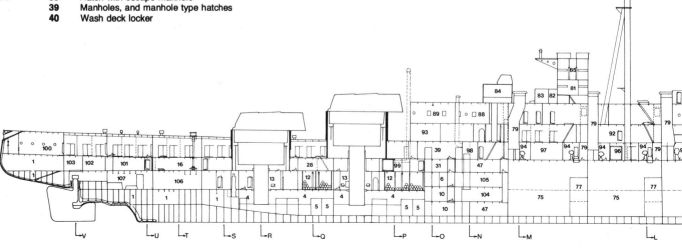

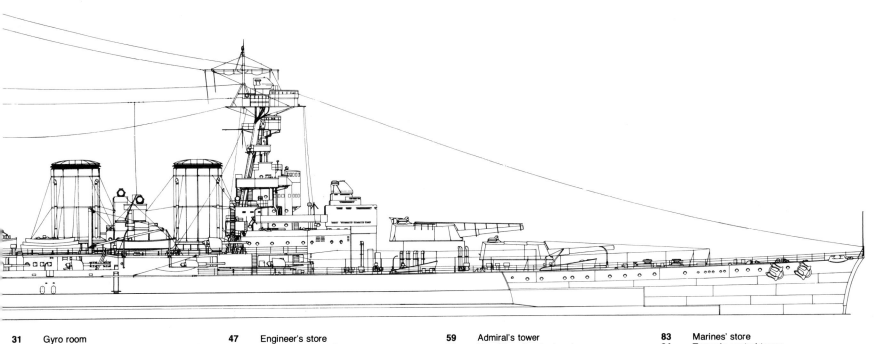

31	Gyro room	47	Engineer's store
32	Torpedo transmitting station	48	Communication tube
33	Lower conning tower	49	Intelligence office
34	Paint store	50	Bakery
35	Torpedo body room	51	Signal distributing office
36	Seamen's mess	52	Watch-keeper's store
37	Gunner's hydraulic gun-gear store	53	Torpedo control tower
38	Searchlight transmitting station	54	Signal house
39	5.5in ammunition working space	55	Admiral's sea cabin
40	Fire brick stowage	56	WC
41	WCs and urinals	57	Upper conning tower
42	Shipwright's working space	58	Admiral's exchange
43	Sick bay		
44	Crew space		
45	Third W/T office		
46	Captain's office		

59	Admiral's tower	83	Marines' store
60	Revolving director hood	84	Torpedo control tower
61	15in gun control tower	85	Searchlight control position
62	Captain's sea cabin	86	Ward room galley
63	Admiral's charthouse	87	Ward room
64	Admiral's signal house	88	Admiral's dining cabin
65	Charthouse	89	Admiral's day cabin
66	Torpedo lookout	90	Ship's scullery
67	15in control top	91	Cooks' mess
68	15in director tower	92	Boat hoist compartment
69	5.5in control top	93	Captain's day cabin
70	Coppersmith's shop	94	Engine room fan compartment
71	Blacksmith's shop	95	Enginesmith's shop
72	W/T office	96	W/T office
73	Ship's galley	97	Central store
74	Cooks' lobby	98	4in ammunition working space
75	Engine room	99	Second W/T office
76	Feed tank	100	Gun room
77	Thrust block recess	101	Admiral's store
78	Disinfector house	102	Gun room store
79	Engine room vent	103	Ward room wine store
80	Secondary battery room	104	4in HA magazine
81	Night defence control position	105	Small arms magazine
82	Oilskin room	106	Carpenter's heavy store
		107	Steering compartment

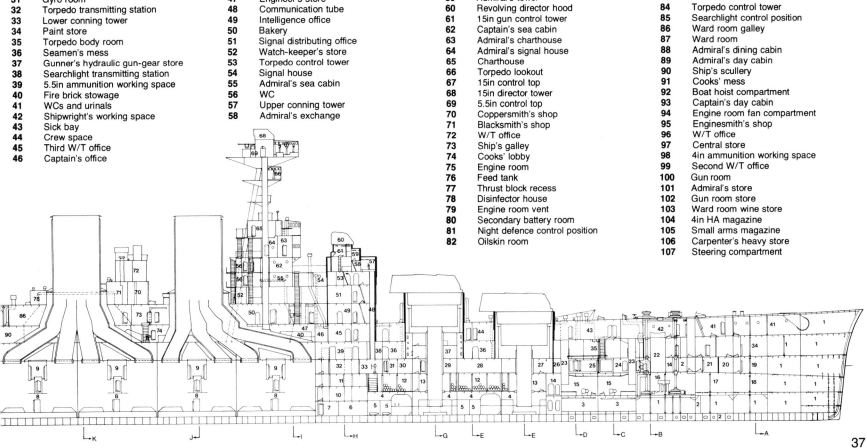

A General arrangements

A2/2 SECTIONS

a Forecastle deck
b Upper deck
c Main deck
d Lower deck
e Platform deck
f Hold
g Shelter deck

1 Engine room
2 Boiler room
3 Oil fuel filling compartment
4 15in handing room
5 15in magazine
6 15in shell room
7 Oil fuel
8 Buoyancy space
9 Water-tight compartment
10 Seamen's heads
11 Paint room
12 Paint store
13 Inflammable liquid store
14 Shipwright's working space
15 Cable locker
16 Capstan engine room
17 Surgeon's examining room
18 Operating room
19 Torpedo body room
20 Refrigerating machinery room

21 Submerged torpedo room
22 Illuminating gear store
23 Drain tank
24 Torpedo head magazine
25 Meat room
26 Sick bay
27 Paravane house
28 Electrical store
29 'A' barbette
30 Isolation ward
31 Awning room
32 Gunner's store
33 POs' mess
34 POs' pantry
35 Seamen's mess
36 CO_2 machinery compartment
37 'B' barbette
38 Provision room
39 Lubricating oil tank
40 Gunner's hydraulic gun-gear store

41 Switchboard room
42 Revolving hood
43 15in gun control tower
44 5.5in gun control tower
45 Torpedo control tower
46 Signal distributing office
47 Watch officer's cabin
48 Intelligence office
49 Gyro adjusting space and electricians' workshop
50 Third W/T office
51 Issue room
52 5.5in ammunition working space
53 5.5in transmitting station
54 Motor generator compartment
55 15in transmitting station
56 Dynamo room
57 5.5in shell room
58 5.5in magazine
59 Hydraulic engine room

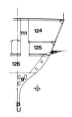
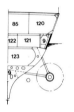
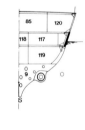

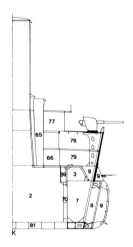
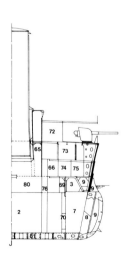
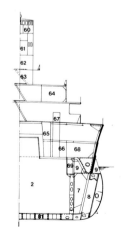

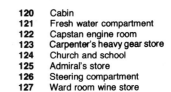

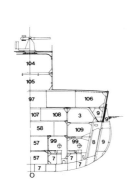
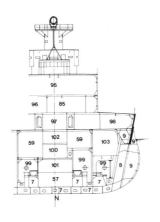
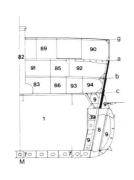
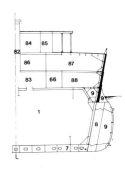

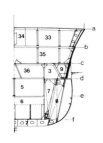
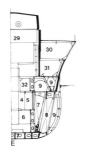
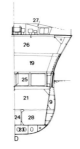
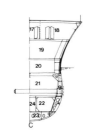

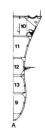

A General arrangements

A3/1 SHELTER DECK

1 Signal distributing office
2 Lobby
3 Boiler room vent
4 Engine room vent
5 Reading room
6 W/T aerial trunk
7 Library
8 Wire rope bin
9 Watch-keeper's store
10 Watch officer's cabin
11 Chaplain's cabin
12 Bakery funnel
13 Navigating officer's cabin
14 Signal officer's cabin
15 Signal house
16 5.5in gun mounting, port and starboard
17 Signal tube
18 5.5in officer of quarters' hood, port and starboard
19 Coppersmith's shop
20 Disinfector house
21 Blacksmith's shop
22 Secondary battery room
23 Night defence control position
24 Oilskin room
25 Marines' store
26 Night lifebuoy
27 4in HA gun mounting, port and starboard
28 4in ready-use ammunition lockers, port and starboard
29 40ft derrick (stowed)
30 40ft derrick and derrick post
31 Main W/T aerial screen
32 Torpedo control tower

A3/2 ADMIRAL'S SIGNAL PLATFORM

1 Torpedo control tower
2 Radio telephone aerial trunk
3 W/T aerial trunk
4 Signal house
5 Admiral's sea cabin
6 Boiler room vent
7 Sounding machine, port and starboard
8 3pdr saluting guns, port and starboard
9 WC
10 Signal lockers, port and starboard
11 Admiral's bathroom.
12 Plumbers' workshop

A3/3 CONNING TOWER PLATFORM

1 Upper conning tower
2 Admiral's exchange
3 5.5in control tower, port and starboard
4 15in control
5 Chief of Staff's sea cabin
6 Captain's sea cabin
7 Submarine lookout, port and starboard
8 WC
9 5.5in director tower, port and starboard
10 Bow light, port and starboard
11 W/T aerial trunk

A3/4 UPPER CONNING TOWER

1 Upper conning tower
2 Admiral's tower
3 5.5in control tower
4 15in control

A3/5 CONNING TOWER ROOF AND REVOLVING HOOD

A3/6 ADMIRAL'S BRIDGE

1 Admiral's charthouse
2 Admiral's signal house
3 5.5in control tower
4 24in signalling searchlight, port and starboard

A3/7 FORE BRIDGE

1 Compass platform
2 Charthouse
3 W/T office
4 Admiral's plotting office
5 Voice pipe cabinet

A3/8 SEARCHLIGHT CONTROL PLATFORM AND COMPASS PLATFORM ROOF

A3/9 FOREMAST SEARCHLIGHT PLATFORM

A3/10 TORPEDO LOOKOUT PLATFORM

A3/11 FOREMAST STARFISH

A3/12 CONTROL TOP

1 15in control top
2 5.5in control top, port and starboard
3 15in director tower
4 9ft rangefinder, port and starboard

A3/13 ROOF OF CONTROL TOP AND 15in DIRECTOR

A3/14 AFTER SEARCHLIGHT CONTROL PLATFORM

1 Searchlight manipulating position
2 Petrol locker, port and starboard
3 Carley raft
4 Range dial, port and starboard

A3/15 AFTER SEARCHLIGHT PLATFORM

A3/16 MIDSHIPS SEARCHLIGHT CONTROL PLATFORM

1 W/T office
2 Searchlight manipulating position
3 15ft rangefinder, port and starboard

A3/17 MIDSHIPS SEARCHLIGHT PLATFORM

A3/18 FORECASTLE DECK

1 5.5in gun mountings, port and starboard
2 5.5in gun support
3 Paravane house, port and starboard
4 Torpedo embarkation hatch
5 Intelligence office
6 Gyro adjusting space
7 Electrical artificers' daylight workshop
8 Boiler room vent
9 Engine room vent
10 Bread cooling room
11 W/T trunks
12 Bakery
13 Gymnastic gear store
14 Boatswains ready-use store
15 Gunner's ready-use store
16 Paravane gear store
17 Drying room
18 Cooks' kitchen
19 Ship's galley
20 Food lift
21 Air compressor compartment (oil fuel tank over)
22 Gun room kitchen
23 Gun room galley
24 WOs' galley
25 Gun crews' urinal
26 5.5in officer of quarters position
27 Potato store
28 Ready-use oilskin store
29 Funnel hatch
30 Coal scuttle
31 Coal bunker
32 Signal tube, port and starboard
33 Ward room galley
34 Admiral's galley
35 Beef screen
36 Admiral's kitchen
37 Ward room kitchen
38 Officers' drying room
39 Ward room
40 Ward room pantry
41 Ward room ante-room
42 Flag lieutenant's cabin
43 Surgeon commander's cabin
44 Engineer commander's cabin
45 Secretary's clerk's office
46 Secretary's cabin
47 Chief of Staff's bathroom
48 Chief of Staff's sleeping cabin
49 Chief of Staff's day cabin
50 Admiral's spare cabin
51 Admiral's bathroom
52 Admiral's pantry
53 Admiral's lobby
54 Admiral's sleeping cabin
55 Admiral's dining cabin
56 Admiral's day cabin
57 Commander's cabin
58 Gunnery officer's cabin
59 Gunner's ready-use store
60 Billiards room
61 Paymaster commander's cabin
62 Squadron commander's cabin
63 Commissioned officers' WCs and urinals
64 Subordinate officers' WCs and urinals
65 Communication tube

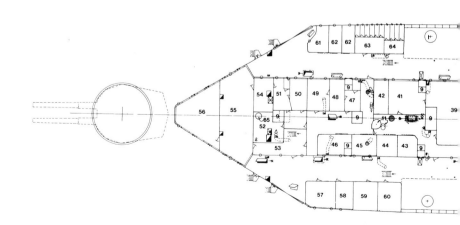

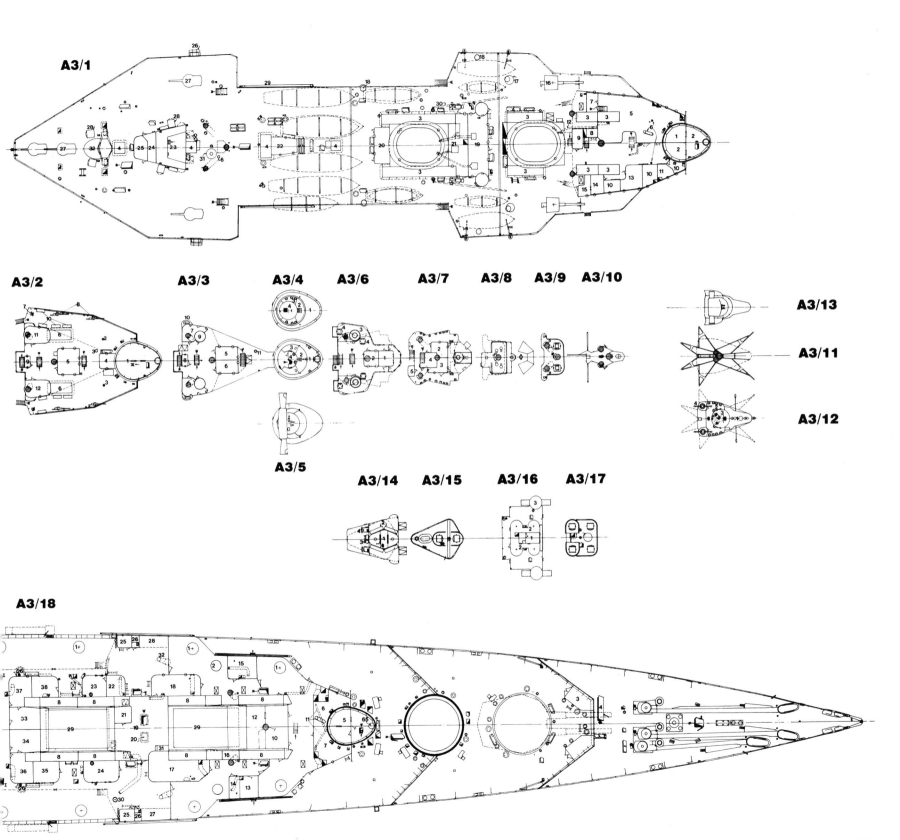

A3/1

A3/2 A3/3 A3/4 A3/6 A3/7 A3/8 A3/9 A3/10 A3/13

A3/11

A3/12

A3/5

A3/14 A3/15 A3/16 A3/17

A3/18

A General arrangements

A3/19

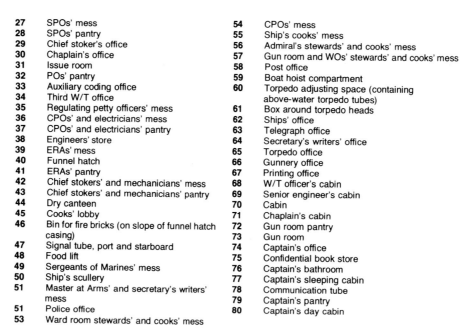

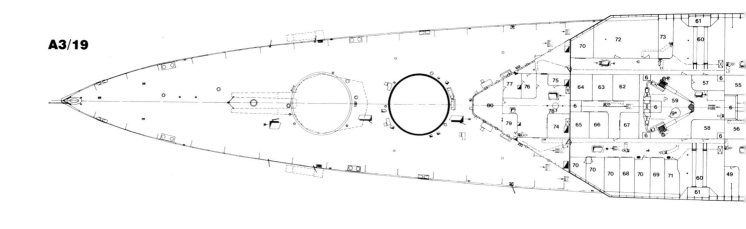

A3/20

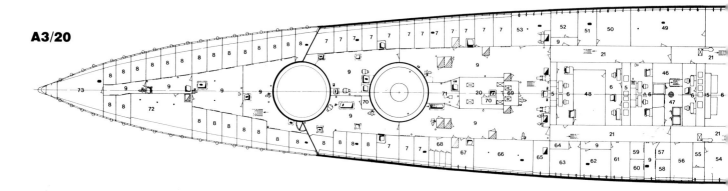

A3/20 MAIN DECK

1	Water-tight compartment	27	Stokers' dressing room	54	Electrical articifers' workshop
2	Seamen's mess	28	Seamen's washplace	55	Electrical articifers' ready-use store
3	Funnel hatch	29	Boys' washplace	56	Engineers' office
4	Boiler room vent	30	Signal station	57	Captain's steward's cabin
5	Engine room vent	31	SPOs' washplace	58	Ward room steward's cabin
6	Engine room vent fan compartment	32	SPOs' dressing room	59	Admiral's steward's cabin
7	Warrant officer's cabin (single and double)	33	Stokers' urinals	60	Admiral's cook's cabin
8	Officer's cabin	34	Chief stokers' and mechanics' washplace	61	Engineers' ready-use store
9	Lobby	35	Chief stokers' and mechanics' dressing room	62	W/T store
10	Paint room			63	Commissioned officers' bathroom
11	Clothing issue room	36	ERAs' washplace	64	Commander's bathroom
12	Lamp room	37	ERAs' dressing room	65	WOs' pantry
13	Cable locker	38	Coal bunker	66	WOs' mess
14	Torpedo body lift	39	Canteen store	67	WOs' bathroom
15	Torpedo body room	40	Cells	68	WOs' urinals and WCs
16	Diving gear store	41	Sentry walk	69	4in ammunition working space
17	Awning room	42	Band instrument room	70	Magazine flooding cabinet
18	Gunner's hydraulic gun-gear store	43	Armourer's workshop	71	W/T trunk
19	Searchlight transmitting station	44	Enginesmiths' shop	72	Church
20	5.5in ammunition working space	45	Auxiliary spare gear store	73	Midshipman's study
21	Ammunition passage	46	Coding office		
22	Stokers' dressing room	47	W/T office		
23	Stokers' washplace	48	Central store		
24	POs' washplace	49	Engineers' workshop		
25	CPOs' washplace	50	Subordinate officers' bathroom		
26	Marines' washplace	51	Subordinate officers' dressing room		
		52	Secondary light store		
		53	Midshipmen's chest room		

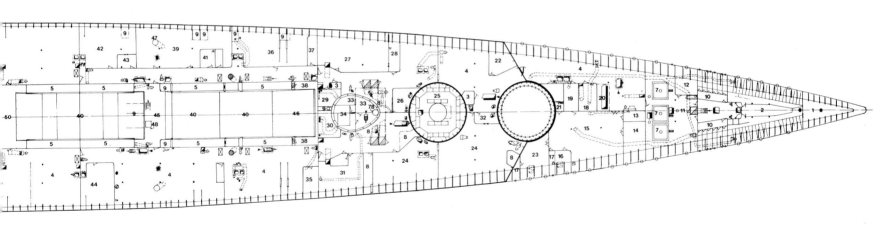

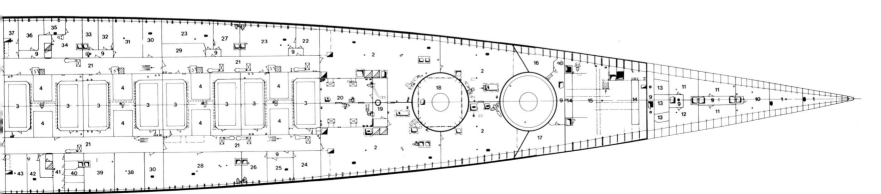

A General arrangements

A3/21

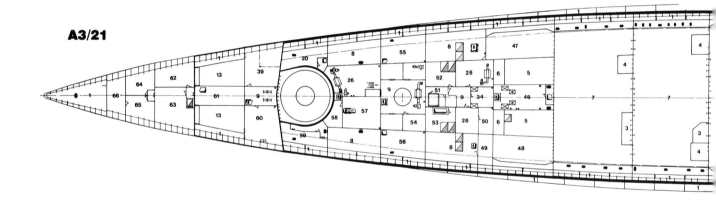

A3/22

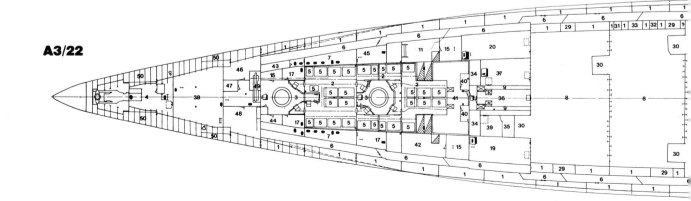

A3/22 PLATFORM DECK

1	Water-tight compartment	25	'B' boiler room
2	15in magazine	26	'X' boiler room
3	15in handing room	27	'Y' boiler room
4	Steering compartment	28	Reciprocating dynamo room
5	15in cordite cases	29	Turbine lubricating oil
6	Buoyancy space	30	Thrust block recess
7	Oil fuel	31	Rape seed oil
8	Engine room	32	Settling tank
9	Air space	33	Mineral oil
10	Inflammable liquid store	34	Hydraulic tank
11	Boatswain's store	35	50 ton pump platform
12	Capstan engine room	36	Small arms magazine
13	Submerged torpedo room	37	Hydraulic engine room
14	Flour store	38	Carpenter's heavy gear store
15	Pump compartment	39	Shaft passage
16	Provision room	40	5.5in handing room
17	Gunner's store	41	5.5in magazine
18	Engineers' store	42	Shipwright's store
19	Turbo-generator compartment	43	Secondary lighting store
20	Diesel dynamo room	44	Gunsight store
21	15in transmitting station	45	Paymaster's store
22	Blank and saluting magazine	46	Marines' store
23	Silent cabinet	47	Dry guncotton magazine
24	'A' boiler room	48	Spirit room
		49	Steering gear – drive from engine room
		50	Palm compartment

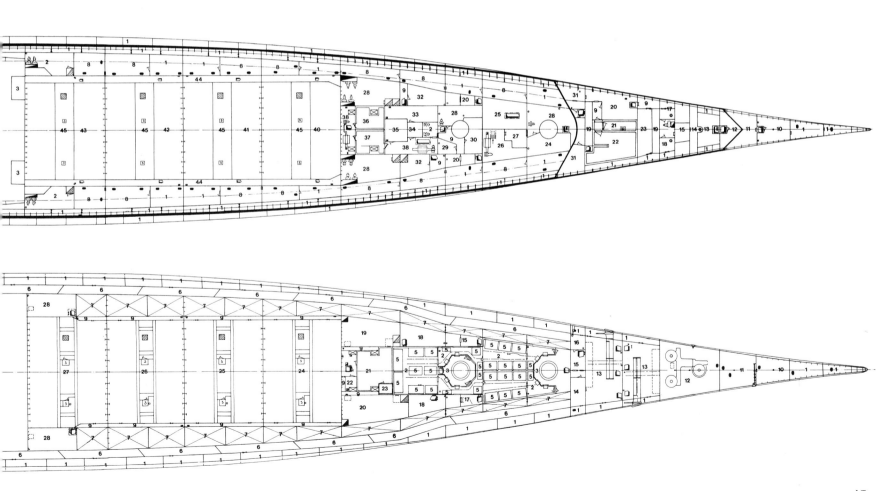

A General arrangements

A3/23 LOWER PLATFORMS

1	5.5in shell room
2	Air space
3	Hand-up
4	4in HA magazine

A3/24 HOLD

1	Water-tight compartment
2	15in shell room
3	Provision room
4	Buoyancy space
5	Air space
6	Shell bins
7	Oil fuel
8	Engine room
9	Air space
10	Torpedo head magazine
11	Mining store
12	Illuminating gear store
13	Torpedo gunner's store
14	Electrical store
15	Gunner's store
16	Engineers' store
17	Hydraulic engine room
18	Hydraulic tank
19	Fresh water tank
20	Drain tank
21	'A' boiler room
22	'B' boiler room
23	'X' boiler room
24	'Y' boiler room
25	5.5in handing room
26	5.5in magazine
27	Feed tank
28	Thrust block recess
29	Central store
30	Shaft passage
31	5.5in shell room

A3/25 DOUBLE BOTTOM

1	Fresh water tank
2	Buoyancy space
3	Oil fuel (including additional tanks fitted 1929-31)
4	Reserve feed water
5	Overflow feed water

A3/23

A3/24

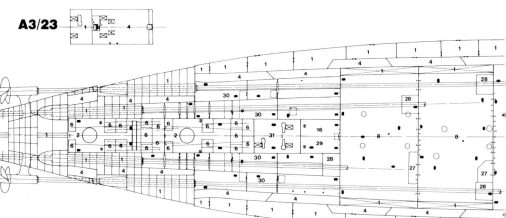

A3/25

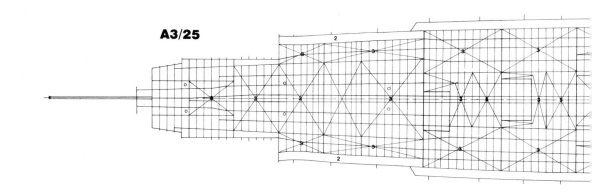

A3/23

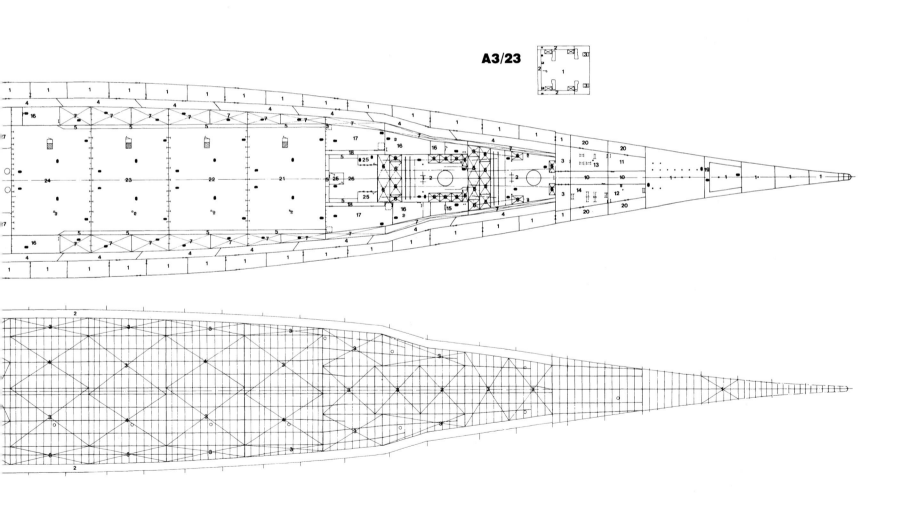

A General arrangements

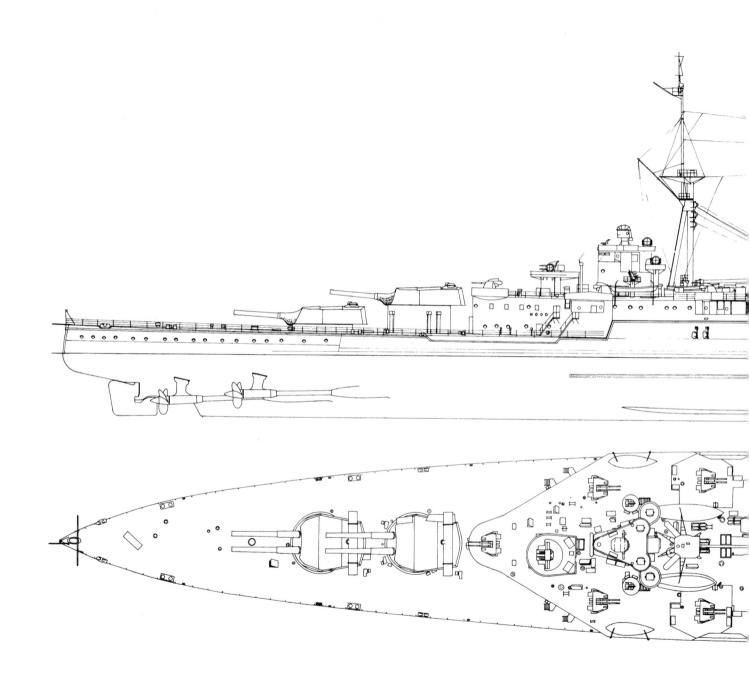

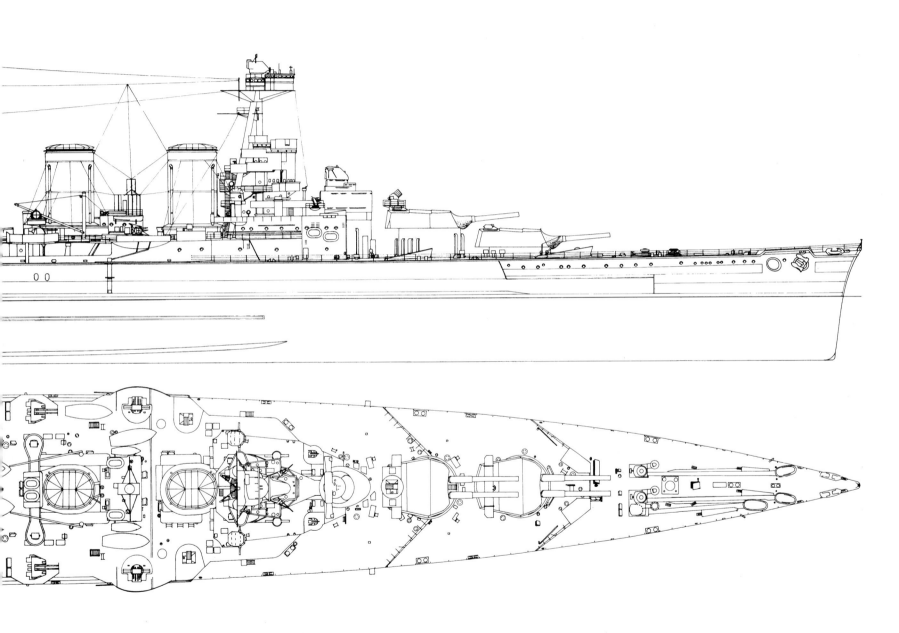

49

B Hull construction

B1 STEEL SECTIONS EMPLOYED IN SHIP CONSTRUCTION

1. Angle bar
2. Tee bar
3. Zed bar
4. Channel bar
5. 'I' (or 'H') bar
6. Angle bulb
7. Tee bulb
8. Built-up 'I' girder

B1

B2 STEEL PLATE RIVETED JOINTS
(note: caulking arrowed)

1. Lap joint (double riveted)
2. Single strapped joint (double riveted)
3. Joggled lap joint (treble riveted)
4. Double strapped joint (single riveted)
5. Double strapped tee bulb (also employed as single strapped, and on angle bulb)
6. Angle strapped joint between longitudinal girder and transverse beam
7. Angle bar joint

B2

B3 TYPES OF TRANSVERSE FRAME

1. Lightened plate frame
2. Water-tight (or oil-tight) frame
3. Bracket frame

B4 TYPES OF LONGITUDINALS AND STRINGERS

A. Vertical keel outside double bottom
B. Water-tight longitudinal
C. Non water-tight longitudinal
D. Oil-tight longitudinal
E. Longitudinal over docking keel
F. Stringer, fore and aft
G. Stringer in bulge structure

1. Limber holes
2. Lightening hole
3. Drain hole
4. Butt strap
5. Lap joint
6. Liner
7. Angle connection to water-tight frame
8. Angle connection to oil-tight frame
9. Angle connection to bracket frame
10. Angle strap
11. Air escape
12. Zed frame
13. Channel frame
14. Intercostal angle bar
15. Continuous angle bar
16. Stringer plate

B3

B5 BOX KEEL (amidships)

1. 4in x 4in angle bar
2. Double strap, over joint
3. ⅝in inner bottom plate
4. 1in inner flat keel plate
5. ⅝in vertical keel
6. 1in outer flat keel plate
7. Angle bar connections

B6 SECTION OF DOUBLE BOTTOM
(showing change from box keel to single keel forward and aft)

1. Box keel
2. Compensating liner
3. Double strap, over joint
4. Single keel
5. Water-tight frame
6. Bracket frames
7. First longitudinal
8. Lightened plate frames
9. Lap joint

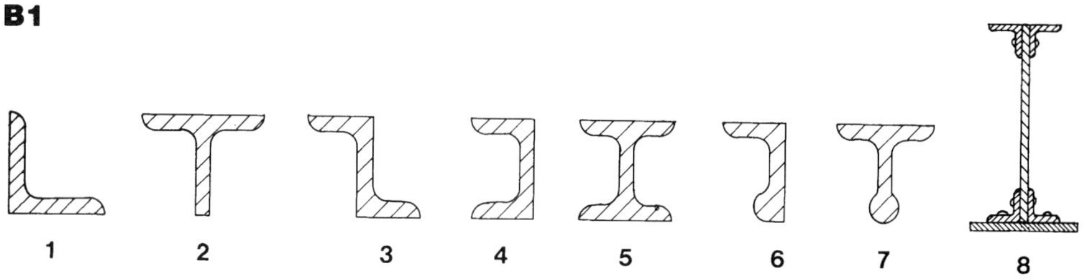

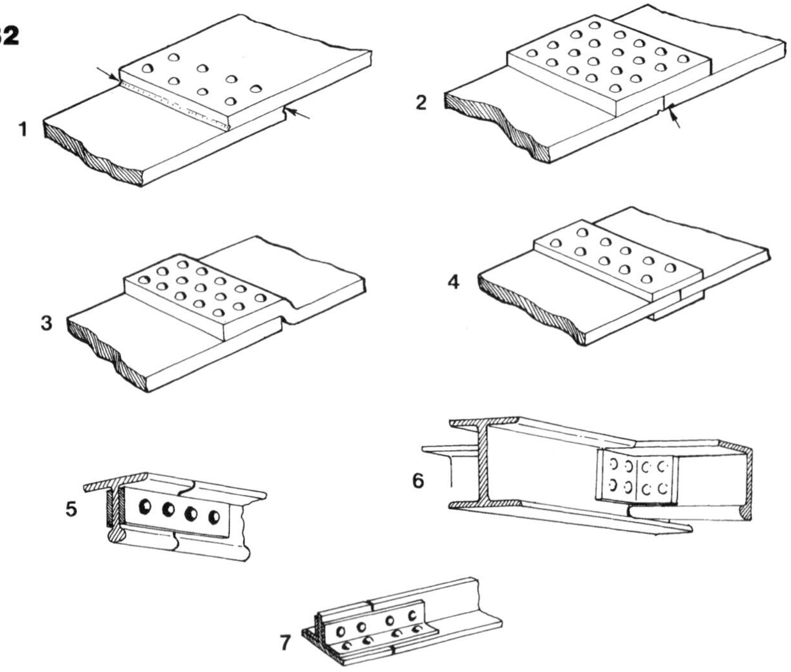

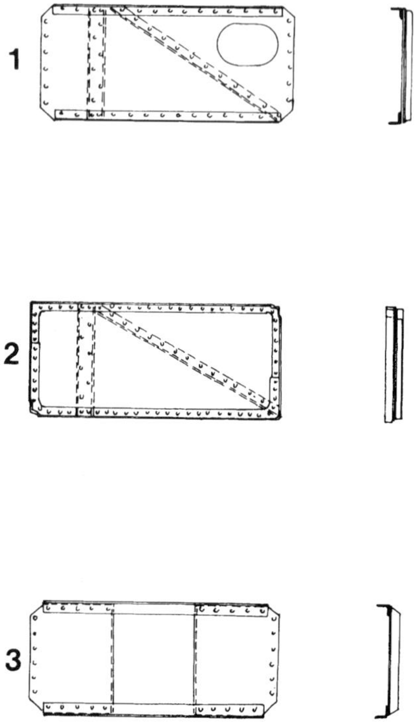

B4

A

B

C

D

E

F

G

B5

B6

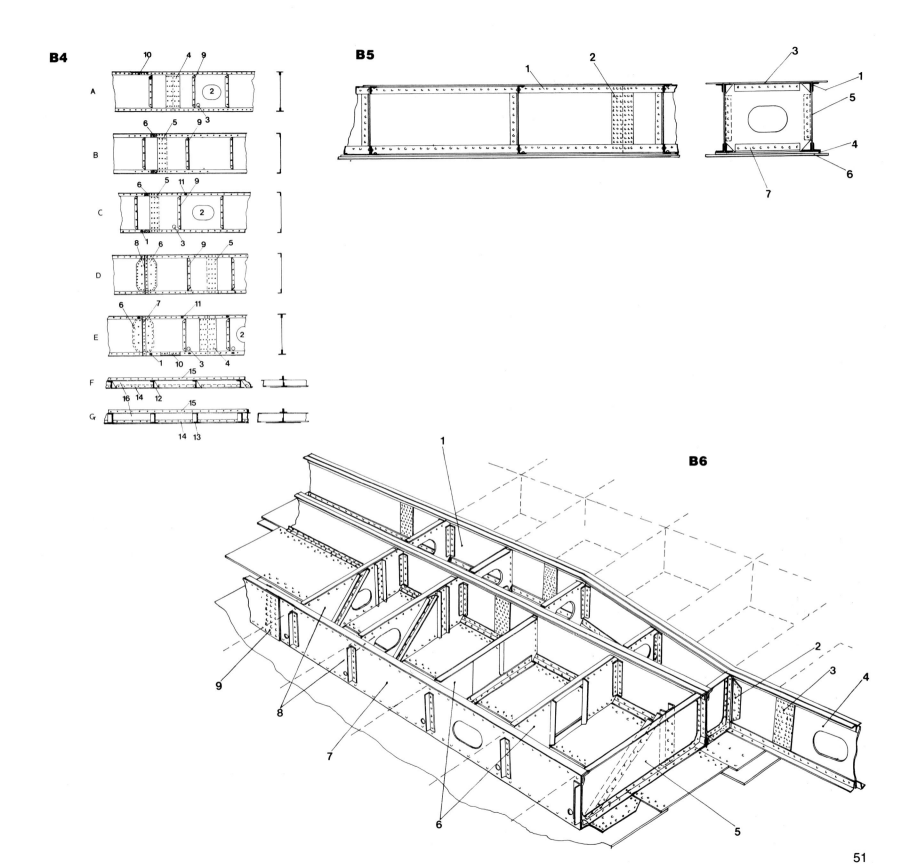

B Hull construction

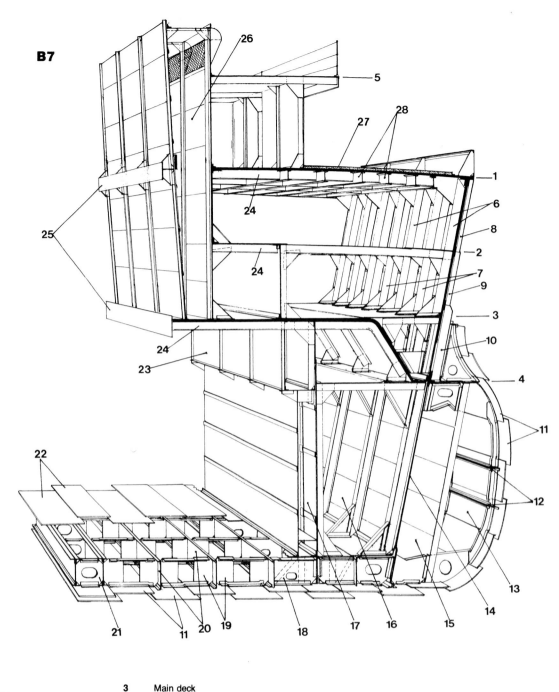

B7

B7 MIDSHIPS HULL STRUCTURE

1	Forecastle deck
2	Upper deck
3	Main deck (protective deck)
4	Lower deck
5	Shelter deck
6	Frames
7	Intermediate frames (behind armour only)
8	5in armour
9	7in armour
10	12in armour
11	Outer bottom plating
12	Longitudinal stringers
13	Water-tight bulge compartment
14	Torpedo bulkhead
15	Buoyancy space (filled with tubes – not shown)
16	Oil-fuel compartment
17	Air space
18	Lightened plate frame
19	Bracket frame
20	Longitudinal frames
21	Box keel
22	Inner bottom plating
23	Ammunition passage
24	Beams
25	Funnel hatch coamings
26	Boiler room vent
27	Wood deck planking
28	Longitudinal beams

B8 FORWARD HULL STRUCTURE

1	Forecastle deck
2	Upper deck
3	Main deck
4	Side plating
5	Lower deck
6	Platform deck
7	Hold
8	Side stringer
9	Frame brackets
10	Side stringer
11	Boundary angle to deck
12	Longitudinal
13	Inner flat keel plate
14	Outer flat keel plate
15	Pillar
16	Zed bar frames
17	deck beams
18	Deck planking
19	Longitudinal girder
20	Vertical keel plate

B9/1 BOW STRUCTURE

1	Contour plate	16	Vertical keel	3	Main deck
2	Stem casting	17	Frames of 'zed' bar	4	Lower deck
3	Keel plates	18	Bulkhead	5	Platform deck
4	Web frames	19	Longitudinal stringers	6	Breast hook
5	Deep beams	20	Outer bottom plating	7	Vertical keel
6	Fairleads	21	Sheer strake	8	Stem casting
7	Hawsepipes	22	Boundary angles	9	Contour plate
8	Forecastle deck	23	Transverse beams of angle bulb	10	Paravane fairlead
9	Upper deck	24	Longitudinal 'I' girder beams	11	Inner flat keel
10	Main deck			12	Outer flat keel
11	Lower deck	**B9/2**	**ARRANGEMENT OF STEM (1/150 scale, except sections which are 1/75)**	13	Outer bottom plating
12	Platform deck			14	Lug
13	Hold flat	1	Forecastle deck	15	Boundary angle
14	Breasthook	2	Upper deck		
15	Floor plate frame				

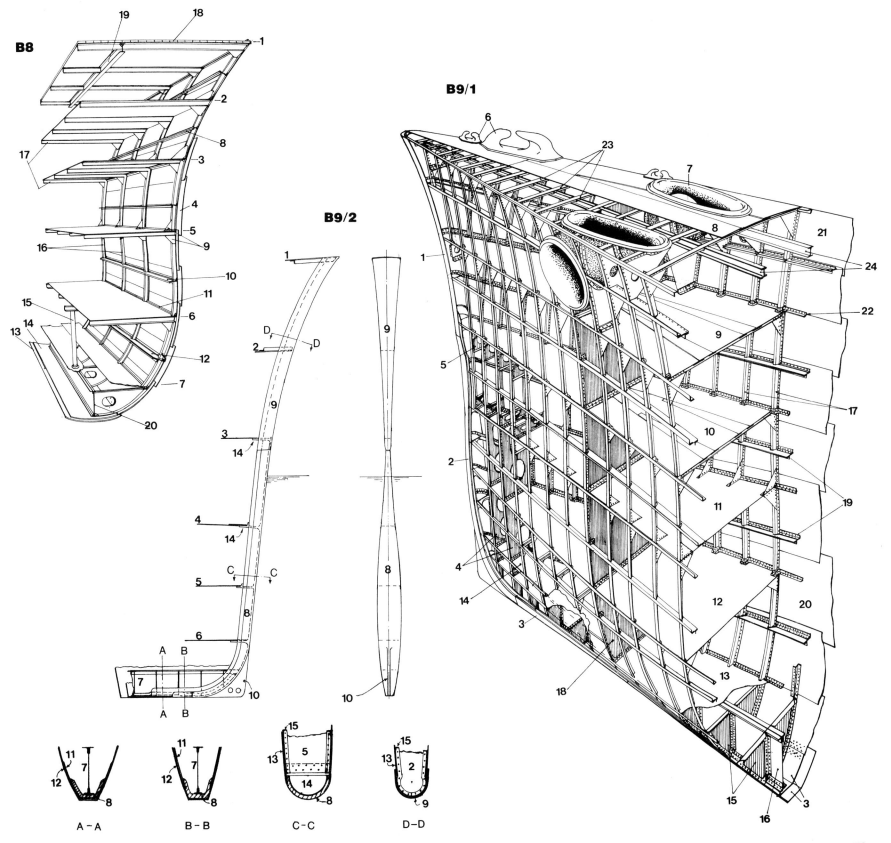

B8

B9/1

B9/2

A – A   B – B   C – C   D – D

53

B Hull construction

B10/1

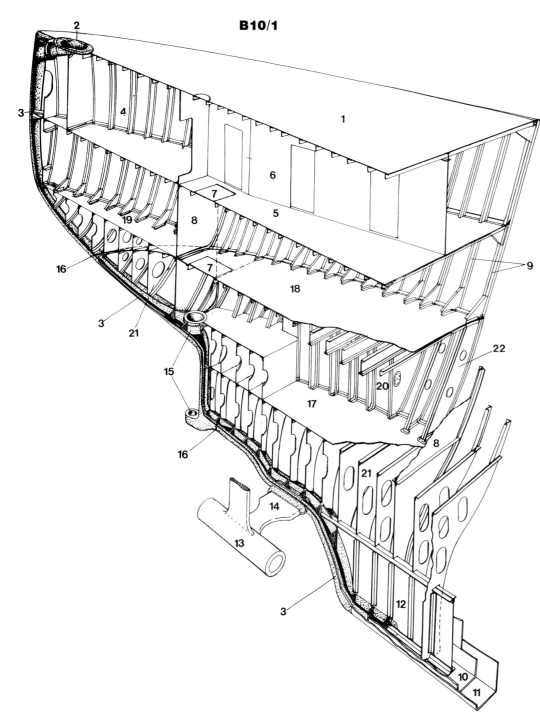

B10/1 STERN STRUCTURE

1	Quarterdeck
2	Hawsepipe
3	Stern castings
4	Midshipmen's study
5	Lobby (main deck)
6	Cabins
7	Portable plate (for lifting rudder)
8	Water-tight bulkhead
9	Zed bar frames
10	Inner flat keel
11	Outer flat keel
12	Vertical keel
13	Starboard inner shaft 'A' bracket
14	Palm
15	Rudder bearings
16	Scarph
17	Steering compartment (platform deck)
18	Store rooms (lower deck)
19	Water-tight compartment
20	Palm compartment
21	Floor plate frames
22	Web frames

B10/2 DETAILS OF STERN CASTINGS
(1/150 scale, except sections A-A and D-D which are 1/75)

1	Upper deck
2	Main deck
3	Hawsepipe (lower section–formed in casting)
4	Lug on casting for connection of deck plating
5	Land for connection of side plating
6	Stern castings
7	Centre-line web on casting
8	Outer bottom plating
9	Water-tight bulkheads
10	Scarph (also provides lug for connection of protective deck)
11	Portable plate for access to rudder crosshead
12	Lower (protective) deck
13	Frame
14	Webs on casting for connection of frames
15	Scarph between forward and middle castings
16	Upper rudder bearing
17	Lower rudder bearing
18	Hardened steel pintle
19	Lower palms of after 'A' bracket scarphed and riveted to casting rabbet
20	Flat keel plates
21	Vertical keel plate
22	Platform deck
23	Inner flat keel
24	Outer flat keel

B11/1 OUTER BOTTOM PLATING AT ENDS
(typical arrangement. 1/150 scale)

1	Longitudinals
2	Vertical keel
3	Inner keel plate
4	Outer keel plate
5	Garboard strake
6	Frame lines
7	Stealers (strakes arranged to double width)

B10/2

A - A

B - B

C - C

D - D

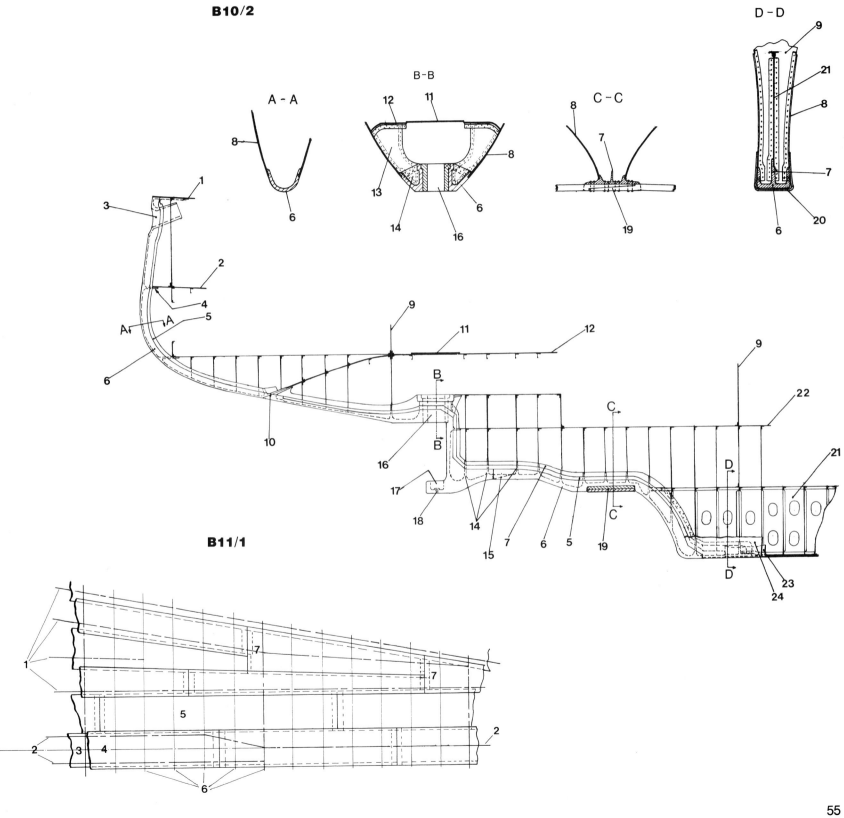

B11/1

B Hull construction

B11/2 OUTER BOTTOM PLATING AMIDSHIPS
(1/150 scale. Note: all strakes of flat bottom amidships, including inner and outer keel and docking keel plates were of 1in thickness)

1 First Longitudinal
2 Second longitudinal
3 Third longitudinal
4 Fourth longitudinal (docking keel)
5 Fifth longitudinal
6 Torpedo bulkhead
7 Vertical keels
8 Inner keel plate
9 Outer keel plate
10 Garboard strake (sunk)
11 Strakes (lettered A, B, C from garboard outwards)
12 Frames
13 Water- and/or oil-tight frames below water-tight bulkheads
14 Triple riveted butt straps joining plate ends
15 Liners under water-/oil-tight frames

B11/3 INNER BOTTOM PLATING ('Y' boiler room. 1/150 scale)

1 First longitudinal
2 Second longitudinal
3 Third longitudinal
4 Fourth longitudinal (bulkhead to oil fuel compartment)
5 Fifth longitudinal
6 Torpedo bulkhead (1½in thick, ¾in + ¾in)
7 Vertical keels
8 Upper keel plate
9 Inner bottom plating
10 Lap joints (double riveted)
11 Frames
12 Main bulkhead between 'X' and 'Y' boiler rooms
13 Main bulkhead between 'Y' boiler room and forward engine room
14 Air space
15 Oil fuel compartment
16 Engineer's store
17 Access manholes to double bottom
18 Boundary angles
19 'I' bar frames (12in x 6in x 6in) to torpedo bulkhead
20 Bulkhead stiffening bars
21 Compensating liners

B12/1 LAPPED DECK PLATING (1/150 scale)

1 Beams
2 Butt straps (under)
3 Plating overlapped and riveted

B12/2 FLUSH DECK PLATING (1/150 scale)

1 Beams
2 Butt straps (under)
3 Edge strips (under)

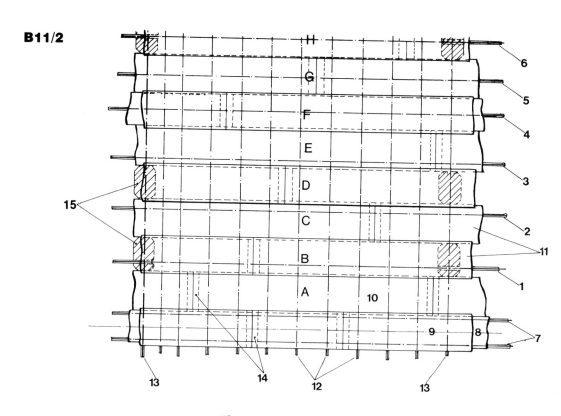

B11/2

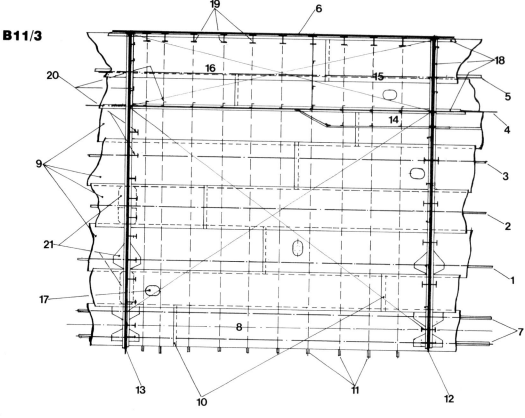

B11/3

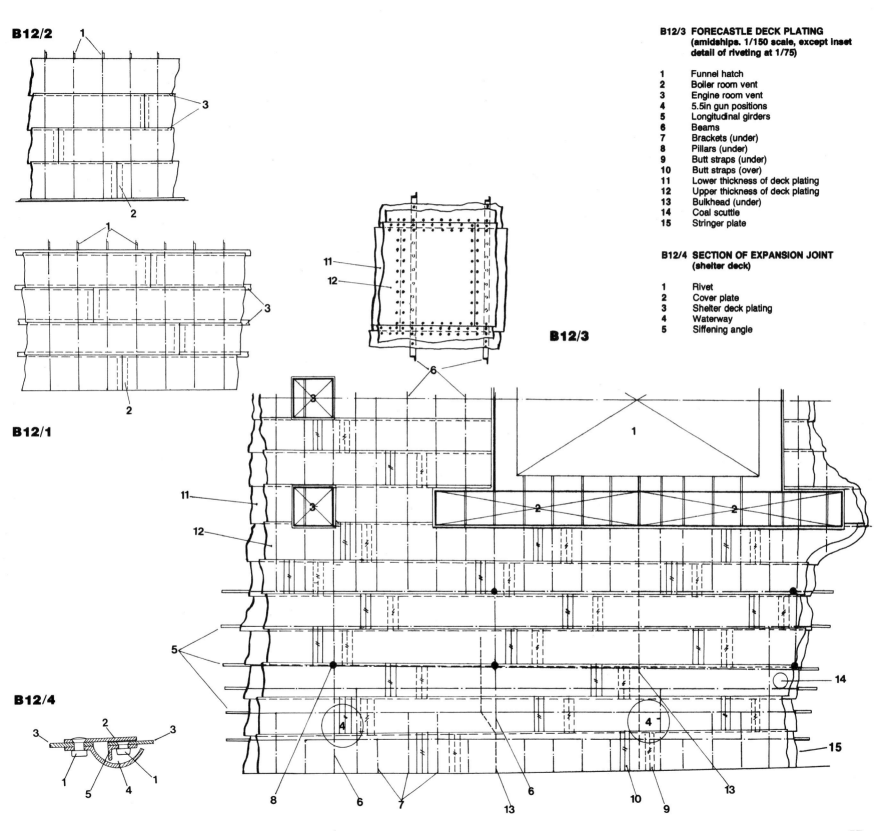

B12/2

B12/1

B12/4

B12/3

57

B Hull construction

B12/5 FORECASTLE DECK, PLATING AT STEM (inset shows typical arrangement of stealer plate joint – the arrangement of stealers in the outer bottom was similar. The arrangement of deck plating, at ends, on the other decks was similar except that these were butt riveted, to be flush, and not lap riveted)

1   Stringer plate
2   Openings for hawsepipes
3   Pillar (under)
4   Longitudinal girders (under)
5   Beams
6   Plate cut away to allow raised plate to pass under stiffening piece
7   Stringer plate

B12/6 DECK BEAMS AND BRACKETS

1   Typical form above forecastle deck level
2   Typical form behind armour on main deck
3   Typical form behind armour on upper deck
4   Modified form of (3) with bracket lengthened to reach second longitudinal girder
5   Typical form outside armour and on internal bulkhead etc
6   Connection of half beam to barbette armour (bolted)
7   Connection of half beam to hatch coaming

a   Angle bulb deck beam
b   Zed bar or angle bar frame
c   Angle connection between bulkhead and deck
d   Bracket (mostly constructed of $\frac{1}{2}$in thick plate)
e   Angle bulb deck beam (9in x 3$\frac{1}{2}$in x $\frac{1}{2}$in thick)
f   Channel bar frame (9in x 3$\frac{1}{2}$in x 3$\frac{1}{2}$in x $\frac{5}{8}$in thick)
g   Longitudinal 'I' bar (12in x 6in x 6in x 1in thick)
h   Angle connection to forecastle deck (8in x 8in x $\frac{7}{8}$in thick)
I   Coaming
j   Angle bar
k   Deck plate
l   Angle strap connection (both sides)
m   Barbette
n   Armour bolts

B13 MAIN WATER-TIGHT BULKHEAD BETWEEN 'X' AND 'Y' BOILER ROOMS (note: arrangement of stiffeners varies from bulkhead to bulkhead. 1/150 scale)

1   'I' girder stiffener
2   Angle bar stiffener
3   Longitudinal bulkhead
4   Brackets
5   Support brackets in double bottom
6   Level of main deck
7   Boundary angle
8   Bulkhead plating joggle lap jointed
9   Liner

B14/1 BODY PLAN (1/150 scale)

A   Line of forecastle deck at side
B   Line of upper deck at side
C   Line of main deck at side
FP   Forward perpendicular
AP   After perpendicular

B14/2 DETAIL OF BILGE KEEL

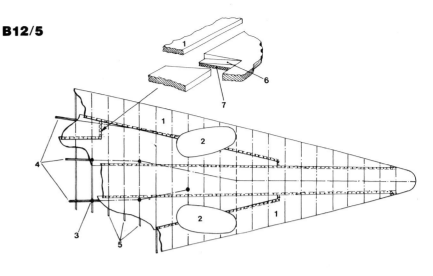

B12/5

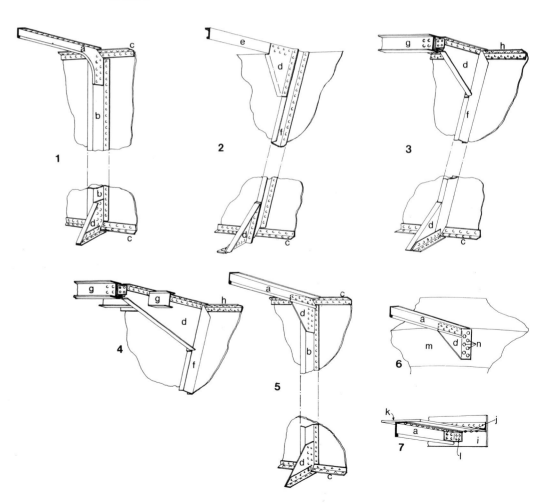

B12/6

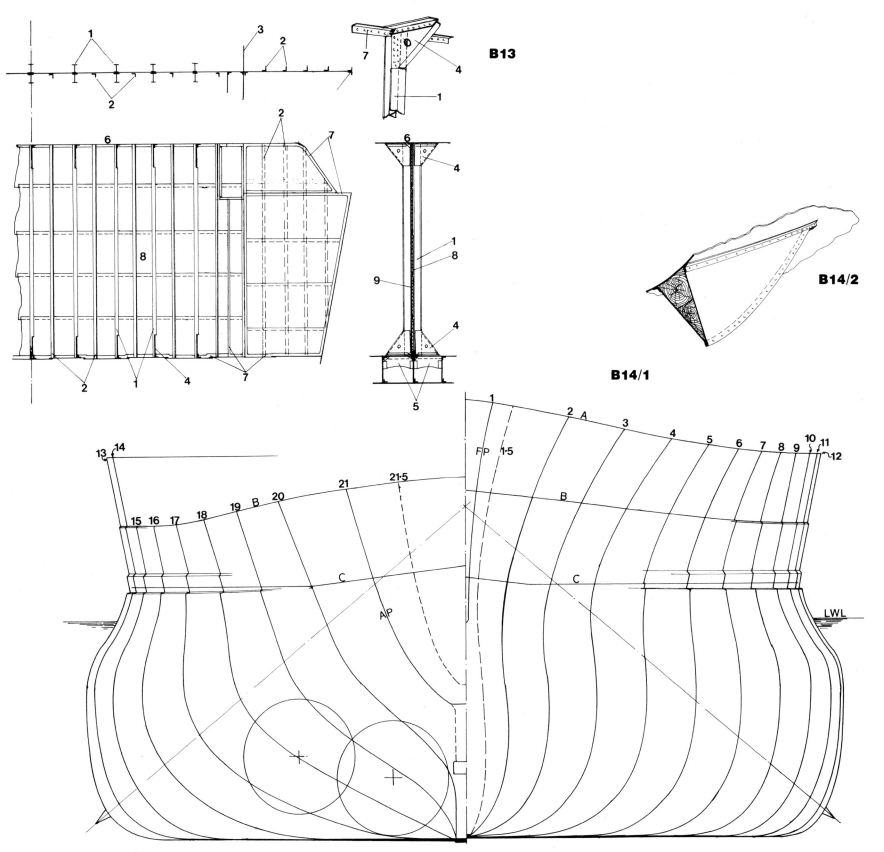

B13

B14/2

B14/1

59

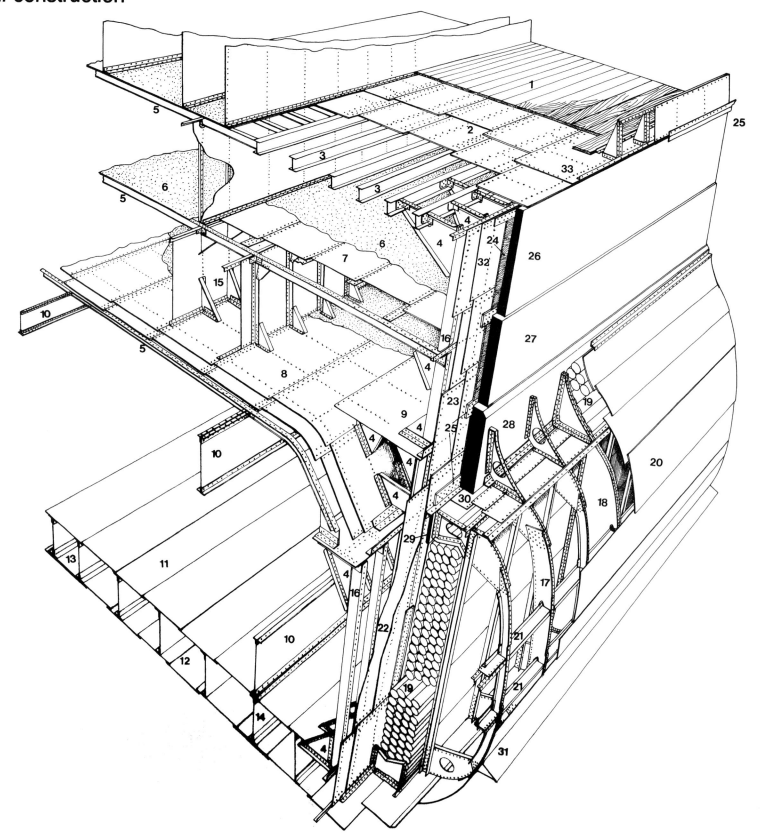

B15   MIDSHIPS STRUCTURE (at forward engine room)

1   Wood deck planking
2   Forecastle deck plating (double thickness)
3   Longitudinal 'I' girders
4   Brackets
5   Transverse beams
6   Corticene deck covering (living spaces only)
7   Upper deck plating
8   Main (protective) deck plating (double thickness)
9   Flat over slope of protective deck
10   Longitudinal girders
11   Inner bottom
12   Double bottom
13   Box keel
14   Docking keel
15   Ammunition passage
16   Frames

17   Web Frame
18   Bulkhead
19   Crushing tubes
20   Outer bottom plating
21   Stringers in bulge compartments
22   Protective longitudinal bulkhead (double thickness)
23   Skin plating behind armour (double thickness)
24   Wood backing
25   Edge strips
26   5in armour
27   7in armour
28   12in armour
29   3in armour (boiler rooms only – ¾in protective plating beyond)
30   Armour shelf
31   Bilge keel
32   Sheer strake
33   Stringer plates

B16   ARMOUR LAYOUT (1/1200 scale)

Numbers give armour and protective plating thicknesses in inches. The larger numbers on the deck plans refer to the deck plating thickness – the double figures on the main deck refer to the thickness on the flat and slope of the deck respectively (ie 3+2 = 3in on flat, 2in on slope). The station numbers on the external profile line up with those on the body plan. The numbers along the keel line of the internal profile are the station numbers of the main water-tight bulkheads.

A   Forecastle deck
B   Upper deck
C   Main deck
D   Lower deck

B16

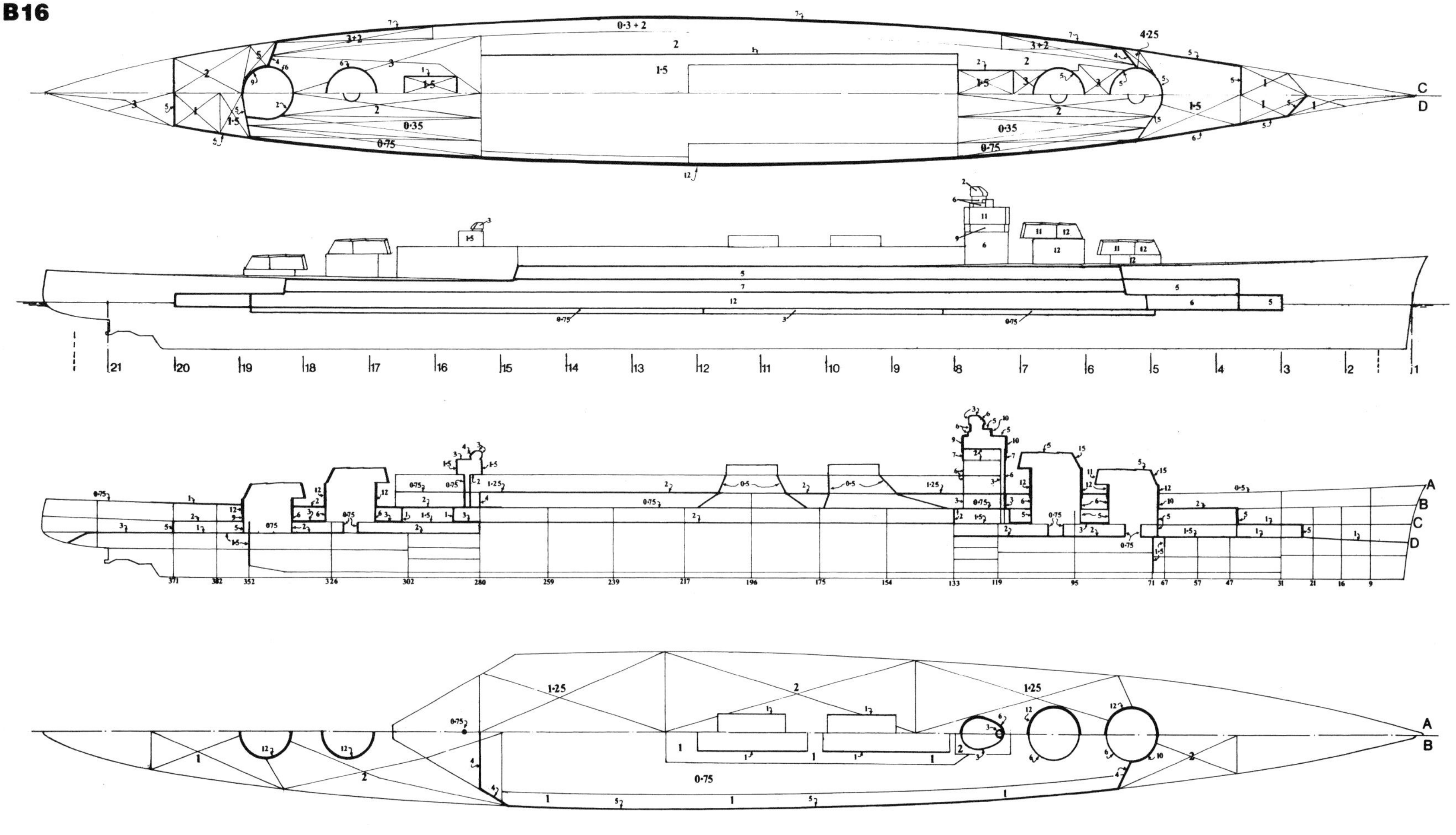

B Hull construction

B17 SECTION OF SIDE ARMOUR AMIDSHIPS (with profile and plan of framing)

1. 5in armour
2. 7in armour
3. 12in armour
4. Brackets
5. Flat over slope of protective deck
6. Deck beams (9in x 3½in angle bulb)
7. Upper deck plating (1in)
8. Frames (9in x 3½in x 3½in channel)
9. Side plating behind armour (1in + 1in)
10. Forecastle deck plating (1¼in + ½in)
11. Angle bar connections
12. Main frames
13. Intermediate frames
14. 3in armour

B18 LONGITUDINAL HOLDING BULKHEAD (at bottom. 1/150 scale)

1. Inner thickness of bulkhead plating
2. Outer thickness of bulkhead plating
3. Edge strips (outboard)
4. Edge strips (inboard)
5. 'I' girder framing, behind bulkhead
6. Double bottom
7. Boundary angle
8. Frames

B19/1 BARBETTE STRUCTURE ('A' turret)

1. Roller path seating
2. Training rack seating
3. 4in armour bulkhead (forecastle to maindeck)
4. 12in barbette armour
5. 6in barbette armour
6. 5in barbette armour
7. 10in barbette armour
8. 5in barbette armour
9. 4¾in armour flat between armoured bulkheads
10. 5in armour bulkhead
11. Forecastle deck
12. Upper deck
13. Main deck
14. Lower deck
15. Platform deck
16. Gunner's store
17. Medical distributing station
18. Magazine
19. Shell bin
20. Shell room flat
21. Hold
22. Shell room
23. Hoist well
24. Water-tight coaming
25. Handing room
26. Oil fuel filling compartment
27. Hoist trunk tube
28. Ring bulkhead

B19/2 DETAIL OF RING BULKHEAD ('Y' barbette. 1/150 scale)

1. Continuous zed bar (7in x 3½in x 3½in)
2. Roller path seating (2 thicknesses of 1½in each)
3. 6in x 6in continuous angle bar (both sides)
4. Training rack seating (1½in thick)
5. Training rack
6. Lower roller path
7. 8in x 5in continuous angle bar
8. Vertical zed frame (5in x 3in x 3in) continous
9. Vertical zed frame (5in x 3in x 3in) continuous
10. Ring bulkhead (1⅛in thick plating)
11. ⅝in thick continuous facing strip (both sides)
12. Horizontal zed frames (5in x 3in x 3in) intercostal
13. Flanged brackets
14. 8in x 8in continuous angle bar (both sides)
15. Angle bar connection to flat
16. Horizontal zed frames (7in x 3½in x 3½in) intercostal
17. ½in thick plating behind armour
18. ¾in thick continuous facing strip
19. Barbette armour
20. Vertical zed frame support to armour

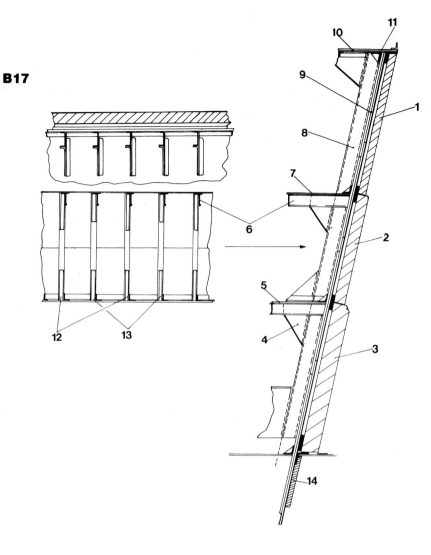

B17

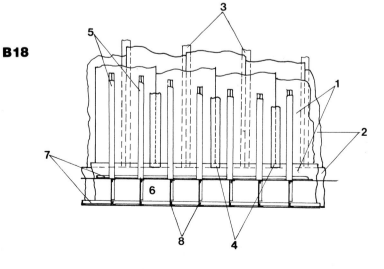

B18

B19/1

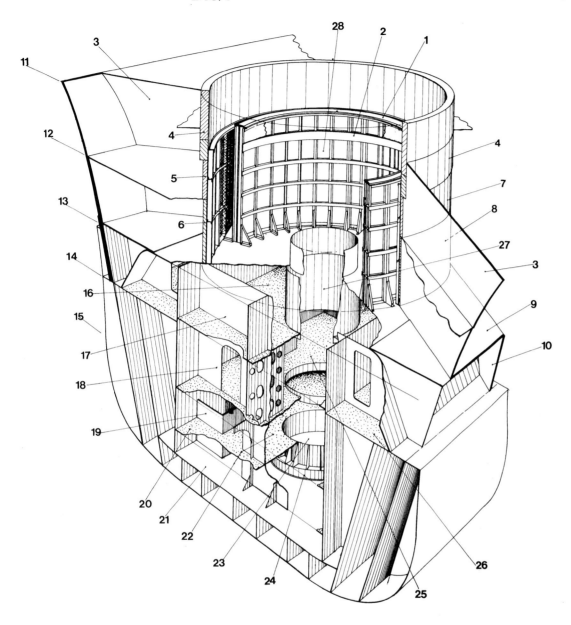

B19/2

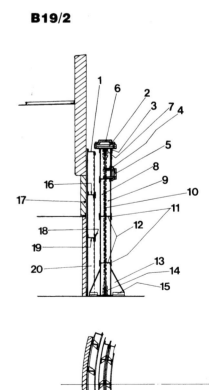

63

C1/1

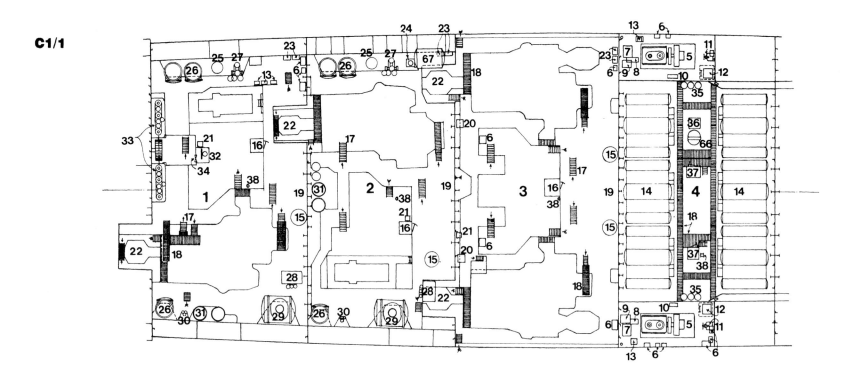

C1/2

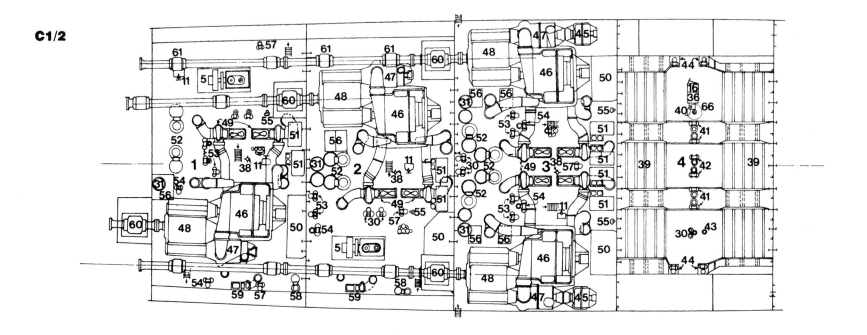

C1/1	**PLAN OF ENGINE ROOMS AND BOILER ROOM AT STARTING PLATFORM LEVEL (main machinery omitted for clarity. All C1 drawings 1/300 scale)**	57	Oil fuel tank pump
		58	Auxiliary air pump
		59	Auxiliary circulating pump
		60	Thrust block
C1/2	**PLAN OF ENGINE ROOMS AND BOILER ROOM AT LOWER PLATFORM LEVEL**	61	Plummer blocks
		62	Deep longitudinal girder
		63	Main condenser
C1/3	**LONGITUDINAL SECTION OF ENGINE ROOMS AND BOILER ROOM (port side)**	64	Fan compartment
		65	Forward bearing of low pressure turbine
		66	Turbo-bilge pump
C1/4	**SECTION AT AFTER END OF MIDDLE ENGINE ROOM (looking forward)**	67	Compressed air tank

C2/1   **YARROW SMALL TUBE BOILER**

C1/5   **SECTION AT FORE END OF FORWARD ENGINE ROOM (looking forward)**

1	After engine room	1	Uptake casing
2	Middle engine room	2	Automatic feed water regulators
3	Forward engine room	3	Smoke observation mirror
4	'Y' boiler room (others similar)	4	Boiler casing stiffeners
5	Steam reciprocating driven dynamo	5	Front casing doors
6	Tanks	6	Safety valve easing gear
7	Transformer	7	Soot door
8	Vent trunk (over)	8	Water drum
9	Drain tank	9	Boiler seating
10	Switch	10	Manhole door
11	Vice bench	11	Drain valve
12	Hatch (down) with escape trunk (over)	12	Sight hole
13	Switch box	13	Oil fuel sprayer
14	Boilers	14	Air doors in air box
15	Feed water heater	15	Drain valve
16	Telephone cabinet	16	Water drum
17	Ladders	17	Casing
18	Gratings	18	Steam drum
19	Starting platform	19	Main steam boiler stop valve
20	Tool box	20	Double full bore safety valve
21	25 gallon issue tank	21	Level of gantry
22	Thrust block recess		
23	Oil tank		
24	Air compressor		
25	Distiller		
26	Evaporators		
27	Air, fresh water and brine pump		
28	Auxiliary feed water heater		
29	Auxiliary condenser		
30	Fire and bilge pump		
31	Oil coolers		
32	Steering cabinet		
33	Steering engines		
34	Sliding door		
35	Oil fuel heaters		
36	Lift		
37	Air lock		
38	Pillar		
39	Boiler bearers		
40	50 gallon issue tank		
41	Main feed pumps		
42	Auxiliary feed pumps		
43	10in seacock		
44	Oil fuel pumps		
45	Cruising turbines		
46	Low pressure turbines (main condenser under)		
47	High pressure turbine		
48	Gear case		
49	Main circulating pumps		
50	Feed tank (30 tons capacity each)		
51	Main feed water filter		
52	Main air pumps		
53	Forced lubrication pumps		
54	Water service pump		
55	Fresh water pump		
56	Oil drain tank (in double bottom)		

C2/1

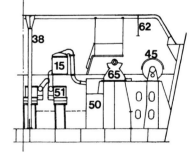

C1/4

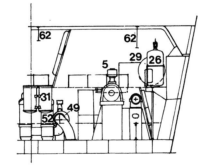

C1/5

C1/3

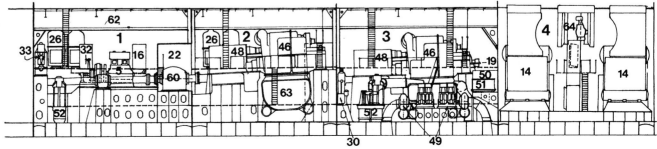

C Machinery

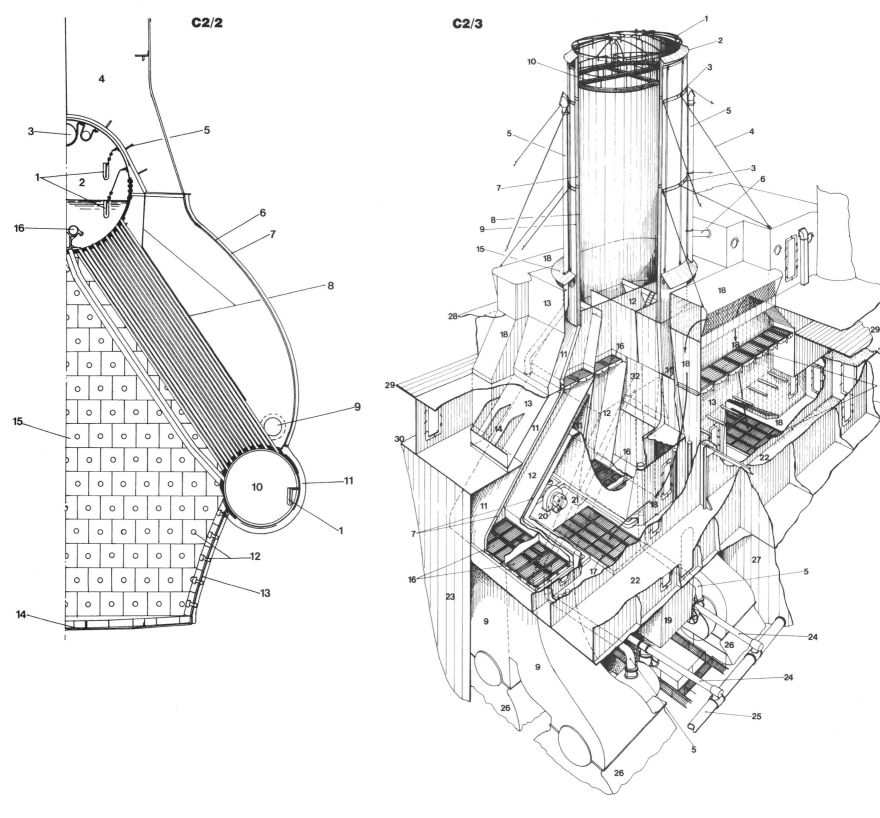

C2/2

C2/3

66

C3

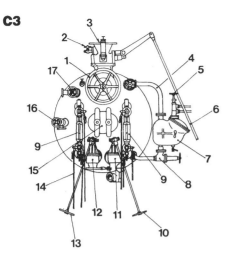

C4

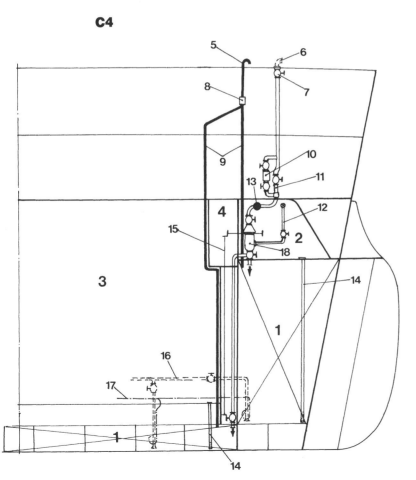

C2/2 HALF SECTION OF YARROW BOILER (1/37.5 scale)

1 Zinc slabs and trays
2 Steam drum
3 Steam pipe
4 Uptake
5 Foot rung
6 Side casing (asbestos sandwiched between two steel plates)
7 Stiffening angles
8 Baffles
9 Soot door (back casing)
10 Water drum
11 Lagging
12 Brick bolts
13 Furnace side casing
14 Brick pans (asbestos between pans and supports)
15 Fire bricks
16 Main feed water pipe (auxiliary feed pipe on left side)

C2/3 GENERAL ARRANGEMENT OF BOILER UPTAKES (after funnel)

1 Cage
2 Hood
3 Stay band
4 Funnel stays
5 Steam pipes from boiler safety valves
6 Funnel from furnace in coppersmith's shop
7 Ventilating air space around funnel
8 Funnel
9 Funnel casing
10 Inspection gantry
11 Insulating air space around funnel casing
12 Boiler uptakes
13 Funnel hatch casing
14 Hammock stowage
15 Air space rain cover
16 Armour gratings in boiler uptakes
17 Armour gratings in boiler room vents
18 Boiler room vent
19 Boiler room fan flat
20 17½in ventilation fan from funnel air space
21 Ventilation fan trunking
22 Ammunition passage
23 Bulkhead between 'Y' boiler room and forward engine room
24 Boiler steam pipe
25 Main steam pipe to forward engine room
26 Yarrow small tube boiler
27 Bulkhead between 'X' and 'Y' boiler rooms
28 Shelter deck
29 Forecastle deck
30 Upper deck
31 Main deck
32 Dividing bulkhead between uptakes from 'X' and 'Y' boiler rooms

C3 YARROW SMALL TUBE BOILER (fittings on face of steam drum)

1 Main steam boiler stop valve
2 Air cock
3 Double full bore safety valve
4 Steam pipe to regulator
5 Feed water height control
6 Rod to safety valve easing gear
7 Automatic feed regulator
8 Water pipe to regulator
9 Water level gauges
10 Feed check valve control handle
11 Main feed check valve
12 Auxiliary feed check valve
13 Auxiliary check valve control handle
14 Control rods to water gauges
15 Manhole door
16 Scum valve
17 Main steam to auxiliaries

C4 DIAGRAMMATIC ARRANGEMENT OF OIL FUEL STOWAGE SYSTEM (1/150 scale)

1 Oil fuel tank
2 Oil fuel working compartment
3 Boiler room
4 Hydraulic pipe and electric lead passage
5 Goose neck vent
6 Portable filling hose connection
7 Shut-off valves
8 Water-tight box
9 Oil fuel tank ventilation pipes (2 per tank)
10 Filter
11 Filter by-pass
12 Connection from fire main (to flood oil tanks)
13 Fore and aft oil fuel filling line
14 Sounding tube (for checking depth of oil and taking temperature)
15 Control rods to shut-off valve
16 Oil fuel suction
17 Steam heating pipes
18 Filling funnel

C Machinery

C5 DIAGRAMMATIC ARRANGEMENT OF OIL FUEL SYSTEM

1 Suction strainer (strainer and filters were fitted in pairs to allow one to be cleaned while the other was in use; no more than one was in use at a time)
2 Pressure and vacuum gauge
3 Pressure gauges
4 Shut-off valves
5 Oil fuel pump
6 Spring loaded relief valve
7 Air vessel
8 Air charging line
9 Cold filters
10 Oil fuel heater
11 Steam to heater
12 Drain from heater to feed tank
13 Hot filters
14 Control rod to upper deck to allow for remote closing of boiler oil fuel shut-off valve
15 Distribution chest
16 Thermometer
17 Pipe to each sprayer
18 Oil fuel sprayer/burner
19 Air doors (adjustable)
20 Air-tight box
21 Air cone (brick lined)
22 Fire bricks
23 Water tubes
24 Steam drum
25 Oil fuel tank

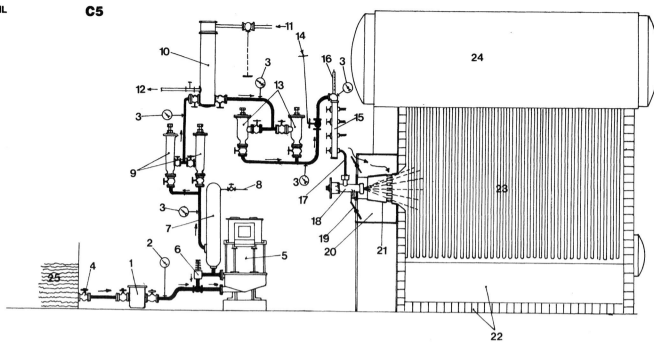

C5

C6 DIAGRAMMATIC ARRANGEMENT OF TURBINE SET (port, forward engine room)

1 Boiler steam to cruising turbine
2 Exhaust from cruising turbine to HP turbine
3 Shut-off valve
4 Boiler steam to HP turbine
5 Boiler steam to astern turbine
6 Cruising turbine
7 HP turbine
8 LP tubine
9 Astern turbine
10 Exhaust to condenser
11 Condenser (under LP turbine)
12 Exhaust from HP to LP turbine
13 Clutch
14 Flexible couplings
15 Shaft gear wheels (392 teeth)
16 HP turbine pinions (55 teeth)
17 LP turbine pinions (75 teeth)
18 Gear case
19 Shaft coupling
20 Port wing propeller shaft

C7/1 MAIN TURBINE SET (port inner, middle engine room)

1 Steam inlet to astern turbine
2 Steam inlet to HP turbine
3 HP turbine nozzle control box
4 LP turbine (astern turbine at forward end)
5 Exhaust from HP to LP turbine
6 HP turbine
7 Face for bolting to turbine seating
8 Gear case
9 Turbine seatings

10 Connection for exhaust for cruising turbine (wing shaft only)
11 Condenser slung under LP turbine
12 HP turbine bearing support
13 Condenser circulating water inlet
14 HP turbine bearing
15 Condenser circulating water outlet
16 LP turbine bearing support
17 LP turbine bearing
18 Level of platform around turbine
19 Astern turbine nozzle control box

C7/2 GEAR CASE AND HP TURBINE FROM AFT

1 HP turbine
2 Exhaust from cruising turbine to HP turbine
3 Nozzle box
4 Main steam to HP turbine
5 Exhaust from HP to LP turbine
6 Expansion joint
7 Pipes of forced lubrication system
8 Cover over after bearing of HP pinion shaft
9 Cover over after bearing of LP pinion shaft
10 Flange of shaft coupling
11 Gear case

C7/3 CROSS SECTION OF GEAR CASE (port side, looking forward – starboard side is mirror image. 1/75 scale)

1 HP turbine pinion (1500rpm, 55 teeth)
2 LP turbine pinion (1100rpm, 75 teeth)
3 Main gear wheel (210rpm, 392 teeth)
4 Propeller shaft
5 Vent
6 Lubricating oil sprayers
7 Oil drain
8 Gear case

C7/4 HELICAL PINION GEAR

C7/5 HALF SECTION OF HP TURBINE (showing principal features of construction – not to scale)

1 Main steam inlet
2 Nozzle control box
3 Control valve
4 First stage nozzle plate
5 Diaphram
6 First and second stage velocity impulse wheels
7 Impulse wheels (third to tenth stages)
8 Segmented brass packing ring (to reduce steam leakage)
9 Cover plate
10 Garter spring
11 Locking ring
12 Shaft
13 Main bearing
14 Thrust collars
15 Steam inlet/outlet to glands
16 Gland case
17 Garter spring
18 Carbon, gland rings
19 Exhaust steam to LP turbine

68

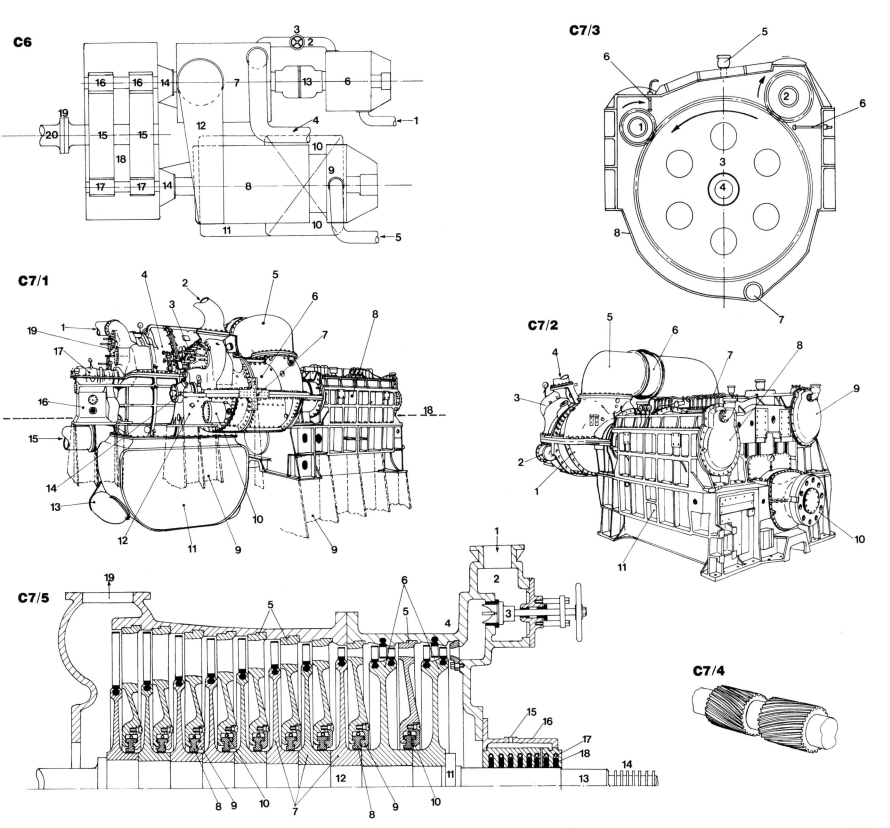

C6

C7/3

C7/1

C7/2

C7/5

C7/4

69

C Machinery

C8/1

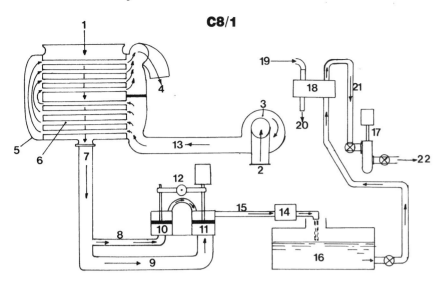

C8/2

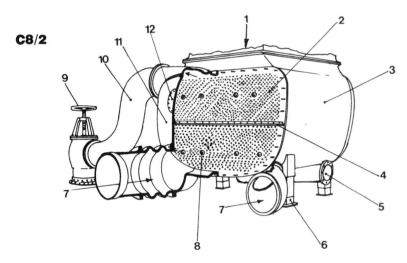

C8/3

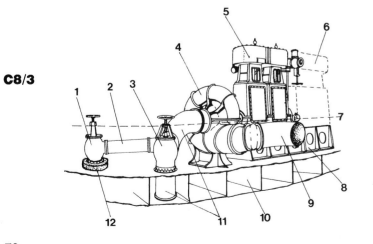

C8/4

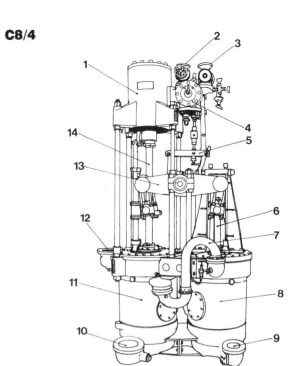

C8/5

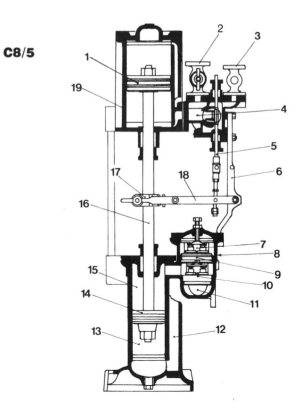

C8/1 DIAGRAMMATIC ARRANGEMENT OF FEED WATER SYSTEM

1 Exhaust steam and air from LP and astern turbine
2 Main sea water inlet (two per condenser)
3 Centrifugal circulating pump (two per condenser)
4 Circulating water outlet
5 Weir 'Uniflex' condenser
6 Circulating water pipes
7 Air pump suction
8 Dry air pump suction
9 Wet air pump suction
10 Dry air pump
11 Wet air pump
12 Weir dual air pump
13 Circulating water to condenser
14 Grease filter
15 Water discharge from air pump
16 Feed water tank
17 Main feed pump
18 Feed water heater
19 Exhaust steam inlet
20 Drain to feed tank
21 Heated feed water suction to feed pump in boiler room
22 Discharge to feed water regulator on boiler

C8/2 MAIN CONDENSER (with front cover cut away)

1 Exhaust from LP and astern turbines
2 Copper sea water tubes
3 Condenser shell
4 Water-tight division plate
5 Outlet to air pumps
6 Spring support (partial support only)
7 Sea water inlet from circulating pump
8 Ends of stays
9 Shut-off valve
10 Main sea water outlet (second outlet not shown)
11 Front cover
12 Inspection door

C8/3 CIRCULATING PUMP

1 Bilge suction shut-off valve
2 Bilge suction
3 Sea suction shut-off valve
4 Centrifugal circulating pump
5 Reciprocating steam pumping engine
6 Engine for second pump
7 Level of platform
8 Engine seating
9 Circulating water to condenser
10 Double bottom
11 Sea water suction
12 Filter

C8/4 WEIR DUAL AIR PUMP

1 Steam piston cylinder
2 Exhaust steam stop valve
3 Steam stop valve
4 Steam slide valve chest
5 Valve gear lever
6 Dry air pump piston rod
7 Dry air pump discharge to wet air pump
8 Dry air pump cylinder
9 Dry air pump suction

10 Wet air pump suction
11 Wet air pump cylinder
12 Main discharge
13 Rocking arm
14 Steam and wet air piston rod

C8/5 WEIR FEED PUMP (in section)

1 Steam piston
2 Steam stop valve
3 Exhaust steam stop valve
4 Steam slide valve chest
5 Slide rod
6 Front stay
7 Discharge
8 Pump valve chest (two on each pump)
9 Discharge valve
10 Suction valve
11 Suction
12 Connection to second valve chest
13 Lower section of pump
14 Pump piston
15 Upper section of pump
16 Piston rod
17 Main crosshead
18 Valve gear levers
19 Steam piston cylinder

C8/6 FEED WATER FILTER

C9/1 COMPOUND EVAPORATOR PLANT (simplified diagrammatic arrangement)

1 Evaporator No 2
2 Evaporator No 1
3 Steam supply to heating coils
4 Steam from first to second evaporator for compound working
5 Evaporated steam to distiller
6 Distiller
7 Distilled water and air
8 Distilled water to feed water tank
9 Steam cylinder of combined air, fresh water and brine pump
10 Fresh water and air pump cylinder
11 Brine pump cylinder
12 Double acting circulating pump cylinders
13 Circulating (cooling) water to distiller
14 Circulating water from distiller to evaporators
15 Water level gauges
16 Blow down discharge to sea
17 Brine discharge overboard
18 Sea suction to circulating pump
19 Diluting water to brine discharge
20 Weed traps
21 Heating coil drains (to feed tank)

C8/6

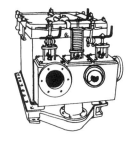

C9/1

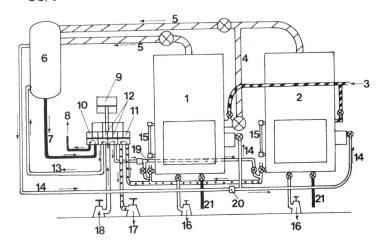

C Machinery

C9/2 WEIR VERTICAL EVAPORATOR (shown with cover door open)

1 Evaporator shell
2 Generated steam outlet valve
3 Gauge
4 Safety valve
5 Safety valve outlet
6 Top connection to water level gauge (hidden on far side)
7 Swinging bar for door
8 Door
9 Evaporating tube heating coils
10 Hand cleaning door
11 Drain valve from coil
12 Blow down discharge to sea
13 Brine valve
14 Inlet steam header
15 Steam inlet valve to coils
16 Inlet steam pressure gauge

C10 FORCED LUBRICATION SYSTEM FOR TURBINES (middle engine room. 1/300 scale)

1 Turbine oil gravity tank
2 Oil drain tank
3 Forced lubrication pumps
4 Oil coolers
5 Supply pipes
6 Return pipes (broken line)
7 Thrust block (oil to bearing and pads)
8 Gear case

9 HP turbine
10 LP turbine
11 Oil to bearings
12 Oil to gear sprayers

C11/1–C11/7 GENERAL ARRANGEMENT OF PROPELLER SHAFTS (starboard side. All 1/300 scale)

1 Thrust block
2 Shaft coupling
3 Plummer blocks
4 Stern tube
5 Shaft bracket
6 Trunk access to shaft passage
7 Bridge over shaft
8 Thrust block recess in after engine room
9 Shaft locking gear
10 Platform for 50 ton pump 'H'
11 Hydraulic engine room
12 Hydraulic tank
13 Oil fuel tanks
14 Pillars (supporting turbo-generator)
15 Palms of shaft brackets
16 Arched openings
17 Hatch (overhead)
18 Platform on inboard side of shafts

C12/1 FIRE AND BILGE PUMP

1 Steam cylinder
2 Air vessel
3 Slide valve chest
4 Steam pipe
5 Fire main screw lift valve
6 Fire main
7 Screw lift valve with hose connection
8 Screw lift valve to pump discharge
9 Pump cylinder
10 Pump valve chest
11 Suction valves, one to sea, one to bilge
12 Valve box
13 Mud box
14 Bilge water strainer
15 Access cover (for cleaning pipe)
16 Cast iron corrosion joint
17 Screw down valve
18 Flood valve (note: operating spindle has no handle)
19 Sea inlet
20 Discharge to sea
21 Non-return valve from water pump discharge
22 Non-return valve from fire and bilge pump discharge
23 Screw down non-return valve with hose connection
24 Flooding pipe
25 Double bottom

C9/2

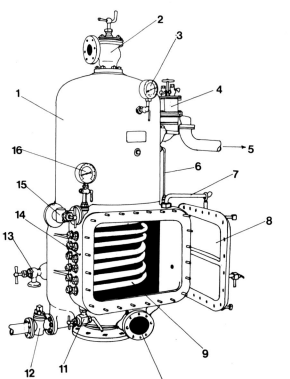

C10

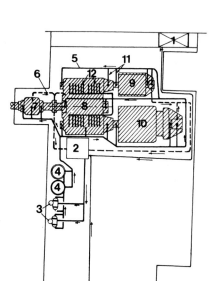

C12/1

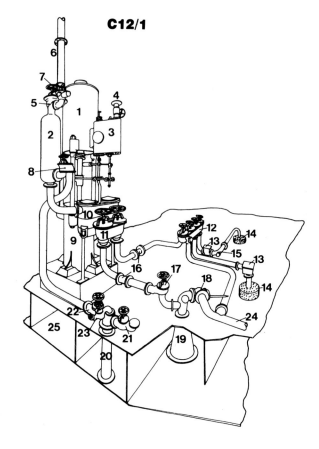

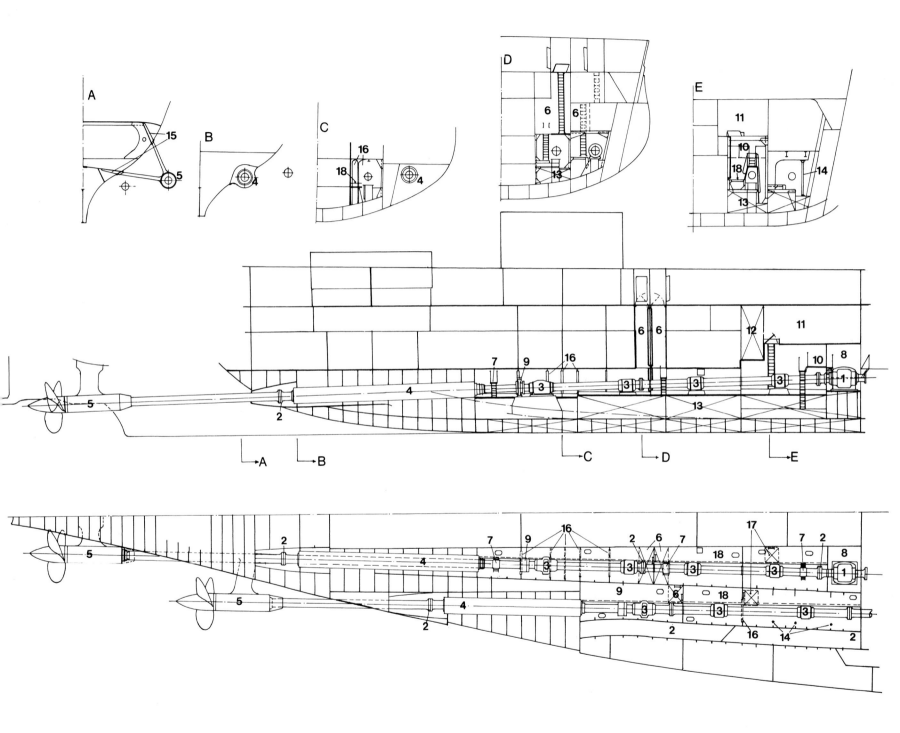

C12/2

C12/3

C13/2

C13/1

C13/4

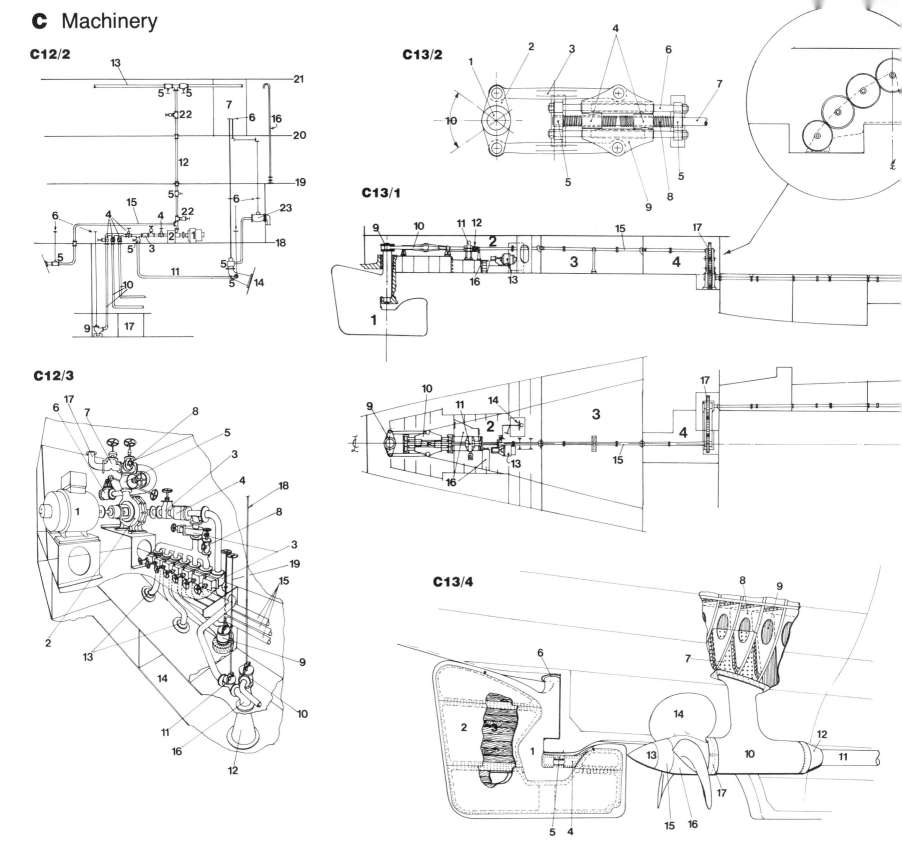

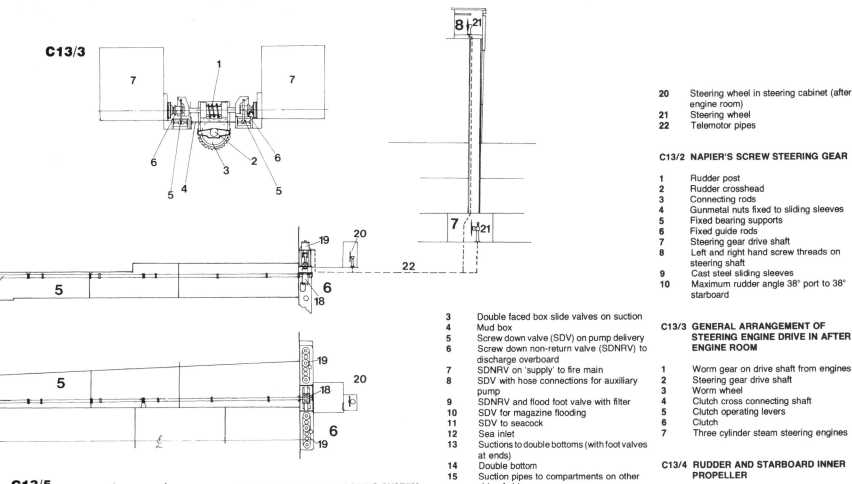

C13/3

C13/2 NAPIER'S SCREW STEERING GEAR

20 Steering wheel in steering cabinet (after engine room)
21 Steering wheel
22 Telemotor pipes

1 Rudder post
2 Rudder crosshead
3 Connecting rods
4 Gunmetal nuts fixed to sliding sleeves
5 Fixed bearing supports
6 Fixed guide rods
7 Steering gear drive shaft
8 Left and right hand screw threads on steering shaft
9 Cast steel sliding sleeves
10 Maximum rudder angle 38° port to 38° starboard

C13/3 GENERAL ARRANGEMENT OF STEERING ENGINE DRIVE IN AFTER ENGINE ROOM

1 Worm gear on drive shaft from engines
2 Steering gear drive shaft
3 Worm wheel
4 Clutch cross connecting shaft
5 Clutch operating levers
6 Clutch
7 Three cylinder steam steering engines

C13/4 RUDDER AND STARBOARD INNER PROPELLER

1 Cast steel rudder frame
2 Covering plates
3 Wood (fir) filling
4 Locking plate
5 Channel bar
6 Gunmetal sleeve running in phosphor bronze bearing (note: 5 and 6 prevented rudder from lifting, hence they were fitted after rudder was installed and had to be removed before the rudder could be lifted out)
7 Palm, riveted to bulkhead and frames of palm compartment
8 Frames of palm compartment
9 Short longitudinal bulkhead of palm compartment
10 Shaft bracket
11 Propeller shaft
12 Wash, or eddy, plate
13 Propeller cone
14 Propeller blade
15 Fairing sleeve
16 Propeller boss
17 Rope guard

---

3 Double faced box slide valves on suction
4 Mud box
5 Screw down valve (SDV) on pump delivery
6 Screw down non-return valve (SDNRV) to discharge overboard
7 SDNRV on 'supply' to fire main
8 SDV with hose connections for auxiliary pump
9 SDNRV and flood foot valve with filter
10 SDV for magazine flooding
11 SDV to seacock
12 Sea inlet
13 Suctions to double bottoms (with foot valves at ends)
14 Double bottom
15 Suction pipes to compartments on other side of ship
16 Seacock
17 Rising main
18 Control rod to magazine flooding cabinet
19 Control rods

C13/1 GENERAL ARRANGEMENT OF STEERING GEAR (1/300 scale, except inset which shows a transverse view of transfer gears looking forward at 1/150 scale)

1 Rudder
2 Steering compartment
3 Carpenter's heavy store
4 Lobby
5 Port inner shaft passage
6 After engine room
7 Lower steering position
8 Conning tower
9 Rudder crosshead
10 Screw steering gear
11 Auxiliary steering gear
12 Main/auxiliary steering clutch
13 Auxiliary steering electric motor
14 Auxiliary steering wheel in cabinet
15 Steering gear drive shaft
16 Platforms
17 Gear wheels
18 Worm and worm wheel drive from steering engines
19 Steering engines

C12/2 PUMPING AND FLOODING SYSTEM (fore and aft of machinery spaces)

1 Electric motor
2 50 ton centrifugal pump
3 Mud box
4 Double faced box slide valves on suction
5 Screw down valve (SDV)
6 Hand wheels for remote operation of valves
7 Magazine flooding cabinet
8 Screw down non-return foot valve (SDNRFV)
9 To SDNRFVs in bilges and double bottom
10 4in bilge suctions
11 4in sea suction
12 4in rising main
13 5in fire main
14 Seacock
15 4in discharge overboard
16 Air escape pipe
17 Double bottom
18 Platform deck
19 Lower deck
20 Main deck
21 Upper deck
22 Hose connections
23 Magazine flood valve

C12/3 50 TON CENTRIFUGAL PUMP

1 Electric motor
2 50 ton centrifugal pump

C13/5 SECTION OF RUDDER (abaft rudder post)

1 Frame
2 Wood packing
3 Covering plates

C Machinery

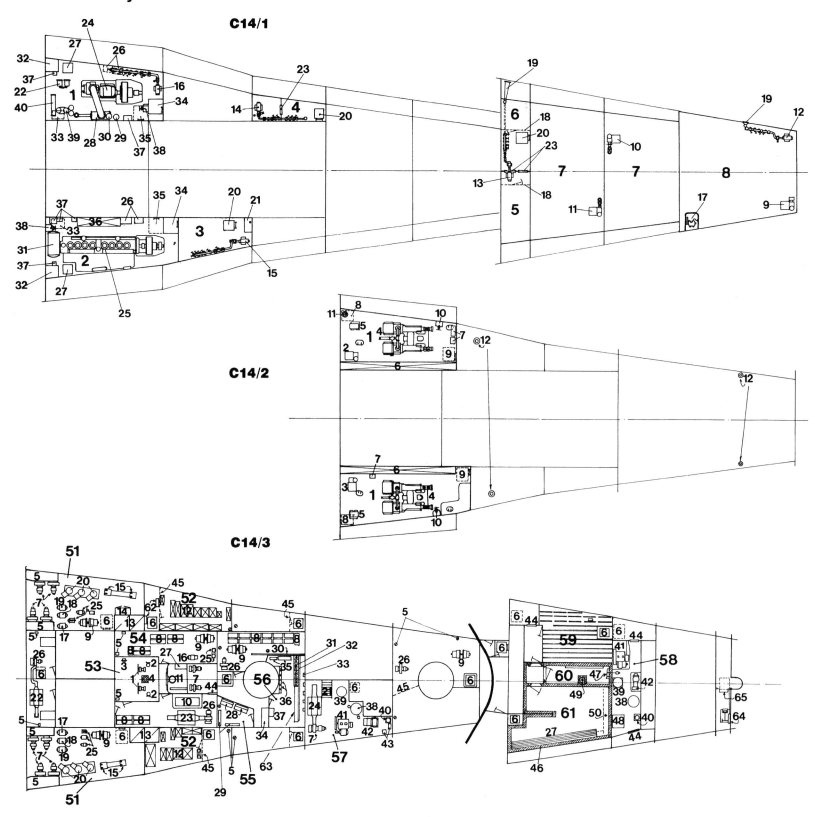

C14/1 AUXILIARY MACHINERY ON PLATFORM DECK FORWARD (1/300 scale)

1 Turbo-generator room
2 Oil dynamo room
3 Engineers' store
4 Pump room
5 Flour store
6 Provision room
7 Submerged torpedo room
8 Capstan engine room
9 350 ton pump No 1
10 350 ton pump No 2
11 350 ton pump No 3
12 50 ton pump 'C'
13 50 ton pump 'D'
14 50 ton pump 'E'
15 50 ton pump 'F'
16 50 ton pump 'G'
17 Fresh water pump (with auxiliary hand crank) added in 1931 when the water-tight compartment in the hold between station 21 and 31 was converted to a fresh water tank
18 Wire mesh bulkhead
19 4in seacock
20 Hatch (and over)
21 Bin
22 Feed water filters
23 Arched openings in bulkheads
24 Turbo-generator
25 Diesel dynamo
26 Switchboards
27 Transformer
28 Condenser
29 Purifier
30 Oil tank
31 Diesel exhaust silencer
32 Vent trunk to hydraulic engine room
33 Vent trunk
34 Access and escape trunk to hydraulic engine room
35 Access and escape trunk
36 Diesel oil tank
37 Tank
28 Vice bench
39 Air and circulating pump
40 Oil cooler

C14/2 AUXILIARY MACHINERY IN HOLD FORWARD (1/300 scale)

1 Hydraulic engine room
2 350 ton pump No 4
3 350 ton pump No 5
4 Hydraulic pumping engine
5 Air compressor
6 Hydraulic tank
7 Tanks
8 Vent trunk (over)
9 Access and escape trunk (over)
10 Vice bench
11 10in seacock
12 11in seacocks (port and starboard)

C14/3 AUXILIARY MACHINERY ON LOWER DECK FORWARD (1/300 scale)

1 Steering wheels
2 Engine room telegraphs
3 Telegraph receiver
4 Compass
5 Vent
6 Hatch (broken line = hatch over)
7 17½in ventilation fan
8 Battery cells
9 15 volt motor generator
10 Ammunition embarkation hatch
11 Gyro compass
12 Storage cabinets
13 Access and escape trunks from auxiliary machinery rooms below
14 Cupboard
15 Searchlight motor generators
16 Milking booster
17 Searchlight and torpedo circuit isolator
18 15in gun circuit isolator
19 5.5in gun circuit isolator
20 Motor generator
21 Ladderway to hatch (over)
22 5.5in magazine cooler
23 'B' 15in magazine cooler
24 'A' 15in magazine cooler
25 Motor alternator
26 12½in ventilation fan
27 Shelves

28 Telephone exchanges
29 Telephone and miscellaneous circuit boards
30 15 volt switchboard
31 Field rheostats (eight, one to control each main generator)
32 Main controlling switchboard
33 Junction boxes
34 Switchboard
35 Switch panels
36 Navyphones (twelve phones for communication with dynamo rooms, etc)
37 Desk
38 CO_2 evaporator
39 CO_2 condenser
40 Brine mixing tank
41 Motor CO_2 compressor
42 Motor brine pump
43 Tank
44 Arched opening
45 Wire bulkhead
46 Insulation
47 12½in fan (overhead) driven by motor in refrigeration machinery compartment
48 Ice making and brine mixing tank
49 Pillar
50 Space for refrigerating coils
51 Motor generator compartment
52 Spare armature room
53 Lower conning tower
54 Low power switchboard room
55 Telephone exchange
56 Main switchboard room
57 CO_2 machinery compartment
58 Refrigerating machinery compartment
59 Provision room
60 Vegetable room
61 Meat room
62 Link boxes
63 Safety rail across front of main switchboard
64 Motor driven 10 ton fresh water pump
65 Auxiliary hand crank for fresh water pump

C14/4 AUXILIARY MACHINERY ON PLATFORM DECK AFT (1/300 scale)

1 Oil room
2 Hydraulic engine room
3 Turbo-generator room
4 Steering compartment
5 Tanks
6 Hatch (escape and access trunk over)
7 Vent trunk (over)
8 Switchboards
9 Hatch (broken line = over)
10 Diesel oil tanks
11 Diesel exhaust silencer
12 Diesel dynamo
13 Vice bench
14 Hydraulic tank
15 Escape and access trunk (over)
16 Outline of fan flat at top of compartment
17 Hydraulic pumping engine
18 Air compressor
19 50 ton pump 'H'
20 50 ton pump 'J'
21 50 ton pump 'K'
22 50 ton pump 'L'
23 50 ton pump 'M'
24 350 ton pump No 6
25 350 ton pump No 7
26 350 ton pump No 8
27 350 ton pump No 9
28 Turbo-generator
29 Air and circulating pump
30 Oil cooler
31 Condenser
32 Oil filters
33 10in seacock
34 4in seacock
35 Transformer

C14/4

77

C Machinery

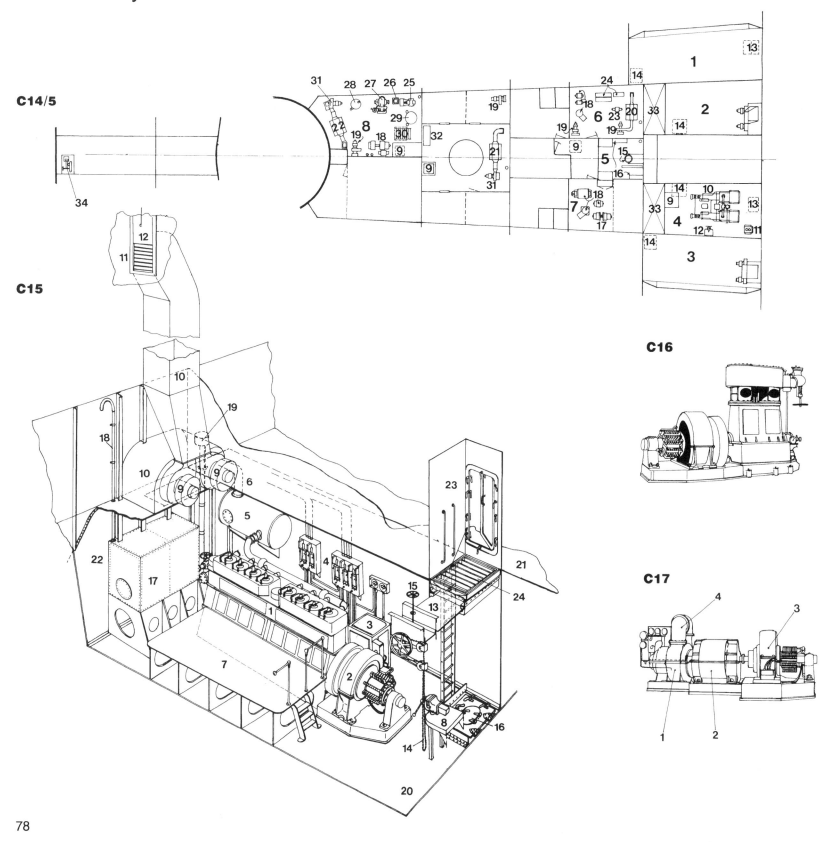

C14/5

C15

C16

C17

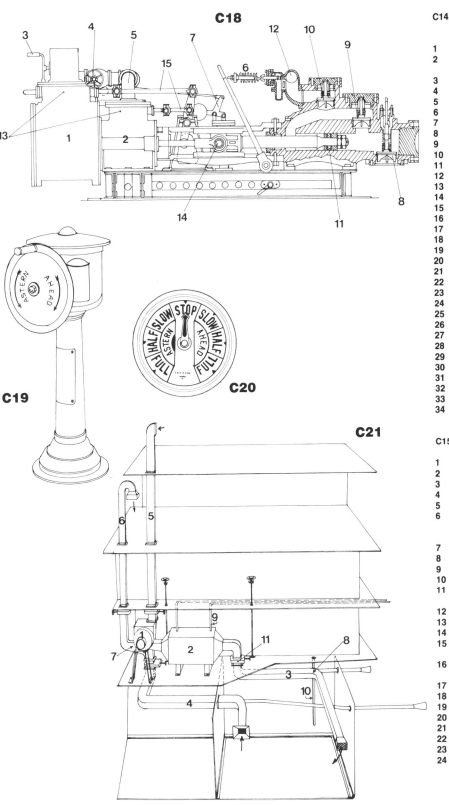

C18

C14/5 AUXILIARY MACHINERY ON LOWER DECK AFT (1/300 scale)

1 Top of oil dynamo room on plaform deck
2 Top of hydraulic engine room on platform deck
3 Top of turbo-generator room
4 Hydraulic engine room
5 Gyro room
6 Motor generator compartment
7 Motor generator room
8 CO_2 machinery compartment
9 Hatch (broken line = over)
10 Hydraulic pumping engine
11 Compressor
12 Vice bench
13 Vent trunk (over)
14 Escape and access trunk (over)
15 Gyro compass
16 Shelves
17 15 volt motor generator
18 Motor generator
19 $12\frac{1}{2}$in ventilating fan
20 5.5in magazine cooler
21 'X' magazine cooler
22 'Y' magazine cooler
23 Milking booster
24 Battery cells
25 Brine pump
26 Brine mixing tank
27 Motor compressor
28 CO_2 condenser
29 CO_2 evaporator
30 Ladder to hatch (over)
31 $17\frac{1}{2}$in fan
32 Switchboard
33 Hydraulic tank
34 10 ton fresh water pump

C15 AFT OIL DYNAMO ROOM

1 Eight-cylinder diesel engine
2 200kW generator
3 Transformer
4 Switchboards
5 Exhaust silencer
6 Diesel exhaust (runs forward and then up port strut of main mast to exhaust above shelter deck)
7 Platform
8 Vice bench
9 $17\frac{1}{2}$in ventilation fans (exhaust)
10 Ventilation trunk
11 Vent opening on side of superstructure at shelter deck level
12 Steel shutter
13 Water-tight scuttle (open)
14 Chain for operating water-tight scuttle
15 Hand wheel for closing water-tight scuttle from lower deck
16 Hatch (with escape manhole) to port outer shaft passage
17 Ready-use oil tank
18 Air escape pipe
19 Vent
20 Platform deck
21 Lower deck
22 After bulkhead of after engine room
23 Access and escape trunk
24 Hinged armour grating

C16 TWO CYLINDER COMPOUND RECIPROCATING ENGINE DRIVEN 200kW GENERATOR

C17 TURBO-GENERATOR SET

1 Steam turbine
2 Gear case
3 200kW generator
4 Exhaust steam pipe from turbine to condenser

C18 PROFILE OF HYDRAULIC ENGINE, WITH HYDRAULIC PUMP IN SECTION (1/37.5 scale. Note: each engine consisted of two sets of cylinders side-by-side)

1 LP steam cylinder
2 HP steam cylinder
3 Exhaust steam stop valve
4 Steam inlet stop valve
5 Steam inlet pipe (cross connected to both HP cylinders)
6 Relief valve
7 Hydraulic governor
8 Hydraulic fluid suction valve (operates on back stroke)
9 Intermediate valve (operates on forward stroke)
10 Delivery valve (operates on back stroke)
11 Hydraulic ram
12 Hydraulic fluid delivery pipe
13 Slide valves
14 Crosshead
15 Slide valve rods

C19 ENGINE ROOM TELEGRAPH TRANSMITTER

C20 ENGINE ROOM TELEGRAPH RECEIVER

C21 MAGAZINE VENTILATION AND COOLING SYSTEM

1 Ventilation fan
2 Cooler
3 Magazine supply trunk
4 Magazine exhaust trunk
5 Fresh air supply trunk
6 Exhaust trunk to atmosphere
7 Throttle valves in supply and exhaust trunks can be shut allowing closed circulation of air through cooler and magazine only
8 Curved baffle within supply trunk to regulate flow
9 Brine pipes from refrigeration plant
10 Temperature tube
11 Rectangular shut-off slide valve controlled from deck above

C Machinery

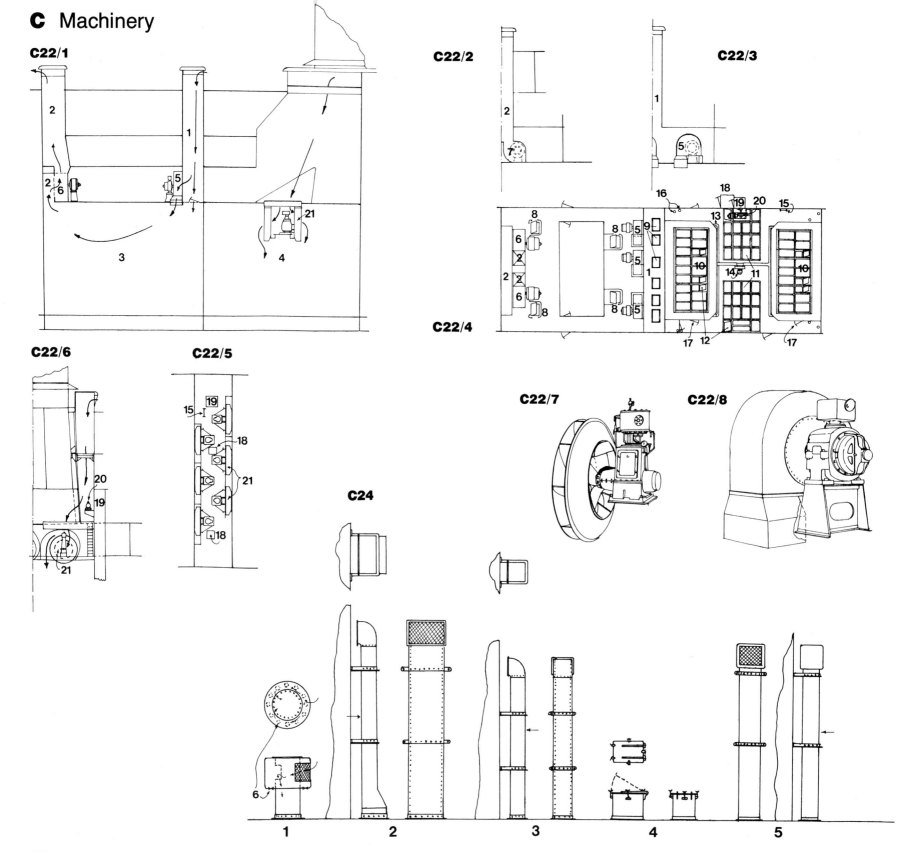

C22/1

C22/2

C22/3

C22/4

C22/6

C22/5

C22/7

C22/8

C24

1

2

3

4

5

C22/1 PROFILE OF 'Y' BOILER ROOM AND FORWARD ENGINE ROOM (note: this key applies to all C22 drawings, which are 1/300 scale)

1 Engine room supply trunk
2 Engine room exhaust trunk
3 Forward engine room
4 'Y' boiler room
5 40in fan driven by electric motor (note other engine rooms 30in)
6 50in fan driven by electric motor
7 35in fan driven by electric motor
8 Hatches to engine room
9 Engine room vents for natural supply
10 Funnel hatch (armour gratings)
11 Boiler room supply vent (armour gratings)
12 Hinged armour grating for access
13 Vent trunk for supplying warm air from funnel casing to fan flat
14 12½in ventilation fan
15 Ladder
16 Vents
17 Air-tight doors
18 Air lock
19 Electric lift
20 Electric lift motor
21 90in supply fans driven by steam reciprocating engines

C22/2 SECTION AT EXHAUST FANS OF AFTER ENGINE ROOM (note: exhaust fans of after and middle engine rooms are smaller than those of the forward engine room)

C22/3 SECTION AT SUPPLY FANS OF FORWARD ENGINE ROOMS (note: forward engine room has three supply fans, other two engine rooms have two)

C22/4 PLAN OF MAIN DECK OVER 'Y' BOILER ROOM AND FORWARD ENGINE ROOM

C22/5 PLAN OF BOILER ROOM FAN FLAT

C22/6 SECTION OF BOILER ROOM VENTILATION SYSTEM

C22/7 90in BOILER ROOM VENTILATION FAN, DRIVEN BY STEAM RECIPROCATING ENGINE

C22/8 ENGINE ROOM SUPPLY FAN DRIVEN BY ELECTRIC MOTOR

C23 TYPICAL VENTILATION ARRANGEMENTS FOR MESS DECKS, STORE ROOMS, ETC

1 Mushroom top supply
2 Mushroom top natural exhaust vent
3 Supply trunk
4 17½in ventilation fan
5 Heater
6 Steam pipes to heater
7 Shut-off valve

8 Distribution trunk
9 Hinged baffles within trunk to regulate supply
10 Air chamber
11 Exhaust vent
12 Supply vent
13 Remote control handwheels for shut-off valves in ventilation trunks passing through decks and bulkheads below

C24 WEATHER DECK VENT TOPS (1/75 scale)

1 Mushroom top vent
2 & 3 Vent trunks as fitted against superstructure and barbettes
4 Vent opening on forecastle deck to capstan machinery compartment
5 Vent trunk with modified tops as fitted against 'X' barbette during 1925–26 refit
6 Drain holes

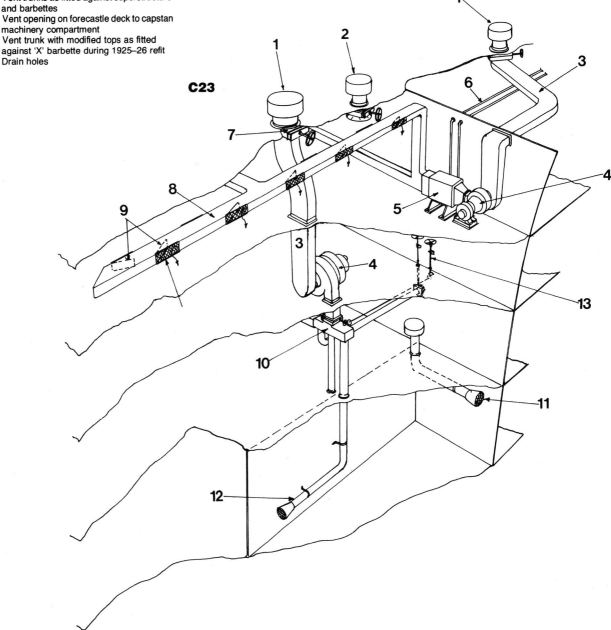

C23

D Accommodation

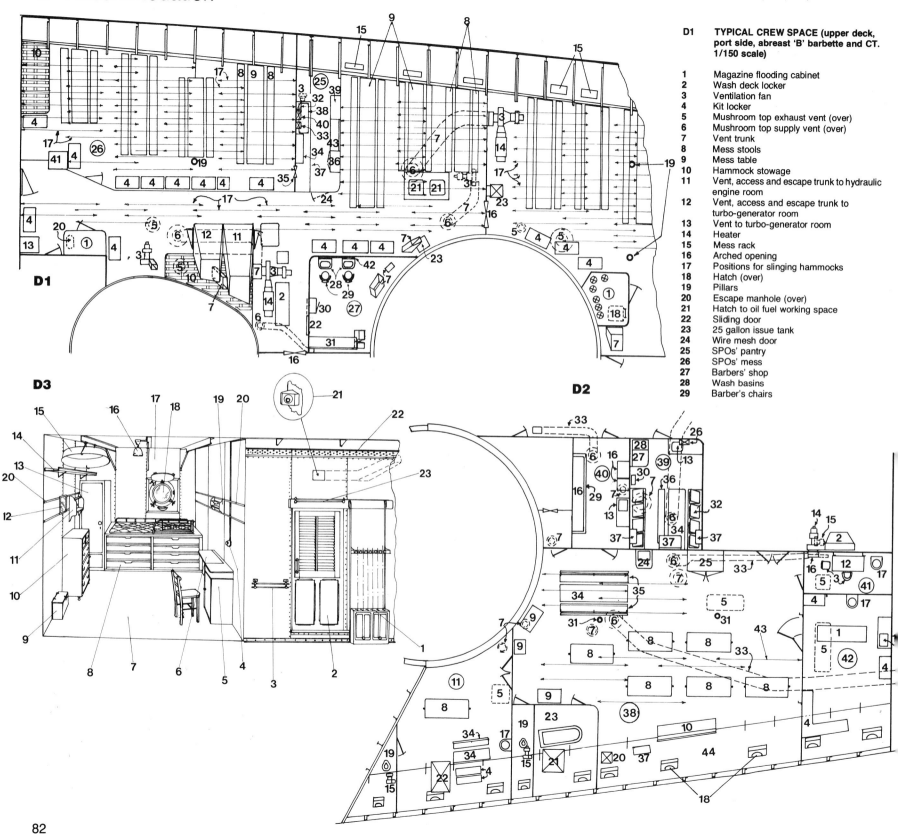

D1

D2

D3

D1 TYPICAL CREW SPACE (upper deck, port side, abreast 'B' barbette and CT. 1/150 scale)

1 Magazine flooding cabinet
2 Wash deck locker
3 Ventilation fan
4 Kit locker
5 Mushroom top exhaust vent (over)
6 Mushroom top supply vent (over)
7 Vent trunk
8 Mess stools
9 Mess table
10 Hammock stowage
11 Vent, access and escape trunk to hydraulic engine room
12 Vent, access and escape trunk to turbo-generator room
13 Vent to turbo-generator room
14 Heater
15 Mess rack
16 Arched opening
17 Positions for slinging hammocks
18 Hatch (over)
19 Pillars
20 Escape manhole (over)
21 Hatch to oil fuel working space
22 Sliding door
23 25 gallon issue tank
24 Wire mesh door
25 SPOs' pantry
26 SPOs' mess
27 Barbers' shop
28 Wash basins
29 Barber's chairs

30 Wall cabinet
31 Seat
32 Drying rack
33 Hot water tank (over)
34 Plate rack (over)
35 Hand-through (serving hatch)
36 Cupboard
37 Dresser drawers and cupboards (under)
38 Sink
39 Shelf (over)
40 10 gallon fresh water tank
41 Vent to hydraulic engine room
42 Wall mirror
43 Hinged seat

D2   SICK BAY (1/150 scale)

1   Operating table
2   Ventilation heater
3   Chairs
4   Shelf
5   Skylight (over)
6   Mushroom top supply vent on forecastle
    deck above
7   Mushroom top exhaust vent on forecastle
    deck above
8   Two cots (one above the other)
9   Kit lockers
10 Hinged seat
11 Isolation ward
12 Kneehole table
13 Sink
14 12½in supply fan
15 7½in exhaust fan (over)
16 Rack (over)
17 Wash basin
18 Side scuttles
19 WC
20 25 gallon issue tank (over)

21 30 gallon fresh water tank (over)
22 100 gallon reserve flushing tank (over)
23 Bathroom
24 Stove
25 Hot cupboard for bedding
26 Fresh water tank (over)
27 Hammock stowage
28 Vent
29 Drawers
30 Foot locker
31 Pillars
32 Hinged seats (lockers under)
33 Ventilation trunk (over)
34 Mess table
35 Mess bench
36 Mess stool
37 Mess tack (over)
38 Sick bay
39 Sick berth staff's mess
40 Dispensary
41 Surgeon's examining room
42 Operating room
43 Positions for slinging hammocks
44 Ceiling on ship's side

D3   TYPICAL OFFICER'S CABIN (main deck aft)

1   Rifle rack
2   Sliding door (slides to right behind rifle rack)
3   Towel rail
4   Light switch
5   Wash stand
6   Hinged table
7   Cork carpet
8   Sliding trays under bunk
9   Foot locker
10 Chest of drawers
11 Book shelf

12 Mirror
13 Wardrobe
14 Shelf
15 Circular bath (stowed)
16 Light
17 Ceiling
18 Side scuttle
19 Water bottle stand
20 Teak mouldings
21 Louvre vents on inside of cabin
22 Ventilation holes

D4   WARD ROOM (and surrounding compartments on forecastle deck. 1/150 scale)

1   Ward room
2   Ward room ante room
3   Table
4   Vent trunk
5   Mushroom top vent on shelter deck above
6   Dresser with drawers and cupboards under
7   Skylight (over)
8   Engine room vent
9   Shelves (over)
10 Dresser with cupboard under
11 Ward room galley
12 Admiral's galley
13 Ward room kitchen
14 Sink
15 Kitchen range
16 Hinged seat
17 10 gallon fresh water tank
18 Hot water tank
19 Ventilation exhaust fan
20 Officer of Quarters hood
21 Rack (over)
22 Drying rack (over)
23 Wash deck locker (added during 1929-31 refit)

24 Pillar
25 Knee hole table
26 Curtain rail over
27 Hinged table
28 Buffet
29 Cushioned settee
30 Cupboard
31 Stove
32 Bookcase
33 Stove pipe
34 Ladderway (down)
35 Ladderway (up)
36 Test tanks (for checking drinking water)
37 Main auxiliary W/T trunk
38 Main W/T trunk
39 Bunk (drawers under)
40 Chest of drawers
41 Bookshelf (over)
42 Bath (over)
43 Wardrobe
44 Engineer commander's cabin
45 Surgeon commander's cabin (as 44)
46 Foot locker
47 Chair
48 Sliding door
49 Square port
50 Hand-through (serving hatch)
51 Ceiling
52 Watch bell (over)
53 Doorway, modified to arched opening by 1931
54 Hot closet (added during 1929-31 refit)
55 Magazine rack

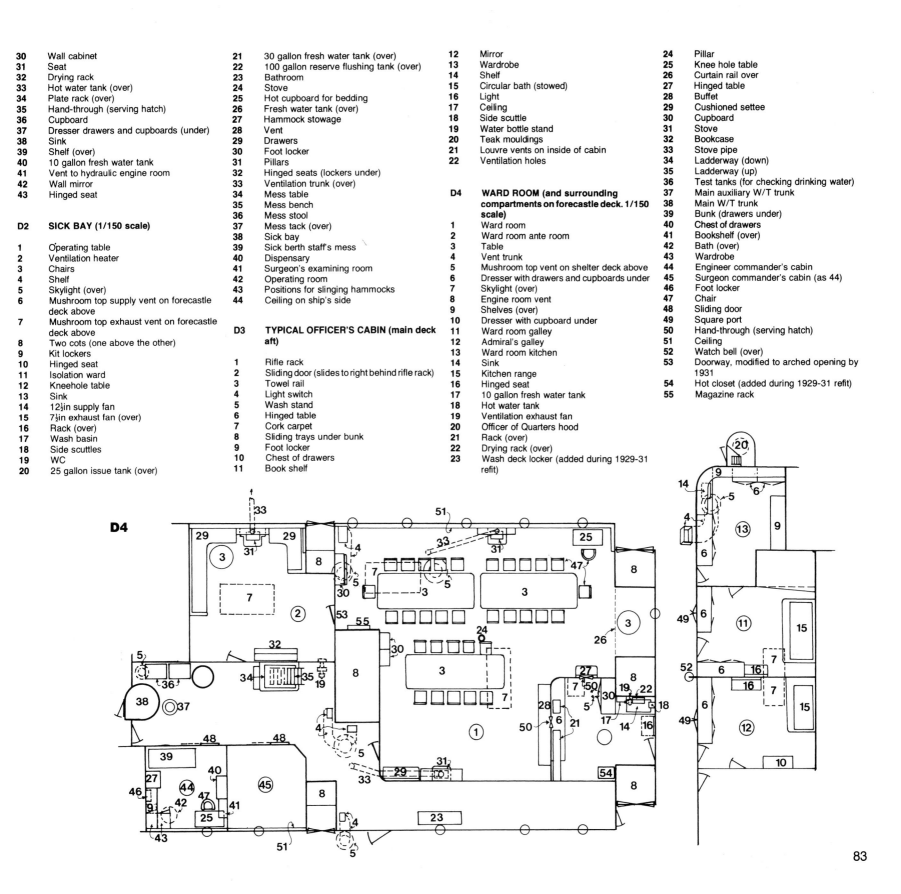

D Accommodation

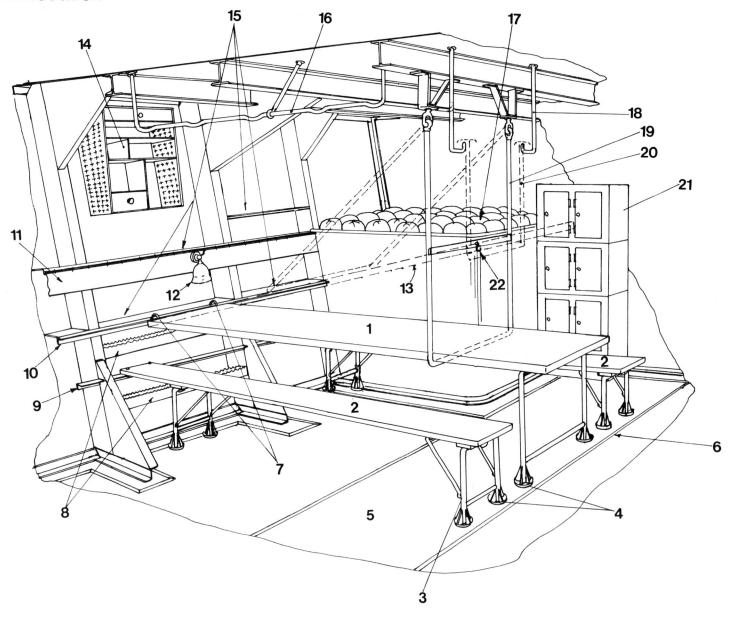

D5

D5	**TYPICAL MESS (note: most of the mess tables were longer than that illustrated and were supported by two bars from the deck head and not one)**	**12**	Light
		13	Stowed position of table (stools on top)
		14	Mess rack (sides perforated)
		15	Shelves for stowage of mess utensils, ditty boxes, etc
1	Pine mess table	**16**	Hammock bar (only one shown for clarity, at least four would normally be visible in this view)
2	Pine mess stool		
3	Folding legs		
4	Cast iron feet	**17**	Hammock stowage
5	Corticene laid on deck	**18**	Hooks for stowing table
6	Brass edging strips to corticene	**19**	Table support bar
7	Table hinges	**20**	Table legs reversed for hanging table on stowage hooks
8	Boot racks		
9	Angle bar for fixing end of stool	**21**	Kit lockers
10	Angle bar for locating table hinges	**22**	Flat bar across table support with hook for mess kettle
11	Steel sheet for fixing lights and their cables		

E Superstructure

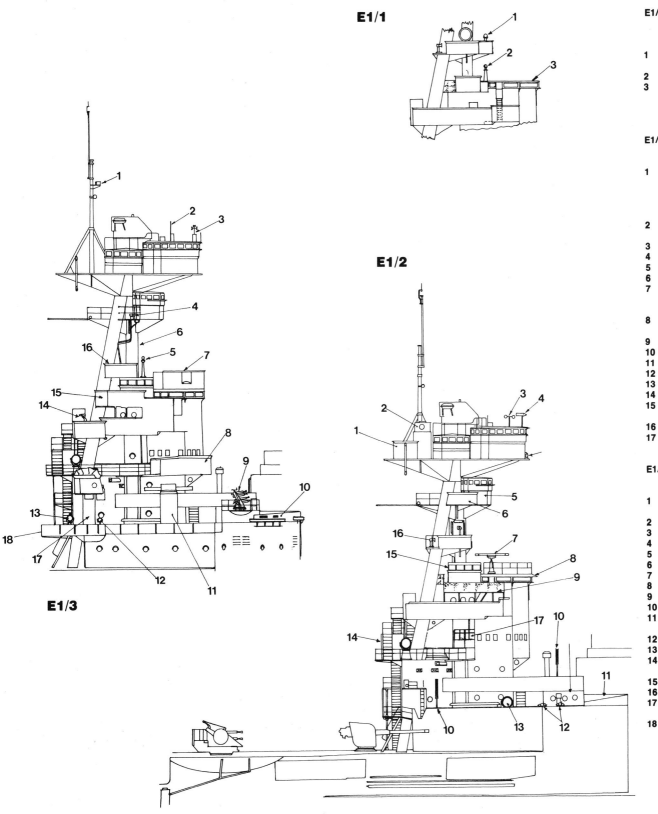

E1/1

E1/1 FORE BRIDGE (late 1920 to 1927. All drawings in section E 1/300 scale unless otherwise noted)

1 Torpedo rangefinder and platform, removed during 1927 refit
2 8ft rangefinder
3 Compass platform built up and new windows provided after trials (roller shutter in roof)

E1/2 FORWARD SUPERSTRUCTURE (after 1929-31 refit)

1 Pom-pom director platforms, moved to position occupied by 5.5in rangefinder during 1934 refit. Port director fitted during 1935 refit – both removed during 1936 refit when directors repositioned on fore bridge)
2 5.5in rangefinder tower (moved to signal deck during 1934 refit)
3 Anemometer
4 Wind vane
5 Torpedo lookout platform
6 Searchlight manipulating platform
7 9ft rangefinder (position after 1927 refit) – roller shutter in compass platform roof plated over
8 Extension to roof added during 1929-31 refit
9 Teak platform added during 1927 refit
10 Semaphore
11 Signalman's shelter
12 3pdr saluting guns
13 24in signalling searchlight
14 Upper tactical plot
15 Torpedo control position added during 1927 refit
16 Syren
17 Windscreen

E1/3 FORWARD SUPERSTRUCTURE (after 1939 refit)

1 Distant reading thermograph added c1935-36
2 Type 75 W/T aerial added during 1936 refit
3 Combined anemometer and wind vane
4 Syren fitted on reduced platform
5 9ft rangefinder
6 Searchlight platform removed
7 Air defence position added during 1936 refit
8 Extension to Admiral's bridge
9 0.5in MG mounting added during 1934 refit
10 Submarine lookouts
11 12ft rangefinder moved down from fore top during 1934 refit
12 Signalling lamp
13 20in signalling searchlight
14 Pom-pom director, moved down from fore top during 1936 refit
15 Upper compass platform enlarged
16 Air defence position added during 1936 refit
17 HACS director MK III added (port and starboard)
18 Admiral's signal platform extended

E Superstructure

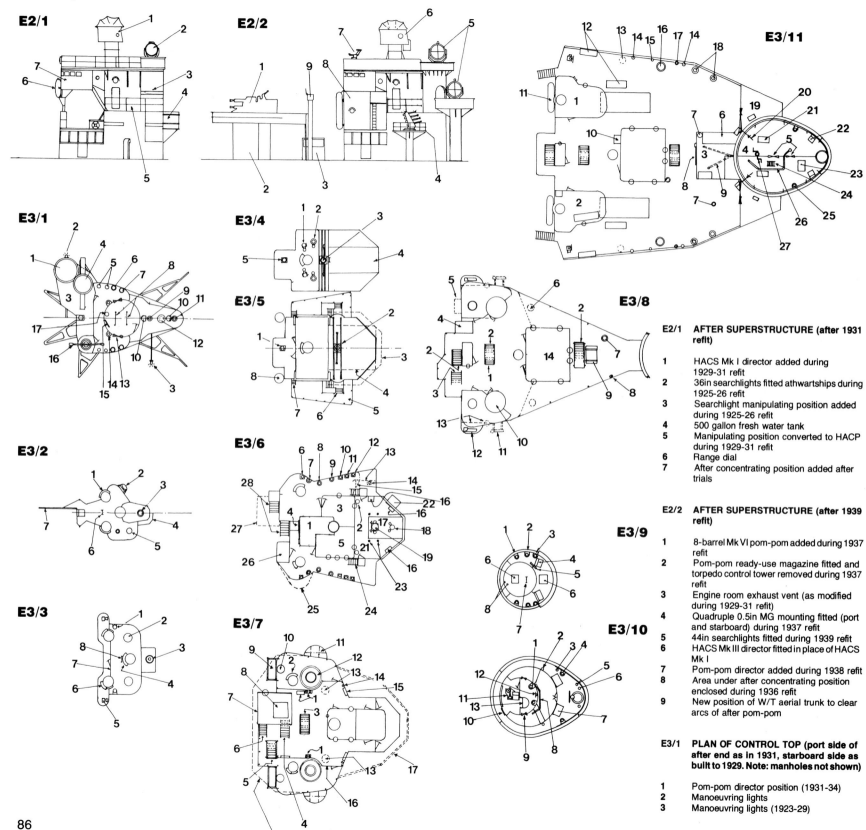

E2/1

E2/2

E3/11

E3/1

E3/4

E3/5

E3/8

E3/2

E3/6

E3/9

E3/3

E3/7

E3/10

E2/1 AFTER SUPERSTRUCTURE (after 1931 refit)

1 HACS Mk I director added during 1929–31 refit
2 36in searchlights fitted athwartships during 1925–26 refit
3 Searchlight manipulating position added during 1925–26 refit
4 500 gallon fresh water tank
5 Manipulating position converted to HACP during 1929–31 refit
6 Range dial
7 After concentrating position added after trials

E2/2 AFTER SUPERSTRUCTURE (after 1939 refit)

1 8-barrel Mk VI pom-pom added during 1937 refit
2 Pom-pom ready-use magazine fitted and torpedo control tower removed during 1937 refit
3 Engine room exhaust vent (as modified during 1929–31 refit)
4 Quadruple 0.5in MG mounting fitted (port and starboard) during 1937 refit
5 44in searchlights fitted during 1939 refit
6 HACS Mk III director fitted in place of HACS Mk I
7 Pom-pom director added during 1938 refit
8 Area under after concentrating position enclosed during 1936 refit
9 New position of W/T aerial trunk to clear arcs of after pom-pom

E3/1 PLAN OF CONTROL TOP (port side of after end as in 1931, starboard side as built to 1929. Note: manholes not shown)

1 Pom-pom director position (1931–34)
2 Manoeuvring lights
3 Manoeuvring lights (1923–29)

4 5.5in gun 12ft rangefinder tower (removed 1932 and replaced by pom-pom director in 1934 and these in turn removed to fore bridge 1936)

5 Searchlight transmitters and receivers, port and starboard

6 5.5in Dumaresq, port and starboard

7 Evershed 5.5in bearing indicator, port and starboard

8 Pillars

9 Evershed transmitter

10 Seat

11 Spotting instrument

12 15in Dumaresq

13 Arched opening, port and starboard

14 5.5in range clock, port and starboard

15 15in range clock

16 9ft rangefinder

17 Dreyer's calculator

E3/2 PLAN OF TORPEDO LOOKOUT (reclassified searchlight manipulating platform after 1927 refit. Port side as built, starboard side after 1927 refit. Note: Torpedo lookout removed during 1940 refit)

1 Vertical casing over cables running down mast strut

2 Range dial, port and starboard (removed during 1927 refit)

3 Torpedo spotting instrument (replaced by rangefinder bearing transmitter during 1927 refit)

4 Extended windshield (added during 1925-26 refit)

5 Searchlight manipulator (added during 1927 refit and removed together with screen and part of platform during 1939 refit)

6 Ladder

7 Spur for signal yard braces

E3/3 FOREMAST SEARCHLIGHT PLATFORM (removed during 1939 refit)

1 Searchlight control

2 36in searchlight, port and starboard

3 Torpedo firing rangefinder and platform fitted during 1921 refit and removed during 1927 refit

4 Cable casing on mainmast

5 Syren, port and starboard (moved to torpedo lookout platform during 1939 refit)

6 Cable casings on mainmast struts

7 Screen

8 Ladder

E3/4 SEARCHLIGHT MANIPULATING PLATFORM (1920-27 refitted as torpedo control position 1927. See E3/5)

1 Searchlight elevating standard, port and starboard

2 Searchlight training standard, port and starboard

3 8ft rangefinder fitted after trials (position originally occupied by gyro compass repeater)

4 Roof with sliding shutter added to compass platform after trials

5 Compass

E3/5 TORPEDO CONTROL POSITION (1927 onwards)

1 Compass

2 9ft rangefinder (removed during 1940 refit)

3 Extension to compass platform roof (added during 1929-31 refit)

4 Outline of air defence position added during 1936 refit

5 Platform around torpedo control position

6 Ladderways to compass platform and fore bridge

7 Ladder (up)

8 Foremast strut

E3/6 PLAN OF FORE BRIDGE (1931)

1 Navigating officer's cabin (formerly Admiral's plotting office converted 1929-31)

2 Chadburn's engine room telegraph, port and starboard

3 Charthouse

4 Sliding door

5 Remote control office (formely W/T office, converted 1925-26)

6 Evershed rangefinder, port and starboard

7 TDS Mk III (torpedo director sight), port and starboard

8 Gyro receiver, port and starboard

9 TDS Mk III, port and starboard

10 5.5in Evershed transmitter, port and starboard

11 Starshell Evershed transmitter, port and starboard

12 15in Evershed transmitter, port and starboard

13 Original outline of platform (modified during 1927 refit)

14 Searchlight Evershed (moved to torpedo control position during 1927 refit)

15 Screen and door removed during 1927 refit

16 Hinged table

17 Raised platform

18 Pelorus

19 Compass

20 Mast strut

21 Compass platform (5ft above level of fore bridge)

22 Chart table

23 Pillars, port and starboard

24 Ladder to compass platform

25 Extension to platform for pom-pom directors (fitted during 1936 refit)

26 Voice pipe cabinet

27 Roof of tactical plot (below)

28 Ladder (down, added during 1929-31 refit)

E3/7 ADMIRAL'S BRIDGE (1931)

1 Signal lamps (stowed)

2 Cable casing on mast strut

3 Ladder (down)

4 Ladder (up, added 1929-31 refit)

5 Ladder (down, added 1929-31 refit)

6 Ladder (up to roof of tactical plot, added 1929-31 refit)

7 Upper tactical plotting position (added 1929-31 refit)

8 Plotting table

9 Teak grating, port and starboard (removed when platform extended, 1939)

10 24in signalling searchlight, port and starboard

11 Guard to bowlight, port and starboard

12 5.5in gun director tower, port and starboard (removed during 1940 refit)

13 Position of 24in signalling searchlights moved to CT platform during 1927 refit

14 Position for signalling lamp, port and starboard

15 Stowage for signalling shutters for 24in searchlights, port and starboard

16 Screen, port and starboard

17 Extension's added to Admiral's bridge during 1939 refit

E3/8 CONNING TOWER PLATFORM (1931)

1 Ladder (up)

2 Ladder (down)

3 Ladder (up, added during 1929-31 refit)

4 500 gallon fresh water tank

5 Tank (added during 1939 refit)

6 Position of 24in signalling searchlight, port and starboard, during 1927 to 1929

7 W/T aerial trunk

8 Semaphore

9 Lewis gun tank

10 5.5in director towers (removed 1940)

11 Bowlight (added after trials)

12 Bowlight (removed during 1939 refit, as blocked by HACS director)

13 Outline of compartment, and added side scuttle, after 1939 refit, port and starboard

14 Captain's sea cabin (was two cabins, see section 'A')

E3/9 5.5in CONTROL AND ADMIRAL'S TOWER

1 Dumaresq, port and starboard

2 Evershed bearing indicator, port and starboard

3 Clear range indicator, port and starboard

4 Hinged table, port and starboard

5 Vent

6 Hatch

7 Ladder to armoured director hood

8 Vents

E3/10 UPPER CONNING TOWER

1 5.5in range clock, port and starboard

2 Periscope, port and starboard

3 Azimuth gyro receiver

4 Bearing sight, port and starboard

5 Engine revolution telegraph

6 Engine room telegraph, port and starboard

7 Hinged table

8 Vent

9 Arched opening between clock space and 5.5in control towers, port and starboard

10 Sliding door

11 Armoured hood training motor

12 15in range dial

13 Hatch to torpedo control tower (below)

E3/11 ADMIRAL'S SIGNAL PLATFORM (1931)

1 Admiral's bathroom

2 Plumbers' workshop

3 Signal distributing office (fitted during 1929-31 refit)

4 Torpedo control tower

5 Arched openings

6 Tables

7 W/T aerial trunk

8 Sliding door

9 Pneumatic tube for transmission of messages

10 3pdr ready-use locker

11 Carley rafts, port and starboard (fitted during 1929-31 refit)

12 Signal lockers, port and starboard (number reduced and rearranged during 1929-31 refit)

13 Original position of foremost 3pdr saluting gun (moved during 1929-31 refit)

14 Davit socket, port and starboard

15 Signalling lamp, port and starboard

16 24in signalling searchlight, port and starboard (fitted during 1929-31 refit)

17 Semaphore, port and starboard

18 3pdr saluting guns, port and starboard

19 Signalman's shelters, port and starboard (added during 1929-31 refit)

20 Frames, port and starboard

21 Table, port and starboard

22 Hinged table, port and starboard

23 Hatch

24 Ladder (up)

25 Torpedo deflection sight, port and starboard

26 Vent (over)

27 Hand training crank for director hood (in case of power failure)

E Superstructure

E3/12 ADMIRAL'S SIGNAL PLATFORM (1939)

1 Signal lockers, port and starboard (added with extended signal deck during 1939 refit)
2 20in signalling searchlight, port and starboard (added 1939)
3 Signalling lamp, port and starboard (added 1939)
4 Sounding machine
5 High angle control position (HACP – provided during 1939 refit)
6 High angle directors (added during 1939 refit)
7 Quadruple 0.5in MG mountings (added during 1934 refit)
8 0.5in ready-use ammunition lockers, port and starboard
9 Submarine lookouts (added during 1939 refit)
10 5.5in rangefinder towers (moved down from fore top during 1934 refit)
11 3pdr saluting guns (removed shortly after the outbreak of war)
12 Semaphore

E3/13 SHELTER DECK (up to 1938)

1 42ft motor launch and 36ft sailing pinnace (1920); 42ft motor launch and 35ft motor boat (c1924 to 1931); 42ft motor launch and 30ft fast motor boat (1931 to 1938)
2 45ft Admiral's barge (1920); 50ft steam pinnace (after trials to 1938)
3 42ft sailing launch (after trials, to 1926); 42ft motor launch (c1926 to 1929); 42ft motor launch and 35ft motor boat (1931)
4 50ft steam pinnace (1920); 45ft Admiral's barge (after trials, to 1938)
5 50ft steam pinnace
6 35ft motor boat
7 Harbour position for 30ft gig (starboard shows position up to 1929 and port the position after 1929-31 refit), provided after trials.
8 32ft cutter and 30ft gig
9 32ft cutter, 30ft gig and 27ft whaler
10 27ft whaler and 16ft dinghy (moved slightly inboard during 1929-31 refit to clear pom-pom)
11 30ft gig and 16ft dinghy (moved slightly inboard during 1929-31 refit to clear pom-pom)
12 32ft cutter (seaboat – in position provided during 1929-31 refit)
13 8-barrel Mk V pom-pom mountings (added during 1929-31 refit)
14 5.5in guns (replaced by 4in HA Mk IV mountings during 1938 refit)
15 4in HA Mk III mountings
16 4in HA Mk IV mountings (added during 1937 refit – estimated position)
17 Two quadruple 0.5in MG mountings (added during 1937 refit)
18 4in ammunition hoist
19 Nine 4in ready-use lockers (added during 1929-31 refit – additional lockers may have been fitted for 4in guns fitted in 1937 and 1938)
20 Jettisonable petrol tank for boats, port and starboard (fitted during 1929-31 refit)
21 Stream anchor (stowed position)
22 Night lifebuoy
23 Cordage reels
24 Locker (removed during 1925-26 refit)

25 Hawser reels (added during 1929-31 refit)
26 Lockers (added during 1925-26 refit and removed during 1929-31 refit)
27 Wash deck locker (removed during 1925-26 refit)
28 Wash deck locker (added during 1925-26 refit)
29 450 gallon fresh water tank
30 5.5in ready-use locker (charges)
31 5.5in gun depression rail, port and starboard
32 Rack over
33 Wash deck locker (removed during 1929-31 refit)
34 Petrol lockers (added during 1925-26 refit and removed during 1929-31 refit)
35 Wash deck locker (removed during 1925-26 refit)
36 Rack
37 Engine room exhaust vents (modified during 1929-31 refit – tops replaced by hinged openings)
38 400 gallon sanitary tank (over)
39 500 gallon fresh water tank (over)
40 Evershed bearing and training receivers, port and starboard (removed when night defence position became sailmaker's shop during 1929-31 refit)

E3/14 SHELTER DECK (1940. No scale)

1 27ft whaler (fitted during 1939 refit)
2 16ft motor dinghy (fitted during 1939 refit and moved forward during 1940 refit)
3 25ft motor boat (fitted during 1939 refit, replaced by 35ft Admiral's barge during 1940 refit)
4 45ft steam pinnace (fitted during 1939 refit, replaced by 35ft fast motor boat during 1941 refit)
5 45ft motor launch and 32ft cutter (fitted during 1939 refit)
6 42ft motor launch (fitted during 1939 refit)
7 50ft steam pinnace (fitted during 1939 refit, replaced by 35ft fast motor boat during 1941 refit)
8 32ft cutter and 30ft gig (fitted during 1939 refit)
9 25ft fast motor boats (fitted during 1940 refit – port position occupied by 32ft cutter and port inner position by 16ft dinghy during 1939-40)
10 16ft motor dinghy (fitted abreast DF platform during 1941 refit)
11 16ft dinghy (fitted abreast DF platform during 1941 refit)
12 16ft motor dinghy (fitted during 1940 refit – occupied by 35ft fast motor boat during 1939-40) moved to position 10 in 1941
13 Torpedo rangefinder tower (removed during 1940 refit)
14 Twin 4in HA/LA mountings (fitted during 1940 refit)
15 Twin 4in HA/LA mountings (fitted during 1939 refit)
16 UP mountings (added during 1940 refit – after pair replaced 32ft cutters fitted during 1939 refit)
17 2pdr pom-pom mountings
18 5.5in gun (refitted during 1939 refit and removed during 1940 refit)
19 0.5in MG mounting platforms (over)

20 Pom-pom magazine (pom-pom on bandstand, over, added during 1937 refit)
21 UP ready-use lockers (as in June 1940)
22 4in ready-use lockers (as in 1940-41)
23 4in ammunition hoists (fitted during 1939 refit)

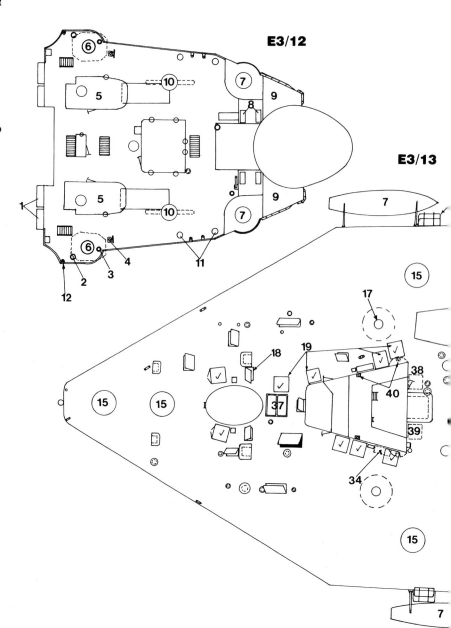

E3/12

E3/13

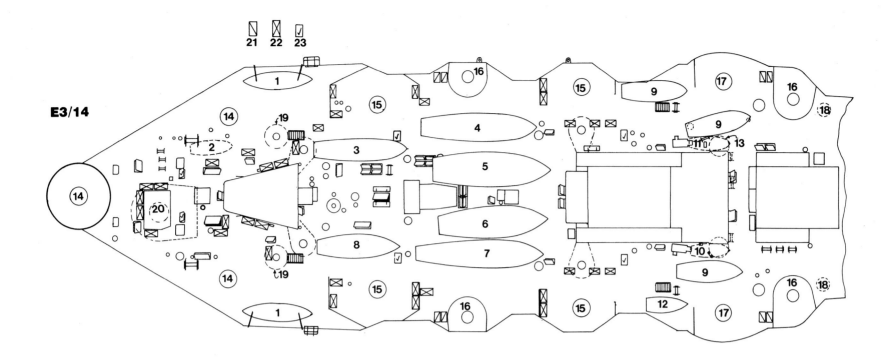

E3/14

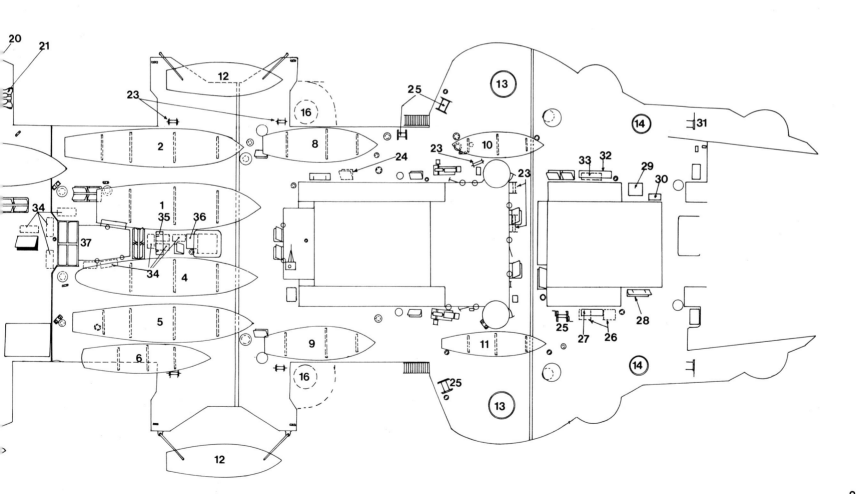

E Superstructure

E3/15

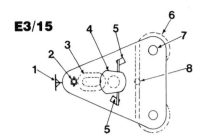

E3/16

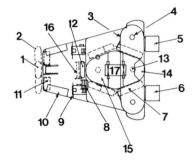

E3/17

E3/18

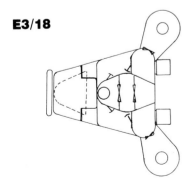

E4/1

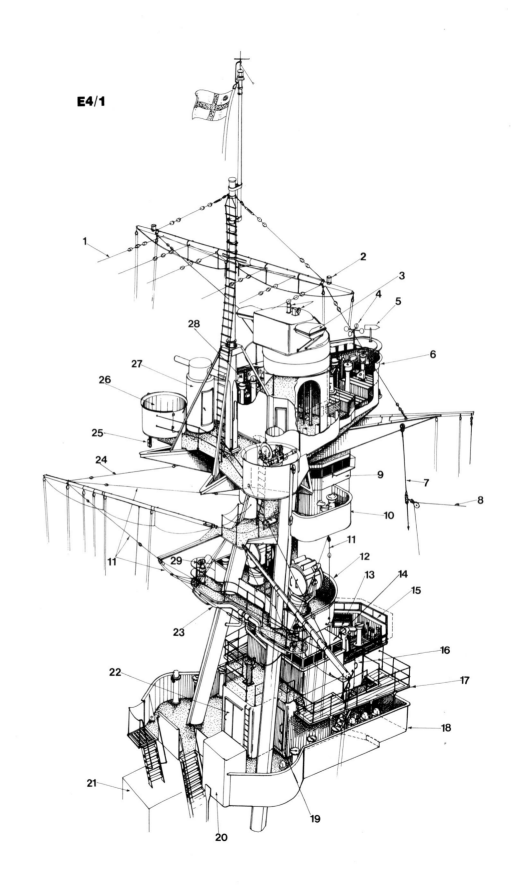

E4/2

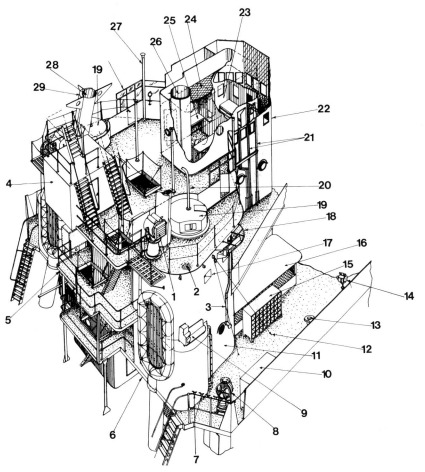

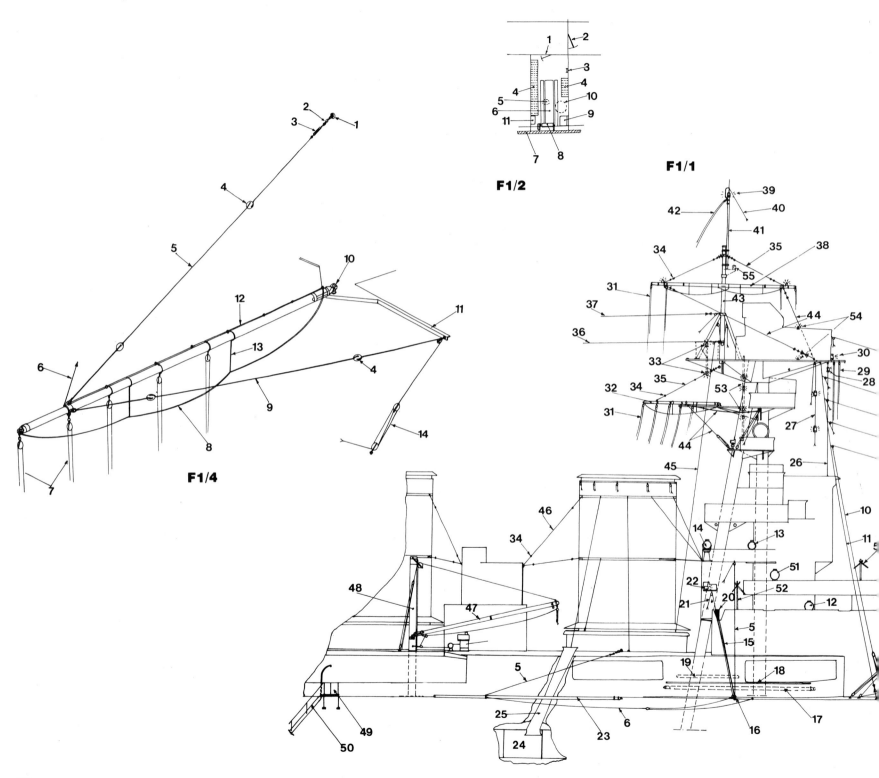

F1/2

F1/1

F1/4

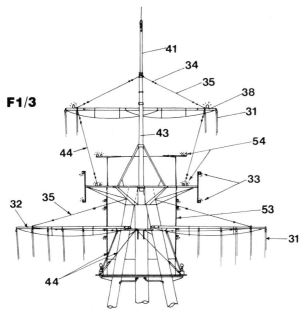

F1/3

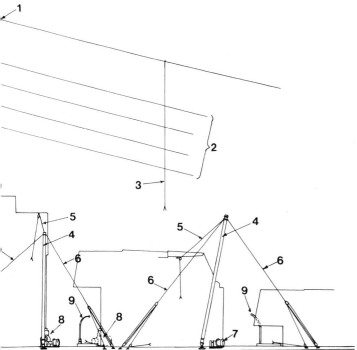

F Rig

F1/6 RIG TO MAINMAST (looking forward. 1/300 scale. key as F1/5)

F1/7 RIG TO MAINMAST (1920 to 1925. 1/300 scale)

As built *Hood* carried a main topgallant mast for the W/T yard. After fitting out and during the world cruise of 1923-24 it was rigged as shown but during most of the remaining period between 1920 and 1925 it was housed down with the W/T yard level with the topmast head. The raised position increased the range of the W/T and hence was used for foreign service, the lowered position was for use in home waters. The topgallant mast was removed during her 1925-26 refit.

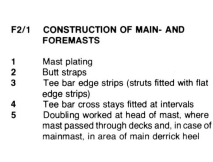

F1/6

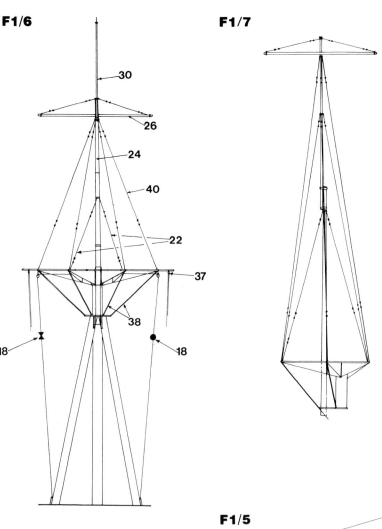

F1/7

F1/5

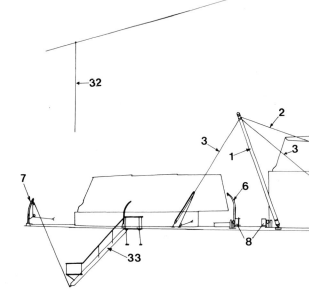

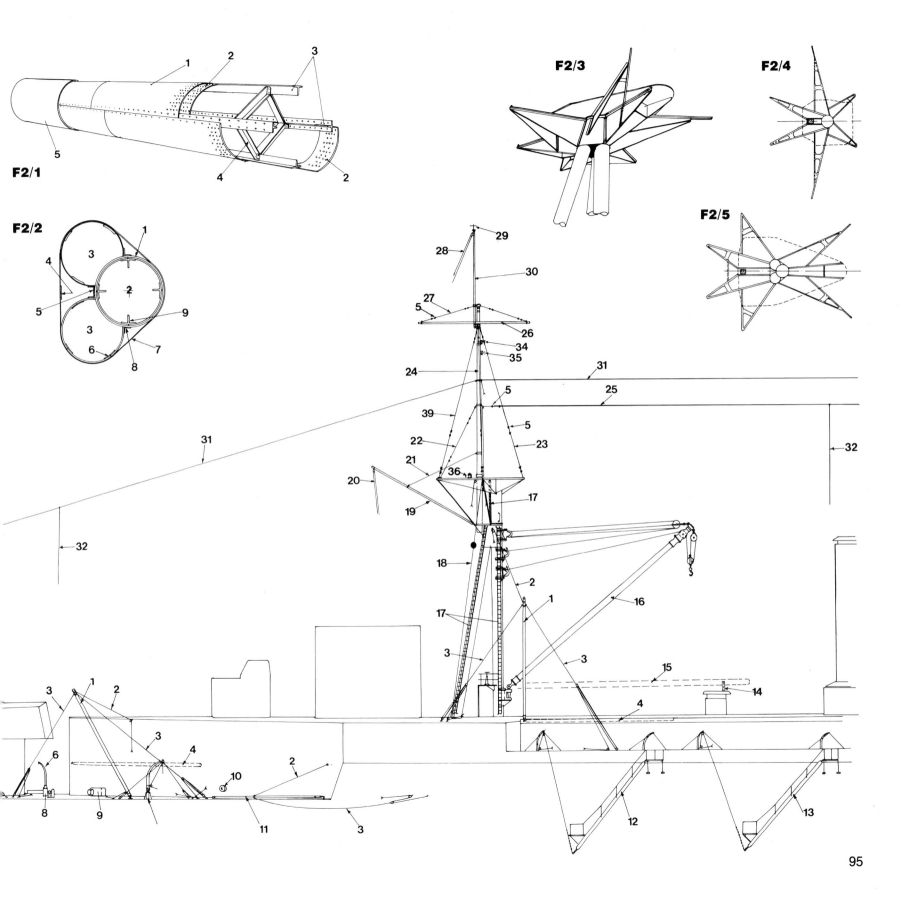

F2/1

F2/2

F2/3

F2/4

F2/5

F3/1

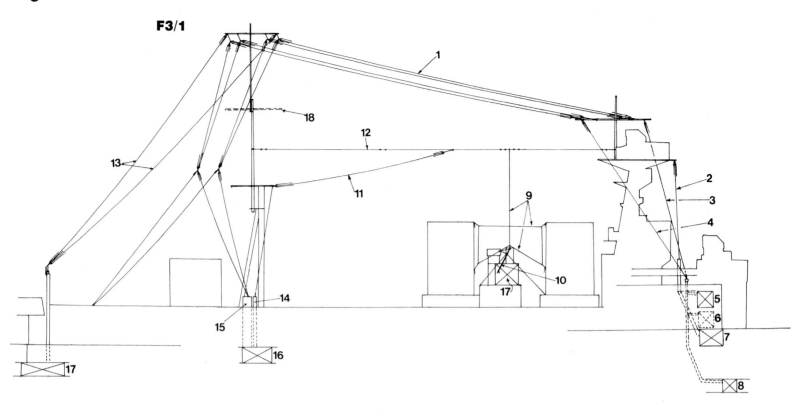

F3/2

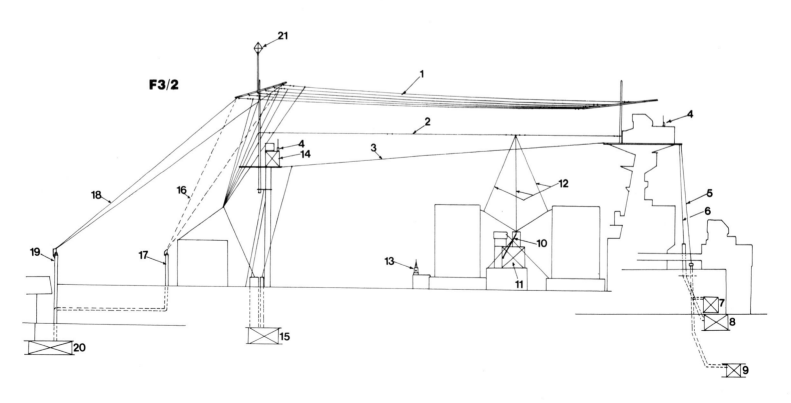

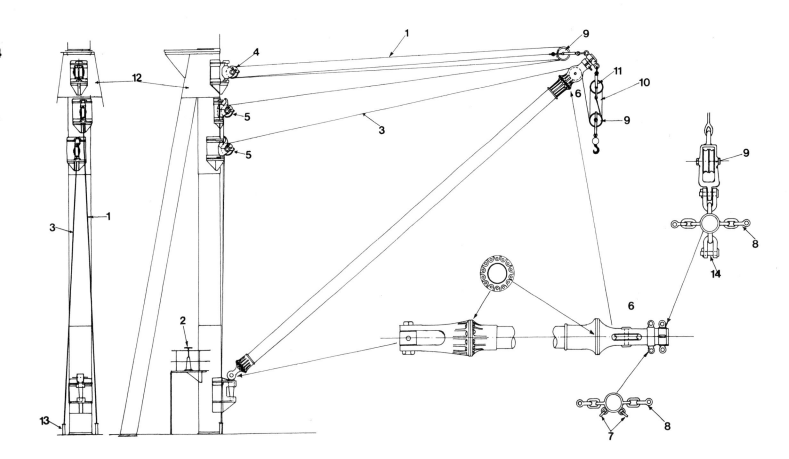

F4

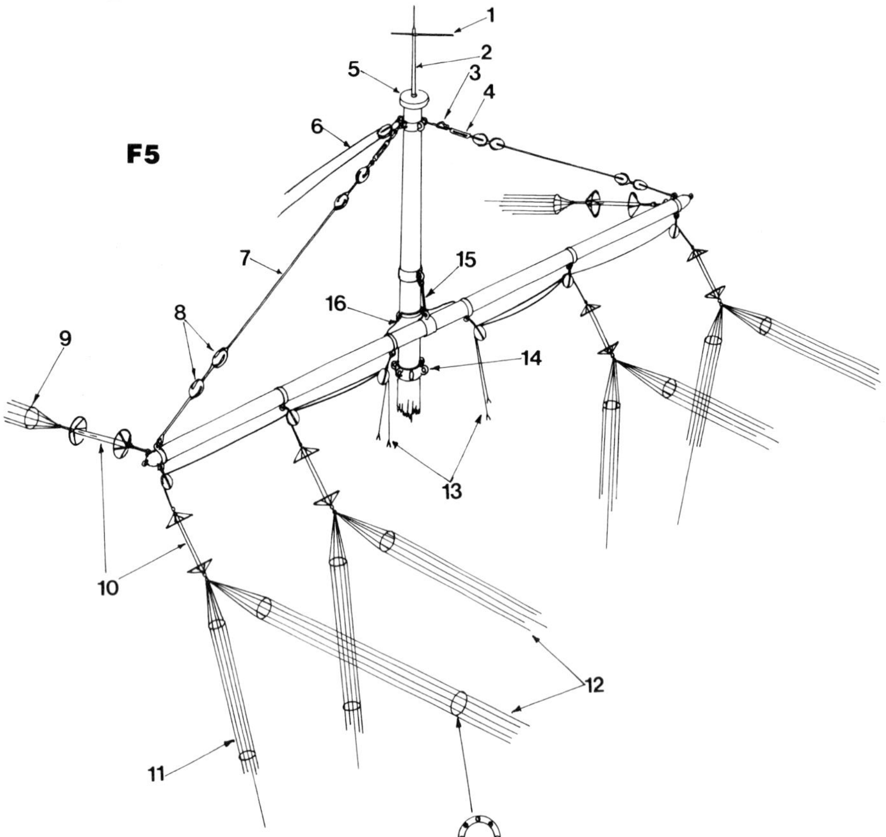
F5
1
2
5
3
4
6
7
15
16
8
9
14
13
10
12
11

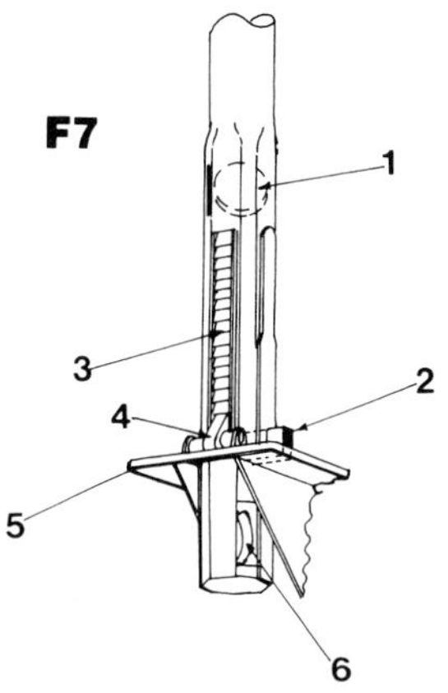
F7
1
3
2
4
5
6

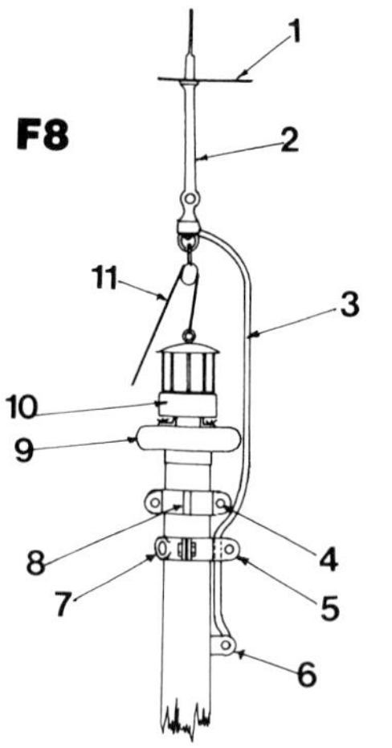
F8
1
2
11
3
10
9
8
4
7
5
6

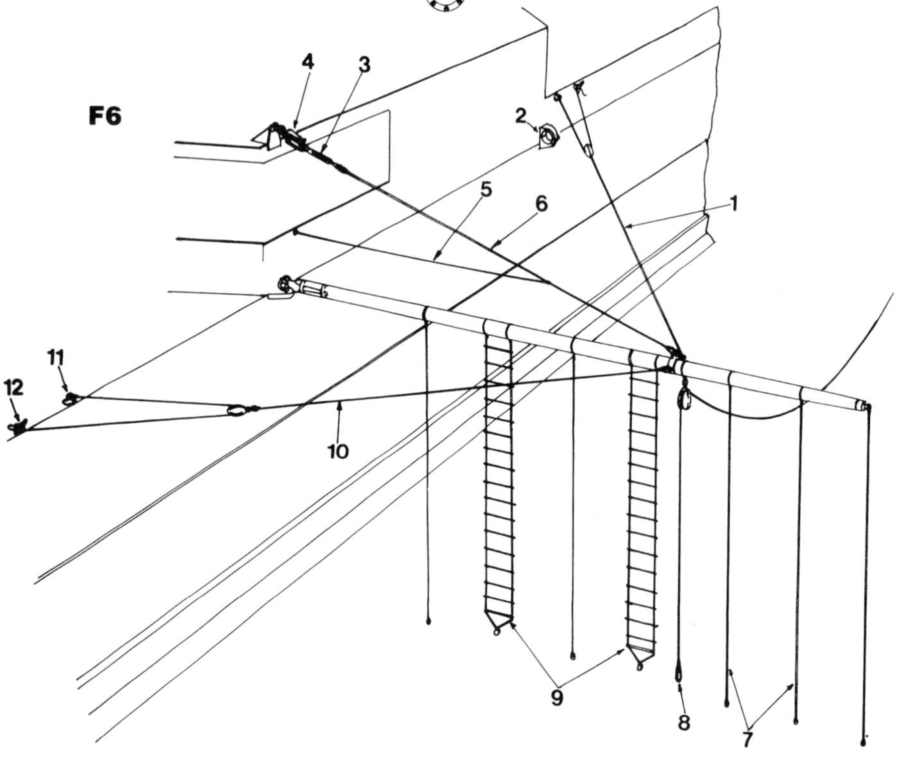
F6
4
3
2
5
6
1
11
12
10
9
8
7

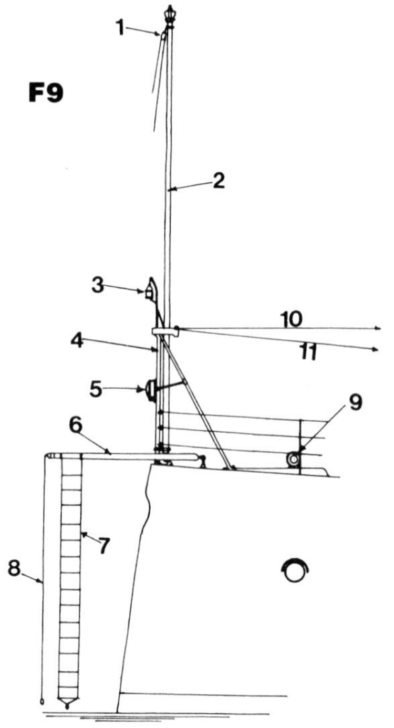
F9
1
2
3
10
4
11
5
9
6
7
8

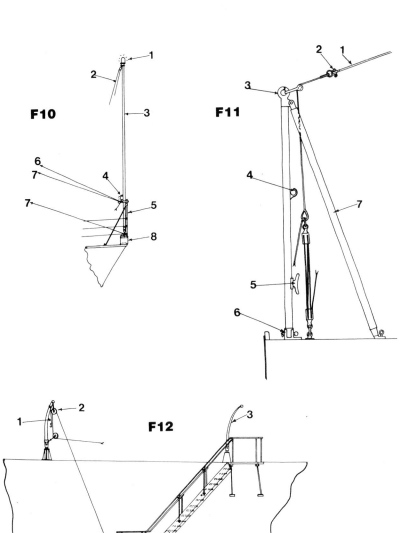

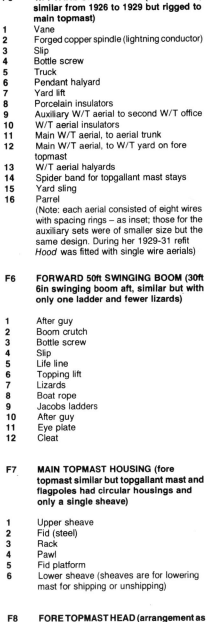

F5 **W/T YARD ON MAINMAST (1920 to 1925, similar from 1926 to 1929 but rigged to main topmast)**

1 Vane
2 Forged copper spindle (lightning conductor)
3 Slip
4 Bottle screw
5 Truck
6 Pendant halyard
7 Yard lift
8 Porcelain insulators
9 Auxiliary W/T aerial to second W/T office
10 W/T aerial insulators
11 Main W/T aerial, to aerial trunk
12 Main W/T aerial, to W/T yard on fore topmast
13 W/T aerial halyards
14 Spider band for topgallant mast stays
15 Yard sling
16 Parrel
(Note: each aerial consisted of eight wires with spacing rings – as inset; those for the auxiliary sets were of smaller size but the same design. During her 1929-31 refit *Hood* was fitted with single wire aerials)

F6 **FORWARD 50ft SWINGING BOOM (30ft 6in swinging boom aft, similar but with only one ladder and fewer lizards)**

1 After guy
2 Boom crutch
3 Bottle screw
4 Slip
5 Life line
6 Topping lift
7 Lizards
8 Boat rope
9 Jacobs ladders
10 After guy
11 Eye plate
12 Cleat

F7 **MAIN TOPMAST HOUSING (fore topmast similar but topgallant mast and flagpoles had circular housings and only a single sheave)**

1 Upper sheave
2 Fid (steel)
3 Rack
4 Pawl
5 Fid platform
6 Lower sheave (sheaves are for lowering mast for shipping or unshipping)

F8 **FORE TOPMAST HEAD (arrangement as built, lamp and spindle were moved to top of flagpole when this was fitted after trials)**

1 Vane
2 Copper spindle (lightning conductor)
3 Hinged gallows
4 Eye for pendant halyard
5 Securing pin
6 Hinge
7 Eyes for Jacobs ladder
8 Eyes for W/T yard lifts
9 Truck
10 Flashing lamp
11 Lamp halyard

F9 **ENSIGN STAFF (1/150 scale)**

1 Ensign halyard
2 Ensign staff
3 Stern and overtaking light
4 Ensign staff stanchion
5 Fog light
6 10ft guest warp boom
7 Jacobs ladder
8 Lizard
9 26ft across stern boom (added during 1929-31 refit)
10 Awning ridge rope
11 Awning rope at deck edge

F10 **JACK STAFF (1/150 staff)**

1 Anchor light
2 Signal halyard
3 Jack staff
4 Shaded stern light
5 Jack staff stanchion
6 Dressing line
7 Hammock girdlines
8 Fairlead (or bullring)

F11 **AWNING STANCHION (1/37.5 scale)**

1 Awning
2 Shackle through cringle (eye fixed into edge of awning)
3 Caliper eye
4 Hook to take awning in lower positon
5 Cleat
6 Heel fitting of similar design to that for guardrail stanchions
7 Stay, normally one but two fitted to corner and ridge rope stanchions

F12 **ADMIRAL'S ACCOMMODATION LADDER (starboard side quarterdeck. 1/150 scale. Note: Other accommodation ladders of same design except handrails of rope instead of wood)**

1 Rope and hook for taking ladder when shifting tackle
2 Ladder davit
3 Ladder and platform working davit
4 Alternate positions for ladder stays to suit ship's draught
5 Portable fender
6 Wood gratings
7 Foot plate

G Armament

G1

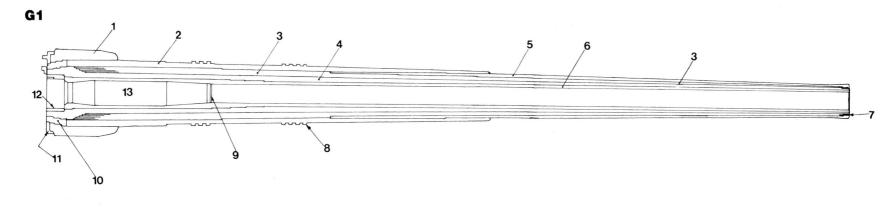

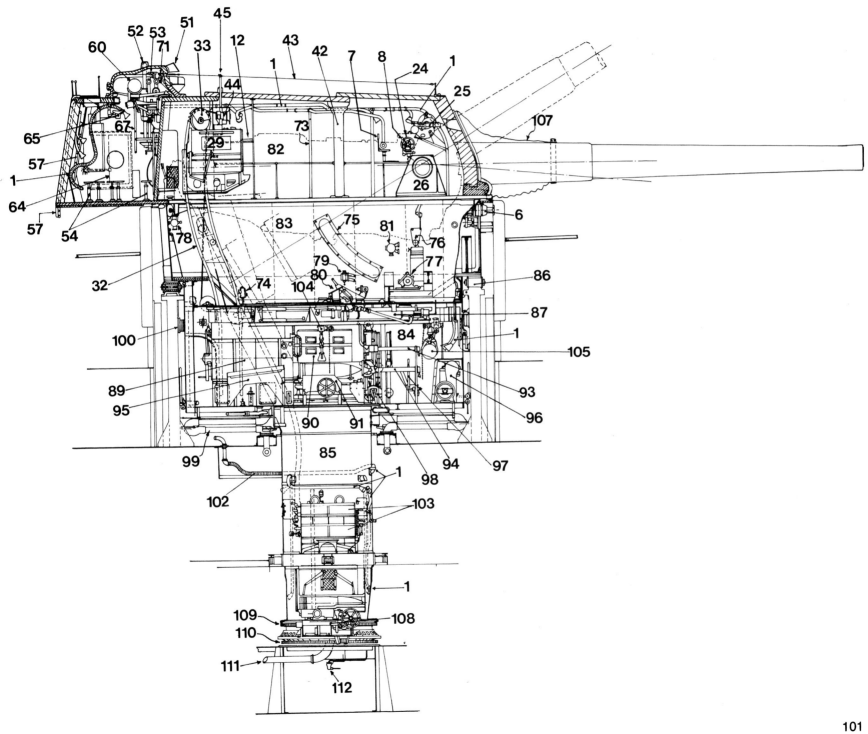

G2/2

G2/4

G2/5

G2/3

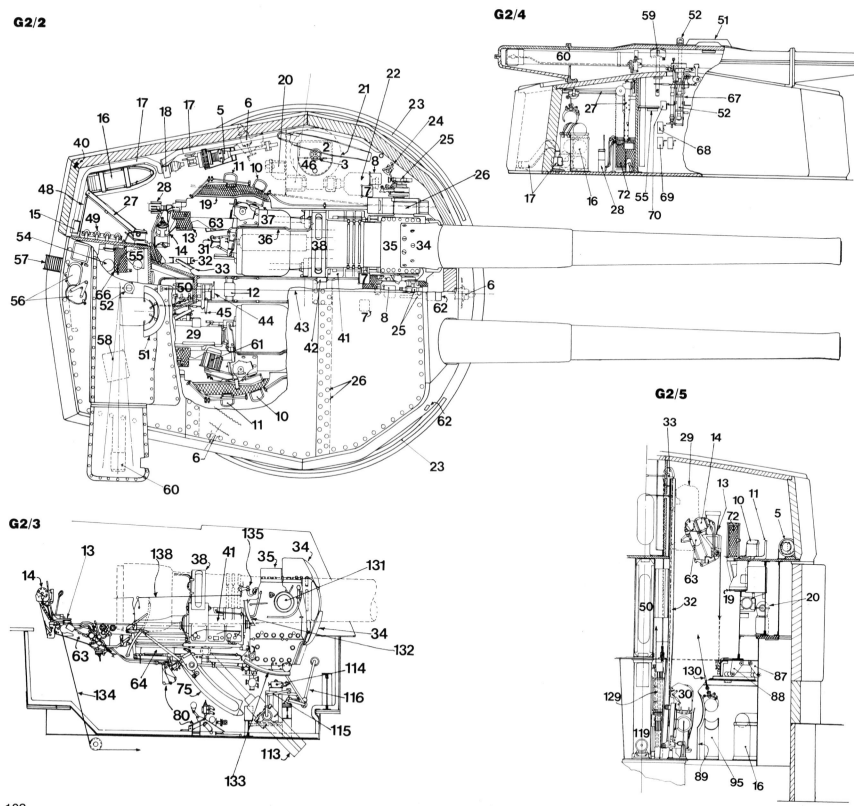

G2/6

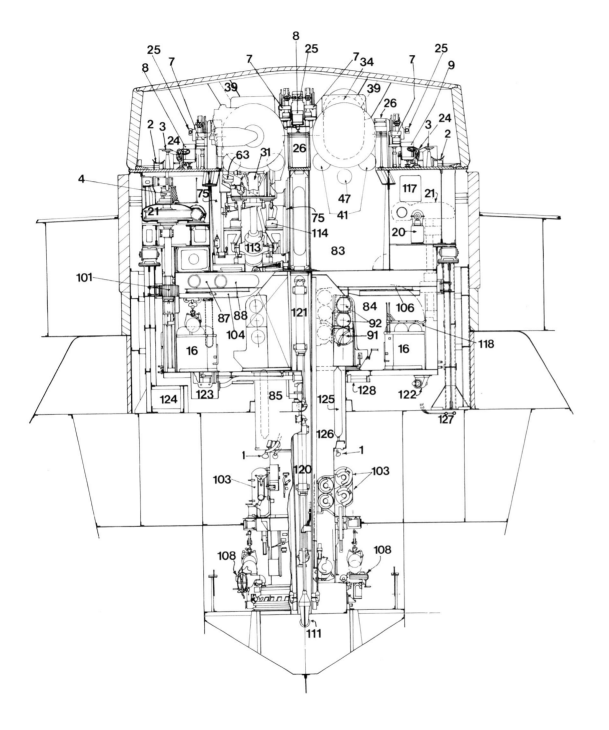

G2/7

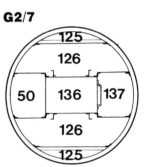

G Armament

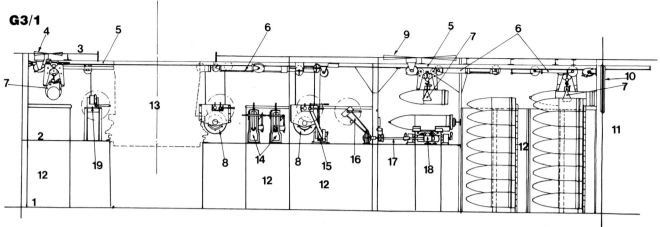

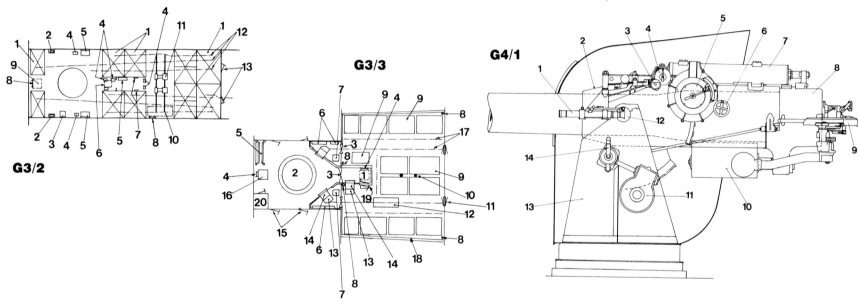

G3/1   PROFILE OF 'Y' SHELL ROOM (1/100 scale)

1	Inner bottom
2	Shell room flat
3	Magazine flat (platform deck)
4	Hatch on centre-line
5	Overhead rail for shell grabs
6	Lifting and traversing hydraulic presses on deck head
7	Shell grab
8	Traversing winch
9	Ammunition embarkation hatch (starboard side)
10	Hatch to 'X' shell room
11	'X' shell room
12	Shell bin
13	Bottom of revolving trunk
14	Hydraulic valve operating standards
15	Lifting winch
16	Hand gear for traversing bogie
17	Clutched shaft from hand gear to transversing bogie
18	Shell traversing bogie
19	Hand operated shell lifting winch

G3/2   PLAN OF 'Y' SHELL ROOM (1/300 scale)

1	Shell bins
2	Hand lifting winch
3	25 gallon fresh water tank
4	Hydraulic valve operating standards
5	Traversing winch
6	100 ton pump (under) – fitted in all shell rooms
7	Auxiliary hand winch to traversing bogie
8	Ladder (up)
9	Hatch (over)
10	Ammunition embarkation hatch (over)
11	Shell traversing bogie
12	Overhead rails
13	Doors to 'X' shell room

G3/3   PLAN OF 'Y' MAGAZINE AND HANDING ROOM (1/300 scale)

1	Hatch (over)
2	Revolving trunk in handing room
3	Arched opening
4	Ladder
5	Stowage for 24 drill charges
6	Stowage for chutes
7	25 gallon fresh water tank
8	Vent
9	Cordite cases in racks
10	Pillars
11	Double doors to 'X' magazine (sealed up during 1929-31 refit)
12	Ammunition embarkation hatch (and over)
13	Hinged cordite tray
14	Flash-tight scuttle
15	Water-tight doors
16	Hatch and over
17	Overhead rails
18	Wood lining
19	Wood door and water-tight door giving access to handing room
20	Voice pipe exchange

G4/1   5.5in Mk II MOUNTING

1	Gun layer's telescopic sight
2	Cradle
3	Deflection handwheel
4	Deflection dial
5	Range dial
6	Range setting handwheel
7	Recuperator spring case
8	Breech
9	Loading tray
10	Recoil cylinder
11	Elevating gear
12	Trunnion
13	Trunnion bracket
14	Elevating crank

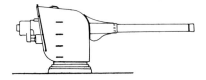

G4/4

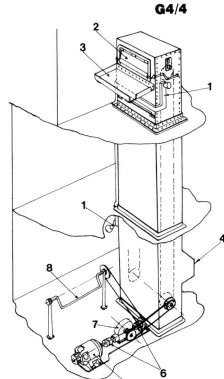

G4/3

G4/2

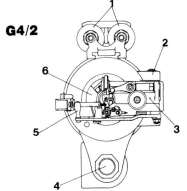

G5/1

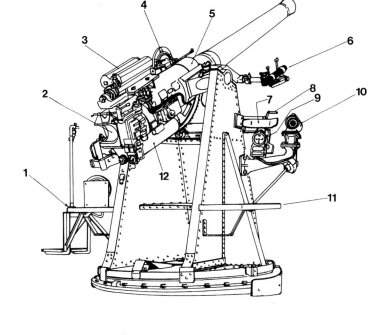

G4/2 5.5in Mk I GUN BREECH

1   Recuperators
2   Carrier hinge
3   Carrier
4   Recoil cylinder
5   Breech operating lever
6   Breech block

G4/3   5.5in Mk II MOUNTING (general arrangement. 1/150 scale)

G4/4 5.5in AMMUNITION DREDGER HOIST (ammunition passage to forecastle deck)

1   Voice pipe
2   Flash-tight scuttle
3   Waiting tray
4   Loading scuttle
5   Electric motor drive
6   Clutches for disengaging and engaging motor or hand drive
7   Worm and wormwheel gear case
8   Hand crank in case of power failure

G5/1 4in HA Mk III MOUNTING

1   Gun layer's platform
2   Sliding breech block
3   Recuperator cylinders
4   Range dial
5   Cradle
6   Gun trainer's sight
7   Gun trainer's rest
8   Traning crank
9   Training indicator
10   Training receiver
11   Trainer's platform
12   Recoil cylinder

G Armament

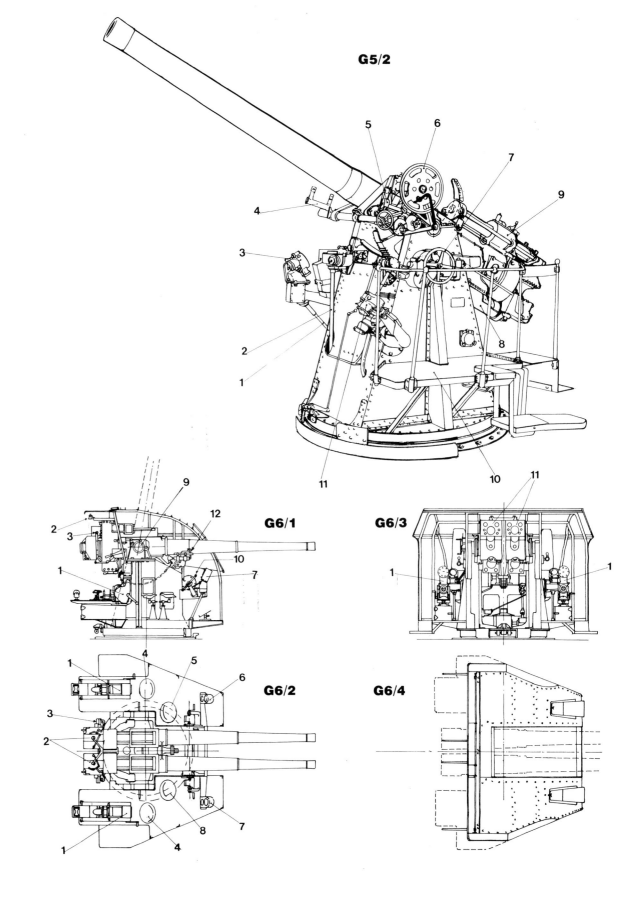

G5/2 4in HA Mk IV MOUNTING

1. Mounting drive to training receiver
2. Training drive spindle
3. Training receiver
4. Trainer's telescopic sight bracket
5. Layer's telescopic sight bracket
6. Range dial
7. Elevating handle
8. Recoil cylinder
9. Recuperator cylinder
10. Gun layer's and sight setter's platform
11. Elevation receiver

G6/1 4in HA Mk XIX MOUNTING (profile, trainer, side. G6/1–G6/7 1/150 scale)

G6/2 (plan)

G6/3 (rear view of mounting)

G6/4 (plan of shield)

G6/5 (profile, layer's side)

G6/6 (profile of shield)

G6/7 (front view of shield)

G6/8 (general view)

1. Fuze setting machine
2. Lights
3. Breech operating lever
4. Fuze setter's seat
5. Gun layer's seat
6. Elevation receiver
7. Training receiver
8. Trainer's seat
9. Trunnion
10. Training crank
11. Counter balance weights
12. Trainer's sight
13. Elevation crank
14. Foot rest
15. Layer's sight
16. Deflection setting wheel
17. Deflection dial
18. Range dial
19. Range setting wheel
20. Breech block

G7/1 EIGHT-BARREL 2pdr POM-POM MOUNTING

1. Voice pipe
2. Elevation crank
3. Open sight
4. Ammunition feed boxes (150 rounds per box, 1200 rounds per mounting)
5. Flash guards
6. Empty cartridge chute (under barrels at front of mounting)
7. Training crank

G7/2 EIGHT-BARREL Mk VI POM-POM MOUNTING (general arrangement. 1/75 scale)

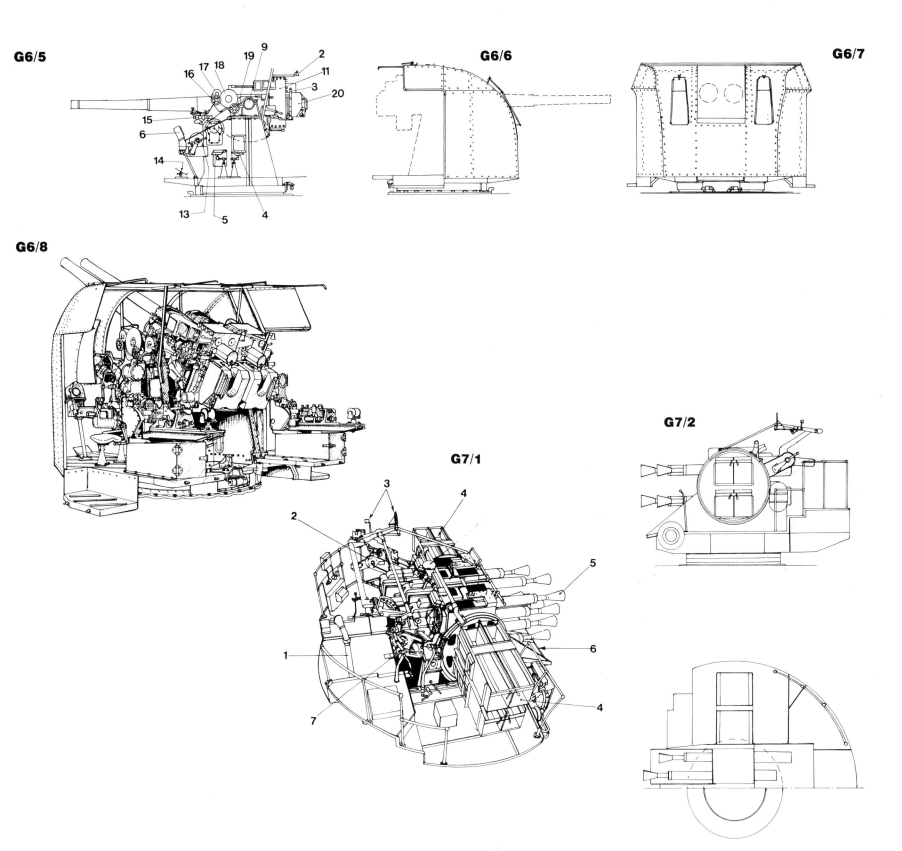

G6/5

16 17 18 19 9 2

15 6 14 13 5 4 11 3 20

G6/6

G6/7

G6/8

G7/1

2 3 4 5 6 1 7 4

G7/2

G Armament

G8   QUADRUPLE 0.5in MG MOUNTING

1   Layer's open sight
2   Sight link motions
3   Elevation arc
4   Layer's body rest
5   Elevation handwheel
6   Elevation gearbox
7   Depression rail
8   Locking bolt
9   Depression control link and follower
10   Ammunition drum guard plate
11   Empty cartridge chute (on left side for guns
     1 (top) and 3 and right side for guns 2 and 4)
12   Ammunition feed drums (on left side for
     guns 2 and 4 and right side for guns 1 and 3)

G9   3pdr SALUTING GUN (1/37.5 scale)

1   Recoil cylinder (one each side)
2   Run out spring (in same casing as recoil
     cylinder)
3   Sliding breech block
4   Shoulder rest
5   Hand grips
6   Firing pistol grip
7   Pedestal (not part of mounting)
8   Carriage

G10   U P MOUNTING

1   Layer's cabinet
2   Mesh frame around tubes
3   Door to layer's cabinet

G11   PARAVANE

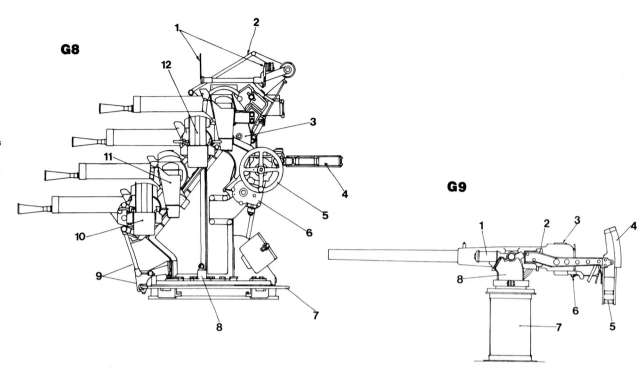

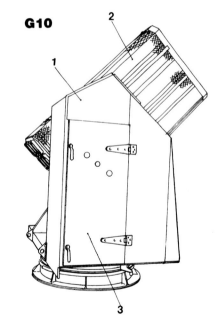

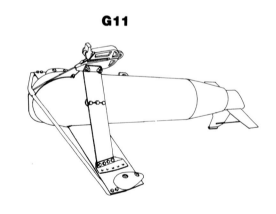

H Fire-control

H1/1 ARMOURED DIRECTOR ON CONNING TOWER (1/150 scale)

1. Training drive shaft
2. Training motor
3. Range taker's seat
4. 30ft rangefinder
5. Ladders
6. Persicopes
7. Manhole cover
8. Telescopic sights
9. Setting dials
10. Tripod type director
11. Roller path

H1/2 ALOFT DIRECTOR TOWER AND 15in CONTROL TOP (1/150 scale)

1. Range clock
2. Dreyer calculator
3. Arched opening to 5.5in control top
4. Pillars
5. Ladders
6. 15in control top
7. Torpedo lookout (1920-29), forward concentrating position (1931)
8. 9ft rangefinder (replaced by 12ft rangefinder during 1929-31 refit)
9. Roller path for director tower
10. 15ft rangefinder
11. Tripod type director
12. Anemometer (1931 – orignally fitted slightly further aft)
13. Wind vane (1931 – originally fitted slightly further aft)
14. Spotting instrument
15. Wood gratings
16. Dumaresq
17. Evershed transmitter
18. Torpedo spotting instrument (replaced by bearing transmitter for rangefinders during 1929-31 refit)
19. Range dial (removed during 1925-26 refit)
20. Manhole
21. Mainmast

H1/3 TRIPOD TYPE DIRECTOR

1. Trainer's seat
2. Training handwheel
3. Slow training handwheel
4. Elevating handwheel
5. Elevation repeater
6. Layer's telescope
7. Trainer's telescope
8. Tilt corrector
9. Range setting handwheel
10. Gun ready board
11. Phone man's seat
12. Layer's seat
13. Firing grips
14. Sight setter's seat

H2/1 AFT TORPEDO CONTROL TOWER (1/150 scale)

1. Ladder
2. Hatch
3. Periscope
4. Torpedo deflection sight
5. 15ft rangefinder
6. Communication tube
7. Seat

H2/2 MIDSHIPS TORPEDO CONTROL TOWER (1/150 scale)

1. Periscope
2. Revolving hood
3. 15ft rangefinder
4. Seats
5. Door
6. Ladder

H3 HACS Mk III DIRECTOR

1. Trainer's sighting port (closed)
2. Glass windscreen
3. Layer's sighting port (closed)
4. Layer's telescopic sight
5. Canvas cover, folded back
6. 15ft HA rangefinder
7. Leg space for range taker

H1/1

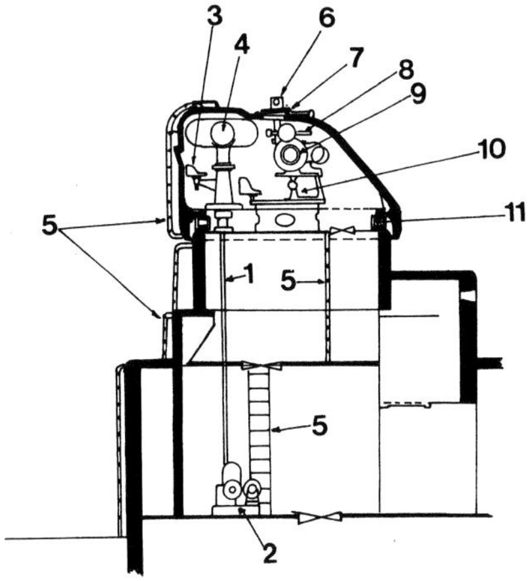

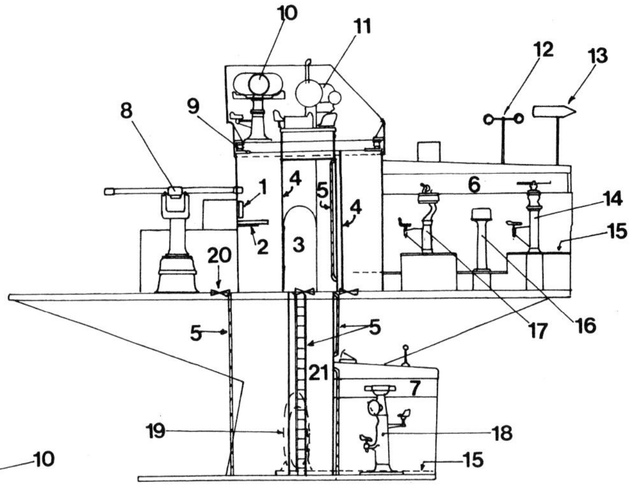

H1/2

H2/1

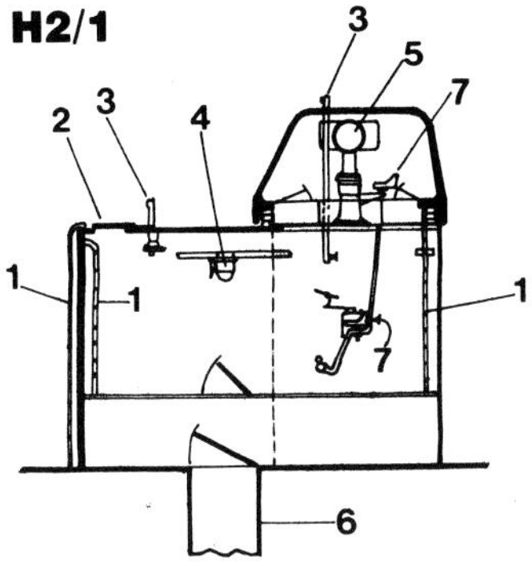

H2/2

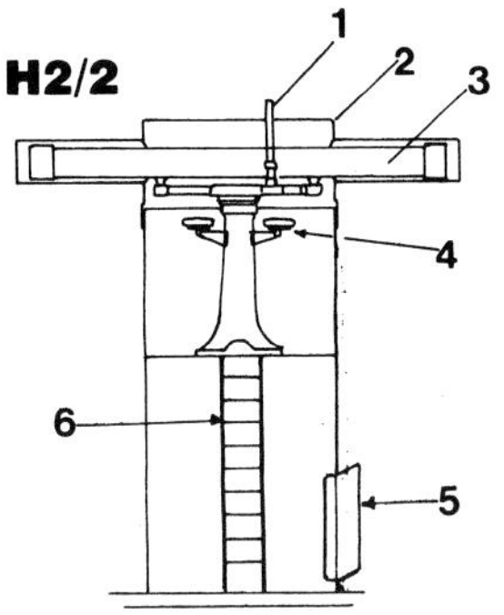

H1/3

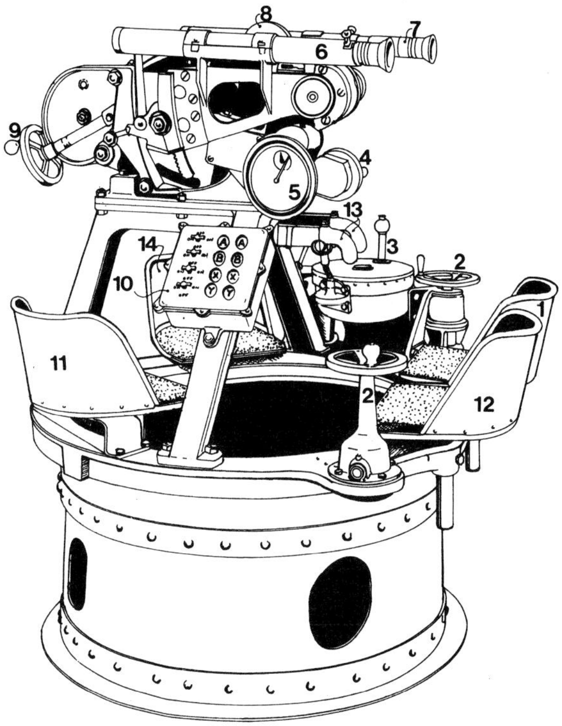

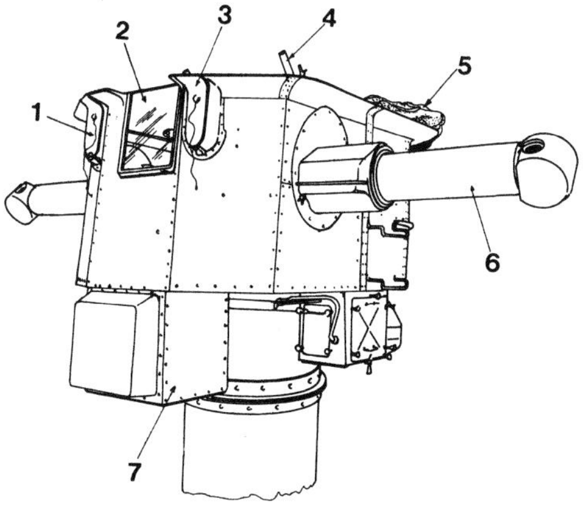

Fittings

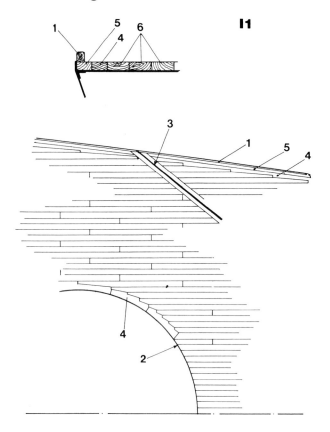

I1

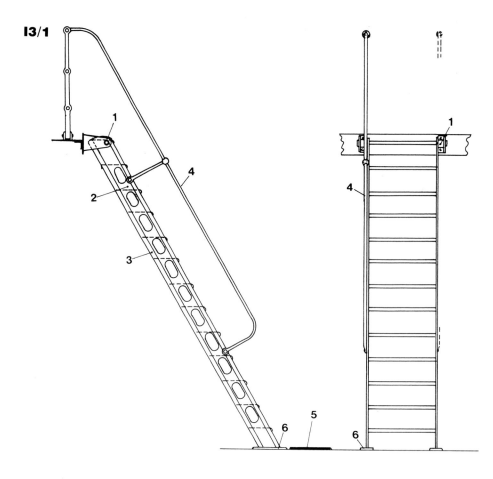

I3/1

I2

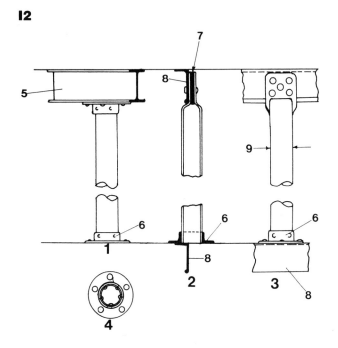

I3/3

I3/4

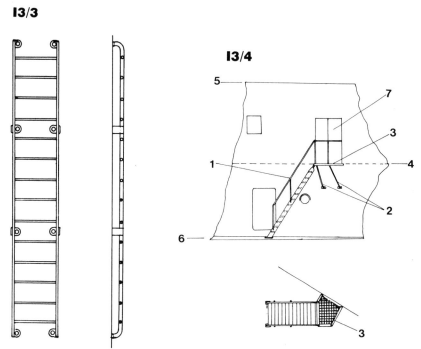

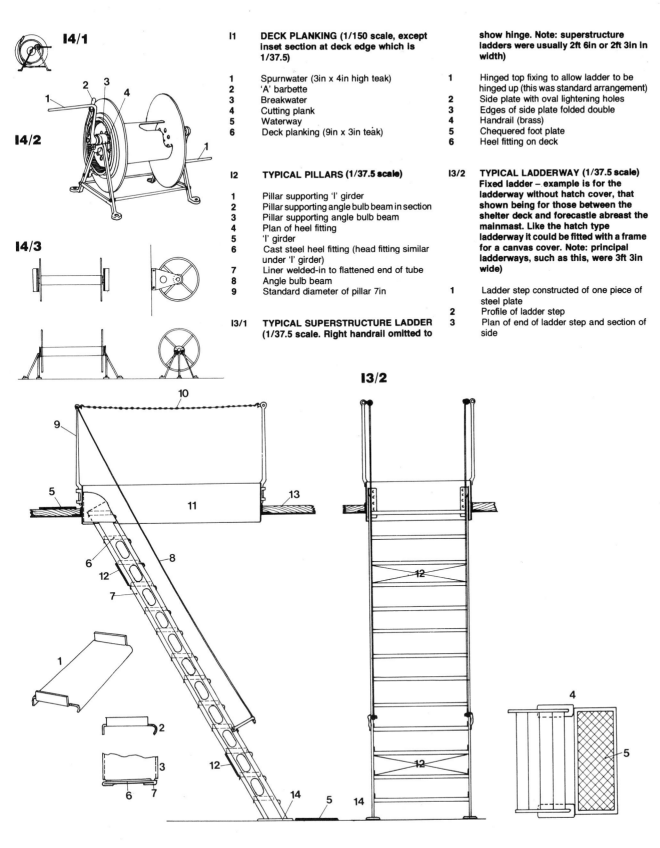

I4/1

I4/2

I4/3

I1 DECK PLANKING (1/150 scale, except inset section at deck edge which is 1/37.5)

1 Spurnwater (3in x 4in high teak)
2 'A' barbette
3 Breakwater
4 Cutting plank
5 Waterway
6 Deck planking (9in x 3in teak)

I2 TYPICAL PILLARS (1/37.5 scale)

1 Pillar supporting 'I' girder
2 Pillar supporting angle bulb beam in section
3 Pillar supporting angle bulb beam
4 Plan of heel fitting
5 'I' girder
6 Cast steel heel fitting (head fitting similar under 'I' girder)
7 Liner welded-in to flattened end of tube
8 Angle bulb beam
9 Standard diameter of pillar 7in

I3/1 TYPICAL SUPERSTRUCTURE LADDER (1/37.5 scale. Right handrail omitted to show hinge. Note: superstructure ladders were usually 2ft 6in or 2ft 3in in width)

1 Hinged top fixing to allow ladder to be hinged up (this was standard arrangement)
2 Side plate with oval lightening holes
3 Edges of side plate folded double
4 Handrail (brass)
5 Chequered foot plate
6 Heel fitting on deck

I3/2 TYPICAL LADDERWAY (1/37.5 scale)
Fixed ladder – example is for the ladderway without hatch cover, that shown being for those between the shelter deck and forecastle abreast the mainmast. Like the hatch type ladderway it could be fitted with a frame for a canvas cover. Note: principal ladderways, such as this, were 3ft 3in wide)

1 Ladder step constructed of one piece of steel plate
2 Profile of ladder step
3 Plan of end of ladder step and section of side

I3/2

4 Plan of foot of ladder and chequered foot plate (5)
5 Chequered foot plate
6 Side plate with oval lightening holes
7 Edges of side plate folded double
8 Rope hand hold
9 Stanchion
10 Chain guardrail
11 Coaming
12 Strengthening strip across back of ladder
13 Wood deck planking
14 Heel fitting on deck

I3/3 TYPICAL VERTICAL LADDER (1/37.5 scale. Constructed from vertical flat bars with round bar rungs)

I3/4 ADMIRAL'S LADDER (1/150 scale. One of four ladders connecting the after end of the forecastle deck with the quarterdeck. Principally used by officers, they were of wood construction. As first completed she carried only two such ladders, the Admiral's ladder to starboard and that for lesser officers to port, but second ladders forward of the originals on each side, were also added after the ship's trials)

1 Teak handrail supported on metal stanchions (Admiral's ladder only)
2 Stays supporting grating
3 Wood grating platform
4 Forecastle deck
5 Shelter deck
6 Quarterdeck
7 Double door

I4/1 HAWSER REEL (1/150 scale. Profile of reel on centre-line of forecastle abaft breakwater – the largest such reel fitted)

I4/2 HAWSER REEL (Hood had only cordage reels as completed but a number of hawser reels had been added on the forecastle by 1931 and others were added on the shelter deck later)

1 Portable hand crank (note: on the smaller hawser reels the hand crank was attached directly to the drum spindle)
2 Brake (one side only)
3 Internal gear wheel attached to drum
4 Pinion

I4/3 CORDAGE REELS (top: bulkhead mounted; bottom: deck mounted)

The reels were supplied in a considerable number of sizes varying in both length and diameter. They varied in detail design; the drum flanges were sometimes of solid construction with circular or elongated lightening holes and the support brackets for the bulkhead mounting could be of similar design to that of the deck mounting shown but without the side strut.

▌Fittings

I5   **FORWARD BREAKWATER (second breakwater of same construction. 1/150 scale, except inset detail of support bracket which is 1/75)**

1   Paravane house
2   Support brackets inside paravane house
3   Roof of lapped plates
4   Portable plate
5   Rollers for ropes passing through opening
6   Mushroom top vents
7   Washdeck lockers
8   Angle bar
9   Cordage reels (removed during 1929-31 refit)
10   Hawser reels (added during 1929-31 refit)
11   Heel fitting for paravane derrick
12   Deck plates for paravane derrick stays (added during 1929-31 refit when design of derrick was modified)

I6   **TYPICAL SMALL EYE PLATE**

I7/1   **DETAIL OF ARMOURED GRATINGS IN FUNNEL HATCH (1/37.5 scale. Armoured gratings in ventilation trunks etc, of same design but coamings not arranged for expansion)**

1   'U' plate connection to allow for expansion
2   Grating retaining clips
3   Hinged grating giving access to ladder
4   2½in space between armour bars
5   Tie bolt with gas pipe spacers
6   Angle bar shelf for grating (3in x 1½in)
7   Funnel casing
8   Funnel hatch coaming
9   Connections made with bolts through elongated holes to allow for expansion
10   Division plate
11   Armoured deck

I7/2   **ARMOURED GRATING IN VENTILATION/ESCAPE TRUNK**

1   Armoured deck
2   Water-tight shutter
3   Pulley
4   Chain for operating shutter
5   Threaded shaft
6   Threaded bars attached to shutter
7   Bevel gears
8   Control shaft
9   Handwheel for closing shutter from above
10   Counter balance weight
11   Ladder
12   Retaining catch for grating
13   Hinged armour grating

I7/3   **WATER-TIGHT MANHOLES (left section typical of manholes in double bottom etc, section on right is typical manhole in vertical bulkhead or in flat if insufficient headroom for coaming. Manholes were 23in by 15in inside coaming)**

1   Nut and bolt fixing
2   Air escape plug (fitted to water-tight compartments only, oil fuel compartments having separate escape vents)
3   Cover retaining chain

4   Deck
5   Stiffening strip
6   Bulkhead
7   Red lead in joint
8   Coaming either 9in or 6in high, with 3½in flange at top and bottom

I7/4   **ARMOURED HATCH WITH DETAIL OF CLIPS (upper clip is standard type which did not involve piercing the deck or hatch cover with its bearing. However, in positions where it was necessary to open the hatch from below (ie for escape from compartment) the clip shown in the lower view was fitted to the cover, or alternatively, the hatch had an escape manhole fitted which also employed clips of this type. Non-armoured hatches, fitted flush with the deck, were of the same design but employed a spring loaded hinge, in place of a counter balance weight)**

1   Hatch cover (of similar thickness to deck)
2   Cover retaining catch (fitted on the bar stanchion if no bulkhead adjacent to hatch)
3   Wire rope to counter balance weight
4   Wedges welded to cover
5   Clips
6   Hinge
7   Foot rungs on under side of cover
8   Coaming 6in high except for flush hatches on forecastle deck amidships where coaming was 12in (not fitted in escape and access trunks)
9   Deck plating
10   Carling
11   Ladder
12   Rubber seal attached to cover by two metal strips held in position by screws

I7/5   **ARMOURED HATCH WITH COUNTER BALANCE GEAR**

1   Hatch cover
2   Clips
3   Coaming
4   Cover retaining clip
5   Top weight
6   Bottom weight
7   Stop for top weight
8   Guide rod
9   Support strap for guide rods
10   Sheave for wire rope
11   Wire rope
12   Wedges for clips
13   Position of top weight with hatch open
14   Position of bottom weight with hatch open

I7/6   **QUARTERDECK HATCH (open, showing frame for canvas cover. 1/37.5 scale)**

1   Stiffening angle bar on underside of hatch cover
2   Hatch cover stay
3   Beam
4   Handrail
5   Ladder

I5

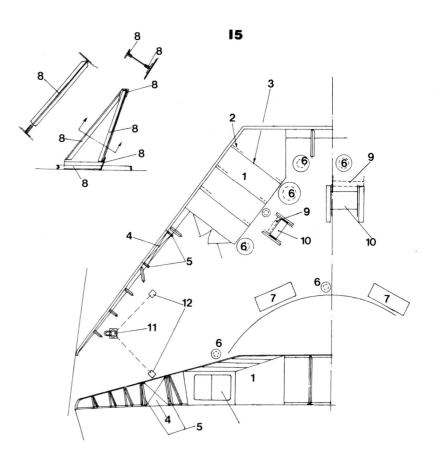

I6

I7/3

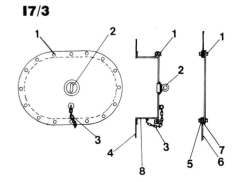

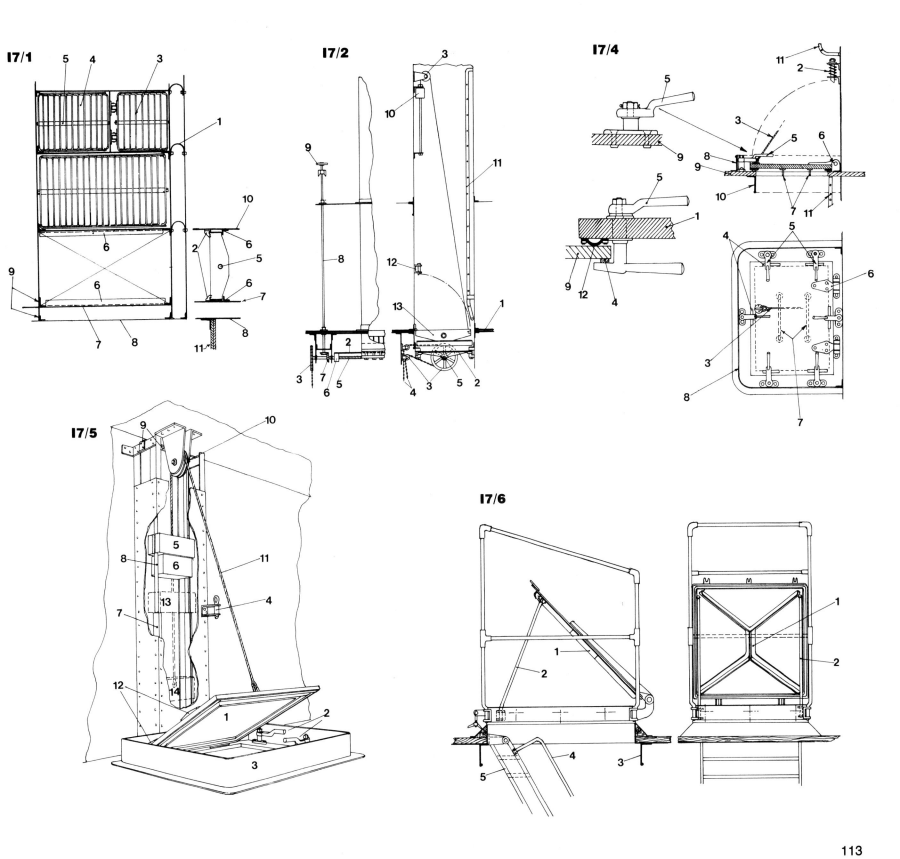

17/1

17/2

17/4

17/5

17/6

▌ Fittings

I7/7

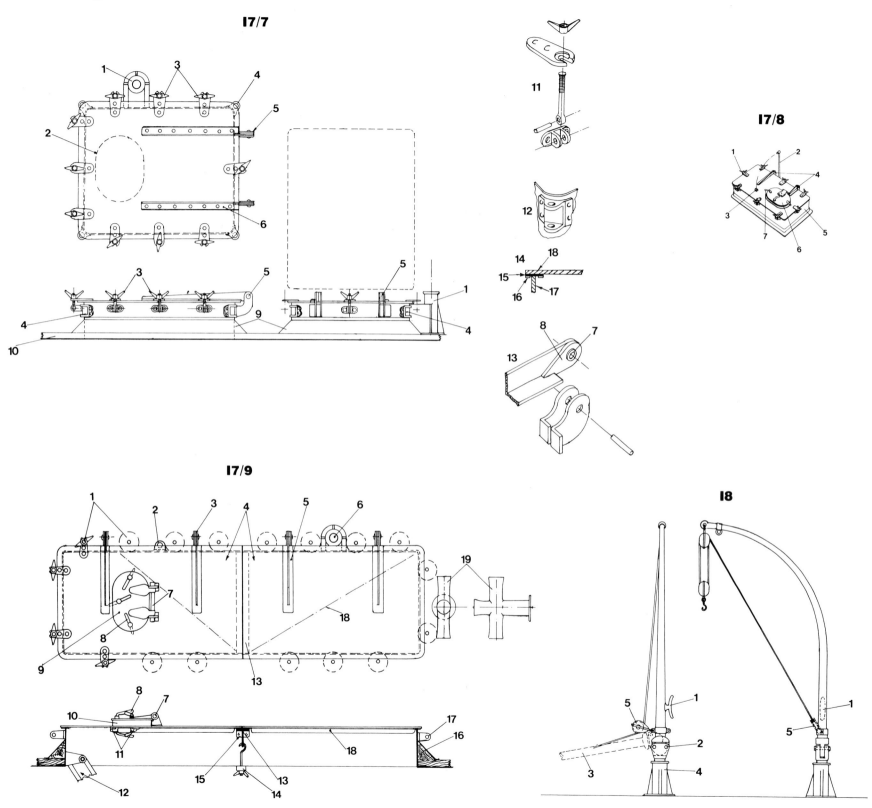

I7/8

I7/9

I8

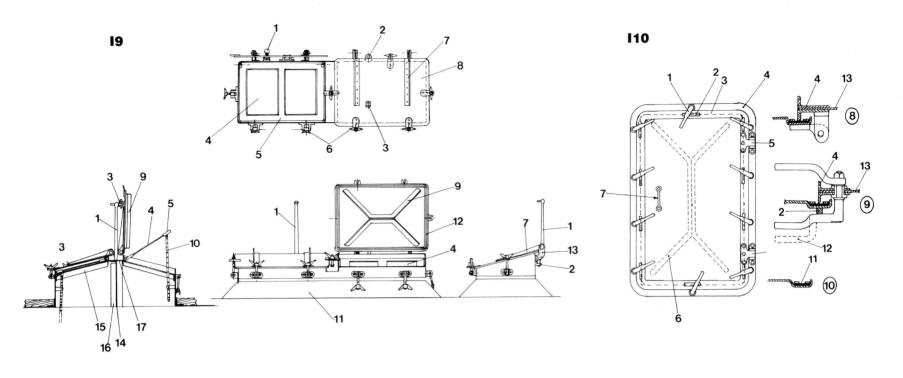

I9   **I10**

I7/7 QUARTERDECK HATCH (1/37.5 scale. Provided access to quarterdeck from officers' accommodation on main deck. Of comparatively large dimensions (5ft x 4ft) for a weather deck hatch but otherwise typical of hatch construction except for being hinged on its narrow side. The hatch on the forecastle, forward of the capstan, was also hinged in this manner and was of similar design except for being only 3ft 6in wide)

1 Davit socket
2 Outline of escape manhole fitted *c*1940
3 Clips
4 Sockets for handrail/cover frame stanchions
5 Hinge
6 Angle bar
7 Bush
8 Strengthening piece
9 Blast plates (fitted to hatches and skylights within blast area of main armament)
10 Wood deck
11 Detail of clips
12 Detail of handrail stanchion socket
13 Detail of hinge
14 Detail of cover seal
15 rubber strip
16 Retaining strips
17 Coaming
18 Hatch cover

I7/8 HATCH WITH ESCAPE MANHOLE

1 Clips
2 Stanchion for holding cover open (replaced

by spring loaded clips when adjacent to bulkhead)
3 Stanchion lug
4 Hinge
5 Coaming 12in deep (exclusive of deck planking) on weather decks 6in deep elsewhere
6 Escape manhole cover (closed)
7 Manhole clips, operable from both sides

I7/9 TORPEDO LOADING HATCH (1/37.5 scale. On forecastle forward of breakwater. Note: The torpedo hatch on the upper deck was fitted flush with deck, details being as in 17/4, but the size and arrangement of split cover shown here was the same)

1 Clips
2 Socket for hatch cover retaining clip stanchion (clip latches over edge of hatch)
3 Hinge on forward facing side of hatch
4 Hatch cover in two sections
5 Tee bar with top web tapered (as with angle bar in I7/7)
6 Davit socket
7 Hinge of escape manhole
8 Clips on escape manhole
9 Escape manhole cover
10 Escape manhole coaming
11 Clip wedges on underside of hatch cover
12 Ladder (port side of hatch used as ladderway – ladder removed when loading torpedoes)
13 Portable Tee bar to provide sealing face and support to joint between hatch covers
14 Strongback across bottom of hatch holding 13 in place

15 Tee bar support brackets
16 Blast plate
17 Clip hinge
18 Stiffening angle in underside of hatch cover
19 Staghorn bollard

I8 TYPICAL DAVIT (1/37.5 scale. As employed for embarking ammunition and stores and for operating accommodation ladder etc. The torpedo davit – fitted adjacent to torpedo hatch – was of the same design but slightly larger being 11ft high, from deck, rather than 9ft)

1 Cleat
2 Bolts
3 Davit stowed by removing one of bolts and hinging down
4 Davit socket
5 Sheave

I9 TYPICAL SKYLIGHT (1/37.5 scale. Skylight to sickbay operating room on forecastle and section of ward room skylight)

1 Stanchion for holding water-tight cover open (when fitted against bulkhead spring clips substituted)
2 Stanchion socket
3 Lug for stanchion
4 Frosted glass windows
5 Window frame (hinged)
6 Clips (sometimes reversed)
7 Angle bar

8 Water-tight cover
9 Angle bar stiffeners on underside of cover
10 Window lifting bar
11 Blast plate
12 Rubber seal
13 Hinge
14 Dividing plate
15 Angle bar for window frame to rest on
16 Angle bar corners
17 Channel bar

I10 TYPICAL WATER-TIGHT DOOR (1/37.5. Example shown is of 5ft 6in x 3ft 6in – size of opening – but sizes varied, the alternative height being 4ft 6in and widths 3ft, 2ft 6in, 2ft 3in and 2ft)

1 Clip
2 Wedge on face of door
3 Edge of door dished
4 Angle bar door frame (both sides of bulkhead)
5 Hinge
6 Angle bar stiffeners on back of door
7 Door handle (both sides)
8 Detail of hinge
9 Detail of clips
10 Detail of dished edge to door
11 Rubber seal
12 Alternative clip to clear hinges
13 Bulkhead

▌ Fittings

I11/1 SIDE SCUTTLE (all these were of the same design the usual diameter being 15in but 9in scuttles were fitted to heads, WCs etc)

1   Scuttle or port
2   Scuttle frame
3   Butterfly clips
4   Deadlight
5   Rubber sealing ring
6   Clip lug
7   Saveall
8   Sidelight frame
9   Sidelight glass
10   Back of deadlight
11   Web
12   Ship's side plating
13   Stay for holding deadlight open (hooks under clip lug)
14   Hinge
15   Rigol

I11/2 SQUARE SIDE PORTS (1/37.5 scale. Fitted to Admiral's apartments and, without the inner window, to some compartments on forecastle deck amidships. Note: square ports with double deadlights were also fitted)

1   Rigol
2   Inside of deadlight
3   Angle bar stiffeners
4   Clips
5   Hinge
6   Window (wood frame)
7   Window frame mounted on ceiling
8   Doubling plate around inside edge of port

I12 STOVE FUNNEL (1/37.5 scale. This entire structure could be dismantled, a cover plate being provided for the deck opening. Note: during, or possibly before her 1940 refit most of Hood's stove funnels were removed so her stoves must have been replaced by electric or steam heaters)

1   Joint (top removable)
2   Stay band
3   Three stays, equally spaced unless other fittings required an unequal spacing
4   Funnel casing to provide air space between funnel and deck and reduce transmission of heat to latter

I13 GUARDRAILS (1/37.5 scale)

1   Guardrails of wire rope (note: some of superstructure and shelter deck guardrails were constructed of metal tube, such fixtures being permanent)
2   Shoe
3   Chain links
4   Bottle screw for adjusting length of guardrail
5   Slip (for dismantling guardrails)
6   Eye fixed to stanchion
7   Stay (normally only one fitted in line with rails and joggled to clear same but corner stanchions on superstructures occasionally had two stays spaced at 90°)

8   Guardrail stanchion of type fitted at ends of guardrail runs and in places where sections of guardrail were frequently taken down (ie in way of bollards, accommodation ladders, fairleads, leadman's platform, etc)
9   Standard guardrail stanchion – heel of stanchions was of square section rest of circular section
10   Removable pin secured to heel fitting by chain
11   Bolt
12   Heel of stay secured by removable pin on chain
13   Heel of stanchion shown in stowed position laid fore and aft on deck
14   Plan of heel fitting

I14 WASH DECK LOCKER (provided stowage for the gear employed in cleaning the decks – mops, brushes, etc)

1   Hinges
2   Padlock

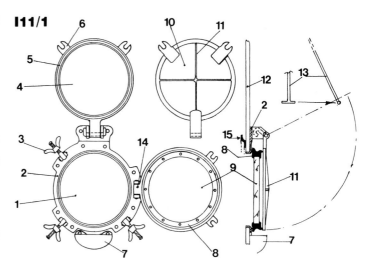

I11/1

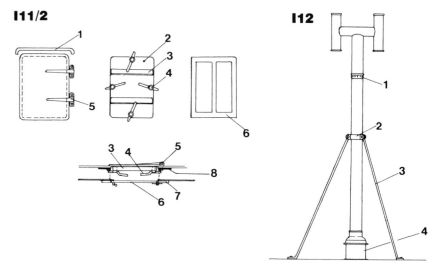

I11/2

I12

I13

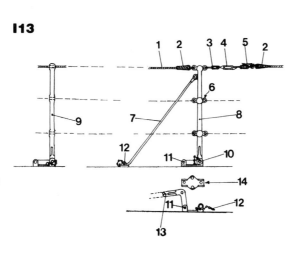

I14

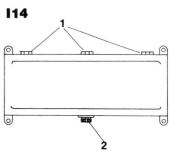

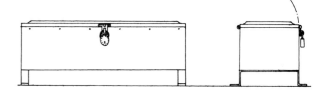

J Ground tackle

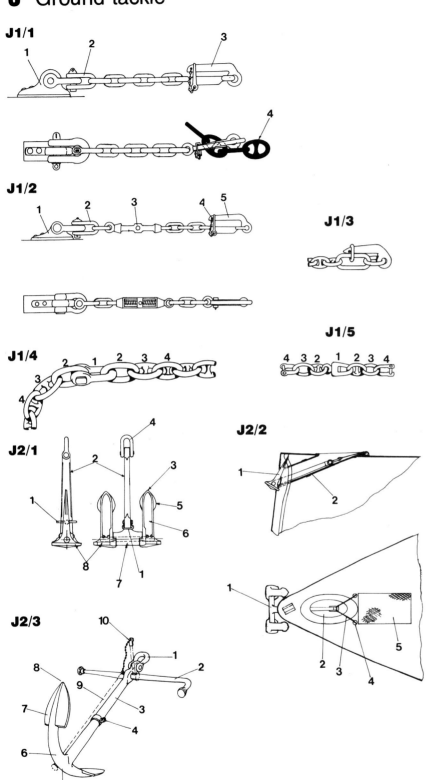

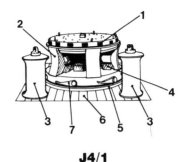

J1/1

J1/2

J1/3

J1/4

J1/5

J2/1

J2/2

J2/3

J3

J4/1

J1/1 BLAKE'S STOPPER (two per anchor cable, one on forecastle and one on upper deck below navel pipes)

1 Stopper lug or eye plate
2 Joining shackle
3 Blake's slip
4 Anchor cable

J1/2 BLAKE'S SCREW STOPPER (one per anchor cable on forecastle deck)

1 Stopper lug or eye plate
2 Joining shackle
3 Bottle screw
4 Retaining pin on chain
5 Blake's slip

J1/3 SENHOUSE SLIP (one per anchor cable attached to base of cable locker)

J1/4 ANCHOR CABLE (showing how each length is joined)

1 Joining shackle
2 Studless long link
3 Enlarged stud link
4 Common stud links (from which rest of 12½ fathom length of cable is made)

J1/5 SWIVEL PIECE

1 Swivel
2 Stud link
3 Studless link
4 Joining shackle

J2/1 WASTENEY-SMITH STOCKLESS BOWER ANCHOR (1/150 scale. Bowers weighed 192cwt 2qtr and the sheet anchor 191cwt 2qtrs but two types were otherwise identical, the difference in weight having only a minor effect in dimensions)

1 Gravity band
2 Shank
3 Bill
4 Anchor ring
5 Fluke
6 Arm
7 Crown
8 Tripping palm

J2/2 STREAM ANCHOR (1/150 scale. Stowed position. Note: The stream anchor was originally stowed in its hawsepipe at the stern as shown but by 1927 stowage was provided on the port side of the shelter deck abreast the mainmast)

1 61cwt Wasteney-Smith stream anchor
2 Stern pipe (a portable covering plate was provided over the deck opening for this during the 1929-31 refit)
3 Anchor strops (these were also provided for the bower and sheet anchors)
4 Eye plate
5 Chequered plate

J2/3 ADMIRALTY PATTERN ANCHOR (Hood carried two kedge anchors of Admiralty pattern, one of 16cwt and one of 12cwt–these were stowed on the forecastle deck amidships just inboard of the chutes to port and starboard. The anchors for the ship's boats were of the same type)

1 Anchor ring
2 Stock
3 Shank
4 Gravity band
5 Crown
6 Arms
7 Flukes
8 Bill
9 Stowed position of stock
10 Wedge for retaining stock in position

J3 NAVEL PIPE WITH WATER-TIGHT BONNET (open)

J4/1 FORECASTLE CAPSTAN

1 Sockets for capstan bars
2 Portable whelp
3 Roller
4 Snug
5 Pawl plate
6 Deck planking under capstan wider than standard planking
7 Pawl

J Ground tackle

J4/2

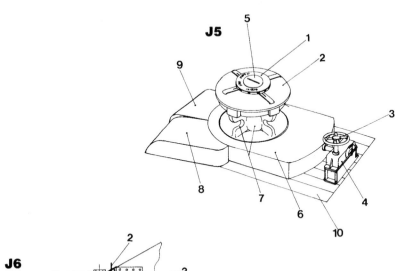

J5

J6

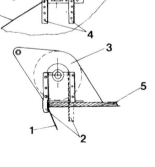

J7

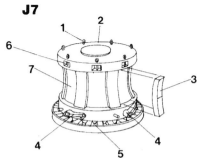

J4/2	CAPSTAN BAR
1	Metal shoe
2	Locating pin hole
3	Wood bar

J5	CABLE HOLDER (port bower)
1	Scroll plate (for engaging and disengaging from drive spindle)
2	Hood plate
3	Brake handwheel
4	Brake operating gear box
5	Centre plate
6	Cover over brake
7	Sprocket and snugs
8	Ramp to navel pipe
9	Ramp to chaffing plate
10	Deck planking under cable holder wider than standard planking

J6	CLUMP CATHEAD (1/37.5 scale)
1	Ship's side
2	Angle bar connection to ship's side
3	Pulley
4	Flange connections to deck
5	Deck planking

J7	AFTER CAPSTAN
1	Locating pin for capstan bars and portable whelp
2	Crown plate
3	Portable whelp
4	Pawl
5	Pawl plate
6	Capstan bar socket
7	Barrel

J8/1	MAIN ANCHOR GEAR, PROFILE (1/200 scale. Note: sheet cable holder not shown for clarity)

J8/2	MAIN ANCHOR GEAR, PLAN (1/200 scale)
1	Bower anchor, port and starboard
2	Sheet anchor
3	Paravane fairlead
4	Bollard (added by 1927)
5	Clump cathead, port and starboard
6	Fairlead
7	Pillars
8	Chequered chaffing plates (*added by 1927)
9	Eye plates (*added by 1927)
10	Awning stanchion
11	Towing fairlead
12	Mooring bollard
13	Hatch and ladderway to heads
14	Portable roller
15	Capstan
16	Rollers (two only but four positions)
17	Cable holder
18	Skylights
19	Scupper
20	9in mushroom top vent
21	Navel pipes with water-tight bonnet

22	Bollard
23	Chequered plate
24	Paravane eye plate
25	Swivel piece
26	Senhouse slip
27	Stopper slip
28	Stopper lug
29	Joining shackle
30	Portable wood cover
31	Cable locker
32	Eye plates for tricing up senhouse slip
33	Cable clench
34	Shackle
35	Exhaust vent from capstan engine room
36	Exhaust vent fan
37	Escape and access trunk
38	Lamp room
39	Capstan spindle
40	Cable holder spindle
41	Hinged hawse pipe cover (on all)
42	Shipwrights' working space
43	Bench against port side
44	Guardrail around cable locker
45	Lobby surrounded by wire bulkhead
46	Stores
47	Lobby
48	Hatches with escape manholes
49	Fresh water compartment
50	Fresh water pump room
51	Flour store
52	Capstan engine room
53	Capstan steam engine
54	Wormwheel drive to spindles
55	Worm drive to cable holder
56	Water-tight compartment
57	Water-tight manhole
58	Anchor cable
59	Screw stopper
60	Blake stopper
61	Davit
62	Cable holder brake handle

J8/1

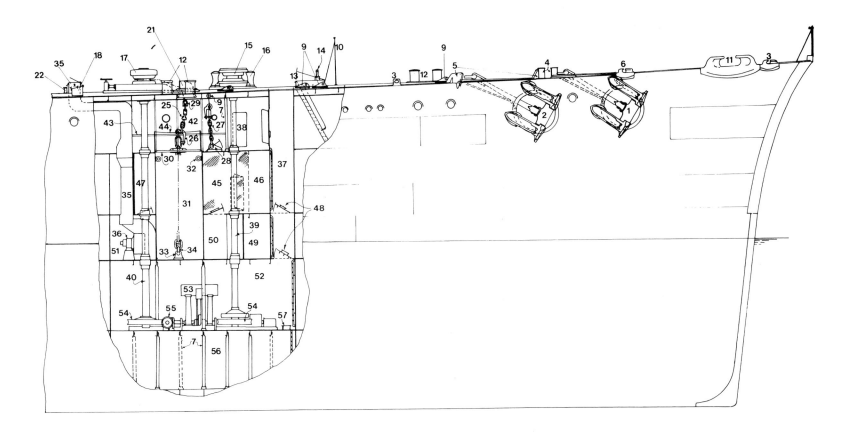

J8/2

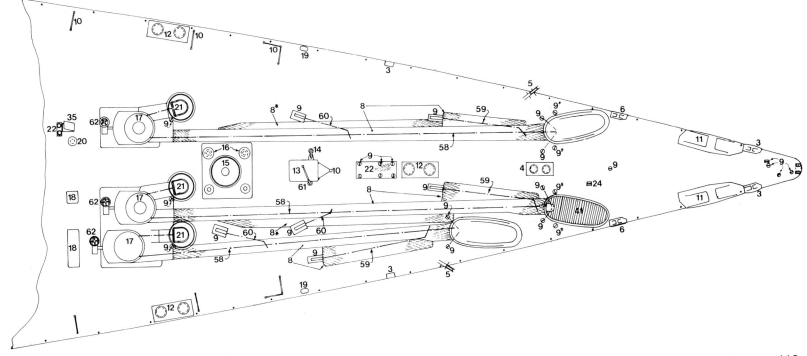

K Ship's Boats

K1

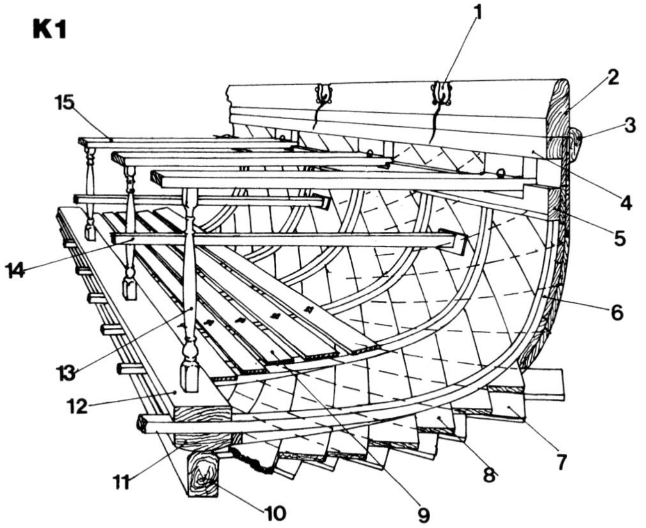

K2

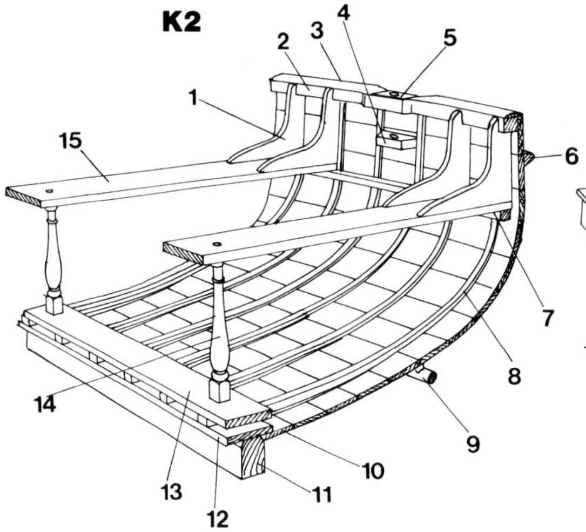

K3

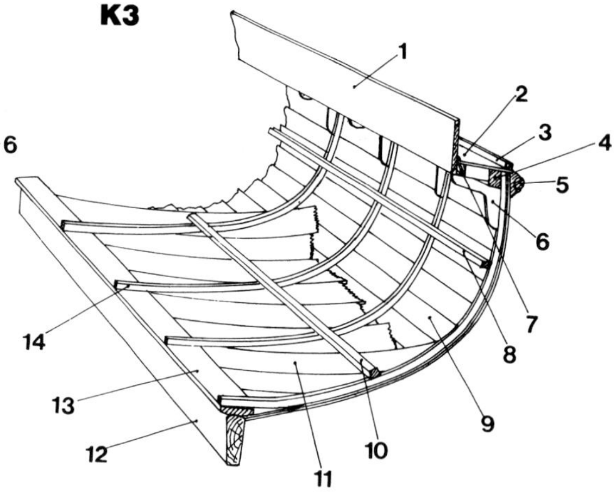

K5

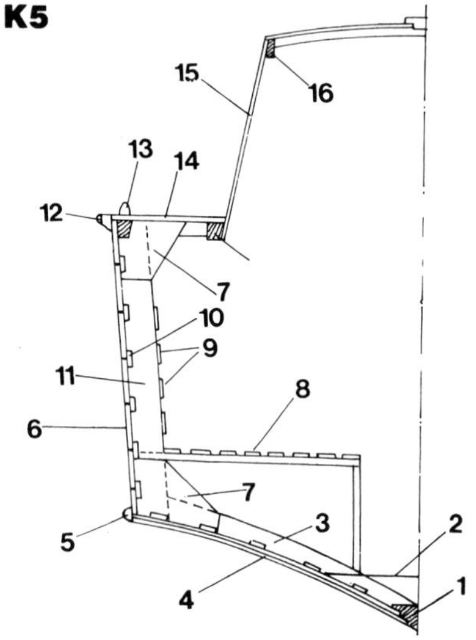

K6

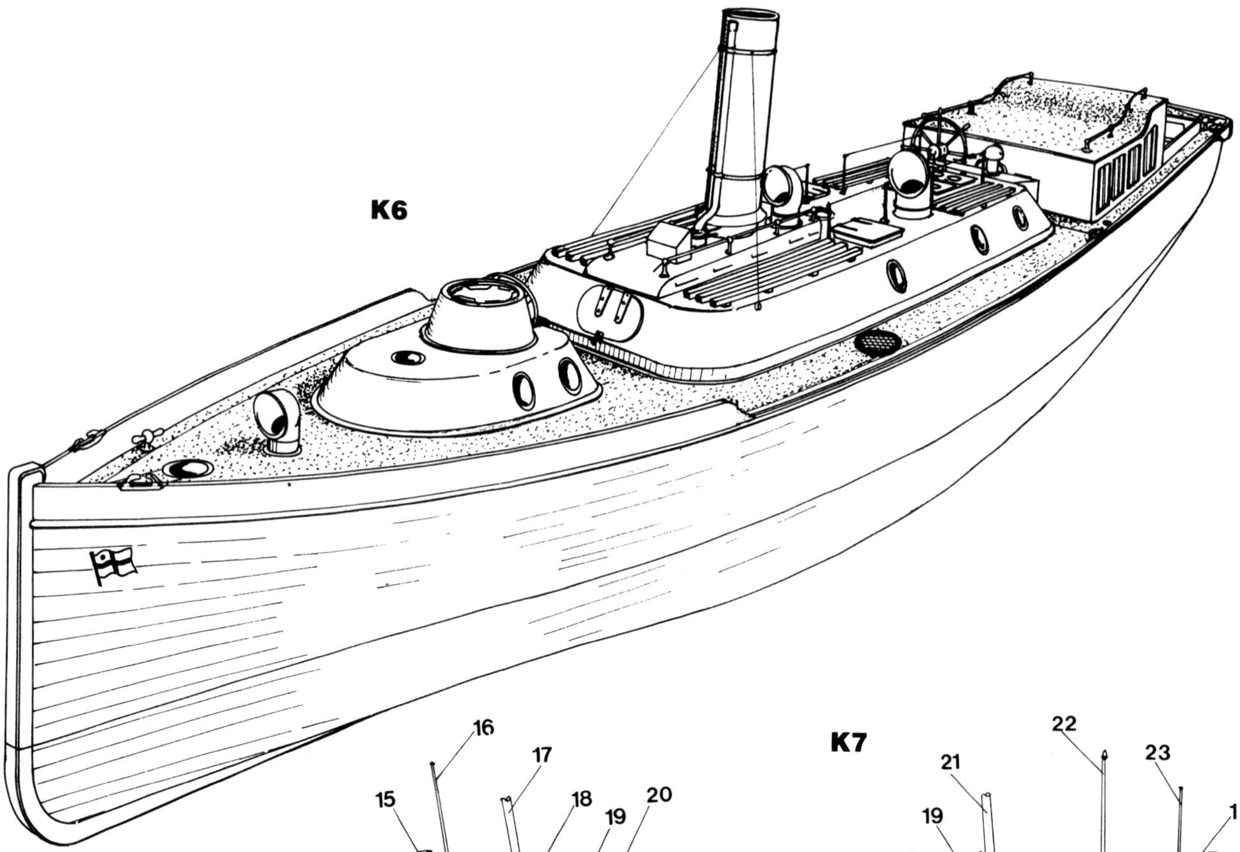

K7

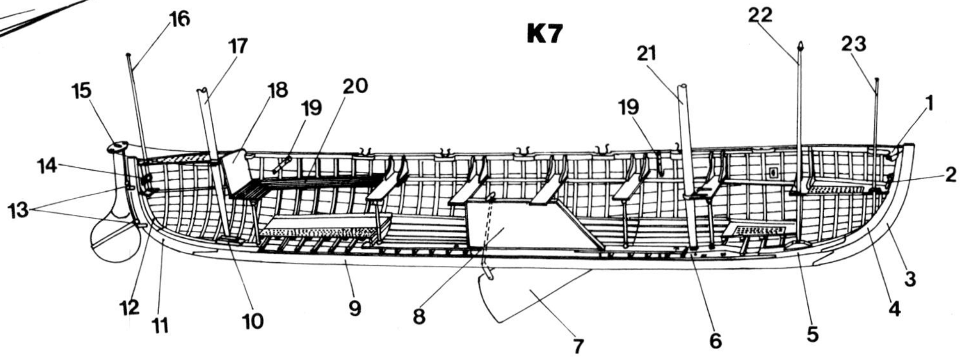

120

K4

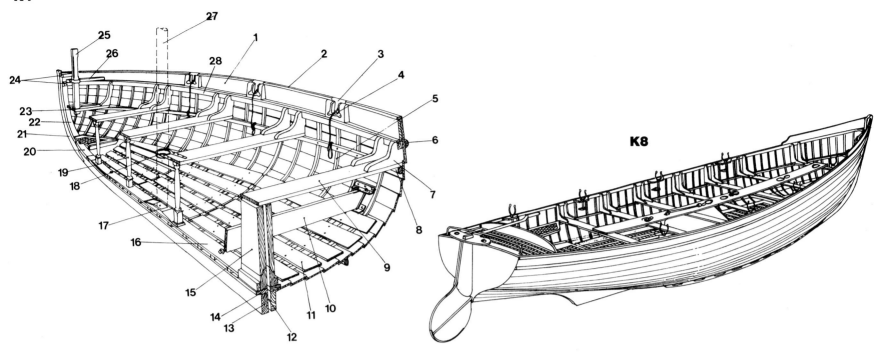

K8

K1	**DOUBLE DIAGONAL CONSTRUCTION (42ft sailing launch)**	K3	**DOUBLE SKIN CARVEL CONSTRUCTION (motor boat)**	15	Box for drop keel	K7	**LONGITUDINAL SECTION OF 27ft WHALER**
				16	Keelson		
1	Wooden shutter in rowlock	1	Coaming	17	Mast heel step	1	Breasthook
2	Washstrake	2	Covering board	18	Mast clamp	2	Stem ring bolt
3	Rubber	3	Footrail	19	Pillar	3	Stem
4	Gunwale	4	Gunwale	20	Deadwood	4	Apron
5	Shelf	5	Rubber	21	Stem	5	Fore deadwood
6	Floor	6	Hanging knee	22	Apron	6	Mainmast step
7	Outer skin planking	7	Carling	23	Towing thwart	7	Centre board or drop keel
8	Inner skin planking	8	Rising	24	Breasthooks	8	Keel box
9	Bottom boards	9	Outer skin, longitudinally planked	25	Towing bollard	9	Keel
10	Keel	10	Bilge stringer	26	Towing strongback	10	Mizzen mast step
11	Hog	11	Inner skin, diagonally planked	27	Mast	11	Stern post
12	Keelson	12	Keel	28	Gunwale	12	After apron
13	Pillar	13	Hog			13	Gudgeons (hinge on stern post) and pintles (pins on rudder)
14	Stretcher	14	Floor			14	Stern ring bolt
15	Thwarts			K5	**HARD CHINE CONSTRUCTION (fast motor boat)**	15	Rudder yoke
						16	Ensign staff
K2	**CARVEL CONSTRUCTION**	K4	**CLINKER CONSTRUCTION (fore end, 32ft cutter)**	1	Keel	17	Mizzenmast
				2	Flat frame	18	Backboard
1	Knee	1	Washstrake (two planks, inner elm, outer teak)	3	Floor	19	Shroud plate
2	Gunwale	2	Capping (Canadian elm)	4	Double diagonal planked bottom	20	Stern benches
3	Capping	3	Poppet	5	Chine	21	Mainmast
4	Rowlock toe piece	4	Rowlock	6	Single planked side	22	Awning stanchion
5	Rowlock socket	5	Floor timbers	7	Floor brackets	23	Pendant staff
6	Rubber	6	Rubber	8	Seat		
7	Rising	7	Knee	9	Back boards	K8	**30ft GIG**
8	Floor timber	8	Rising	10	Plank edge strips		
9	Bilge rail	9	Thwart	11	Floor		
10	Garboard strake	10	Stretcher	12	Rubber		
11	Keel	11	Bottom boards	13	Spurnwater		
12	Hog	12	Drop keel channel	14	Deck		
13	Keelson	13	Keel	15	Wood canopy		
14	Pillar	14	Hog	16	Shelf		
15	Thwart						
				K6	**50ft STEAM PINNACE**		

121

K Ship's boats

K9 THE SEABOAT (a 32ft cutter on davits)

1 After guy
2 Jackstay
3 Davit sling
4 Robinson's disengaging (quick release) gear
5 Fore guy
6 Griping spar
7 Gripes
8 Griping spar bracket
9 Jumping net
10 Staghorn bollard
11 Pudding

K10 42ft SAILING LAUNCH

K11 50ft STEAM PINNACE (K11–K24 1/150 scale)

K12 45ft ADMIRAL'S BARGE

K13 42ft SAILING LAUNCH

1 Gratings
2 Mast
3 Stretcher
4 Mast carlings
5 Lumber rack
6 Thwart
7 Bottom boards
8 Tiller
9 Stern benches
10 Chain locker

K14 45ft MOTOR LAUNCH (note: 42ft motor launch was similar but had only a single rubber, like the 42ft sailing launch from which it was derived)

1 Portable wood and canvas covers, usually removed or partially removed to allow stowage of boats on top of launch
2 Petrol engine

K15 36ft SAILING PINNACE (of generally similar design and construction as 42ft launch)

1 Lumber rack
2 Mast
3 Chain locker
4 Vickers MG mounting
5 Thwart
6 Stretcher

K16 35ft MOTOR BOAT

K17 35ft FAST MOTOR BOAT

K18 35ft MOTOR PINNACE

K19 32ft CUTTER

1 Hawser reel
2 Stretcher
3 Mast
4 Keel box
5 Awning stanchion
6 Pendant staff
7 Centre board, on drop keel
8 Handrail

K20 30ft FAST MOTOR BOAT

K9

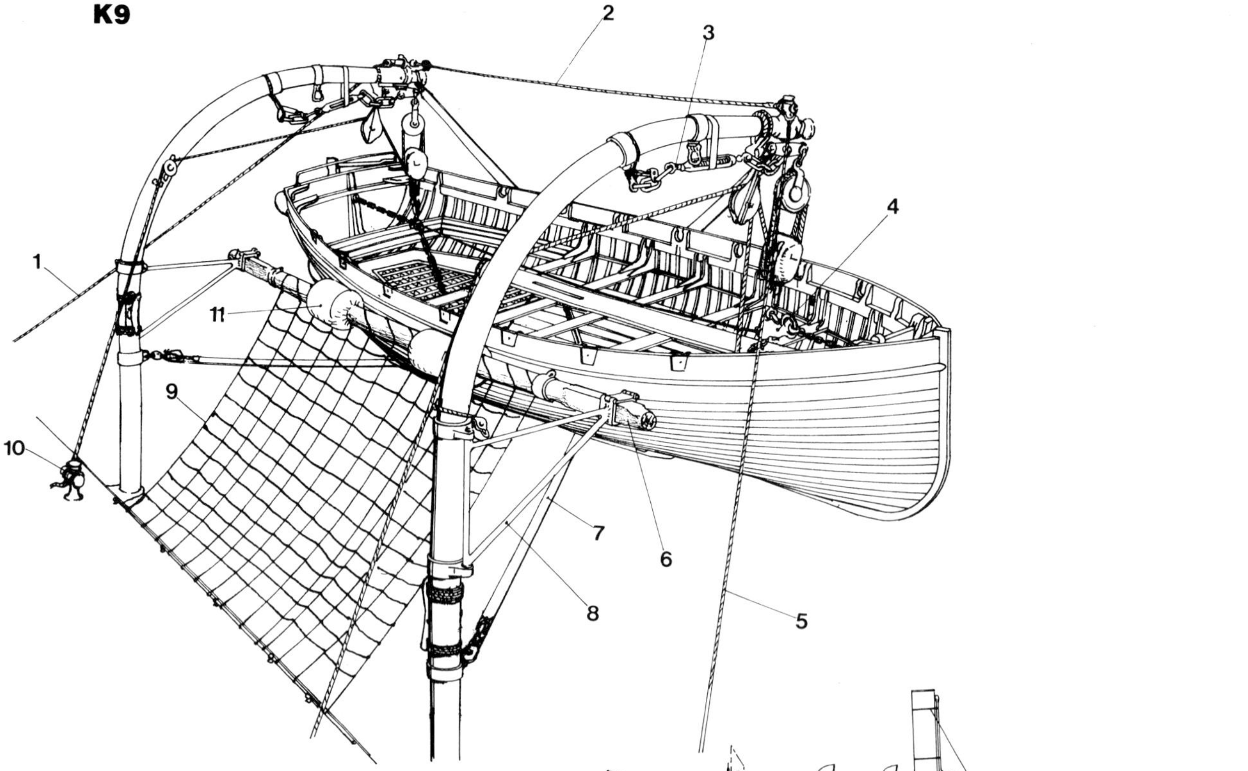

K11

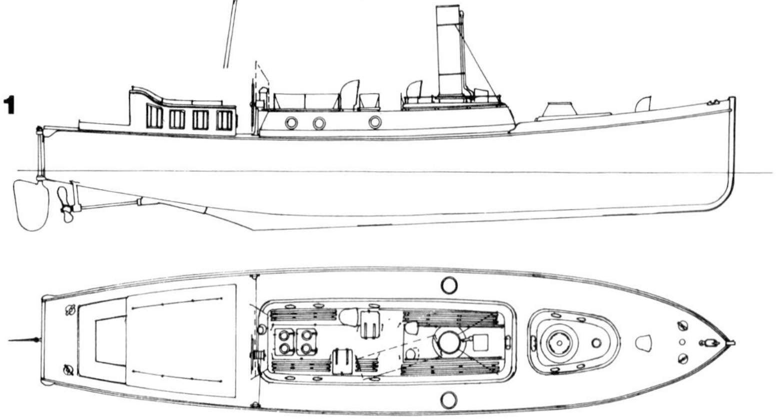

K12

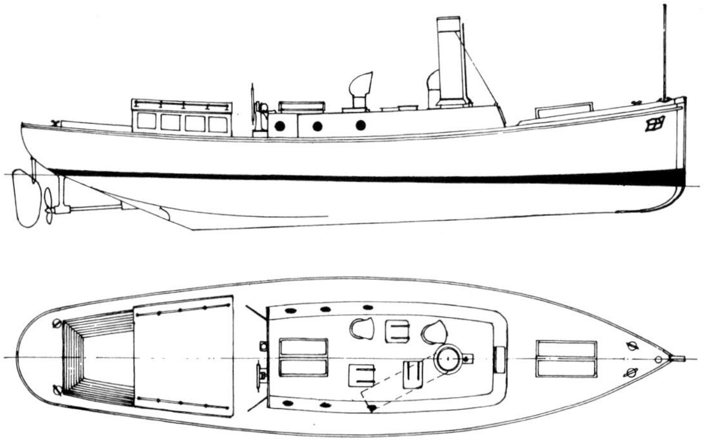

K10

K13

K14

K15

K16

K17

K18

K19

K20

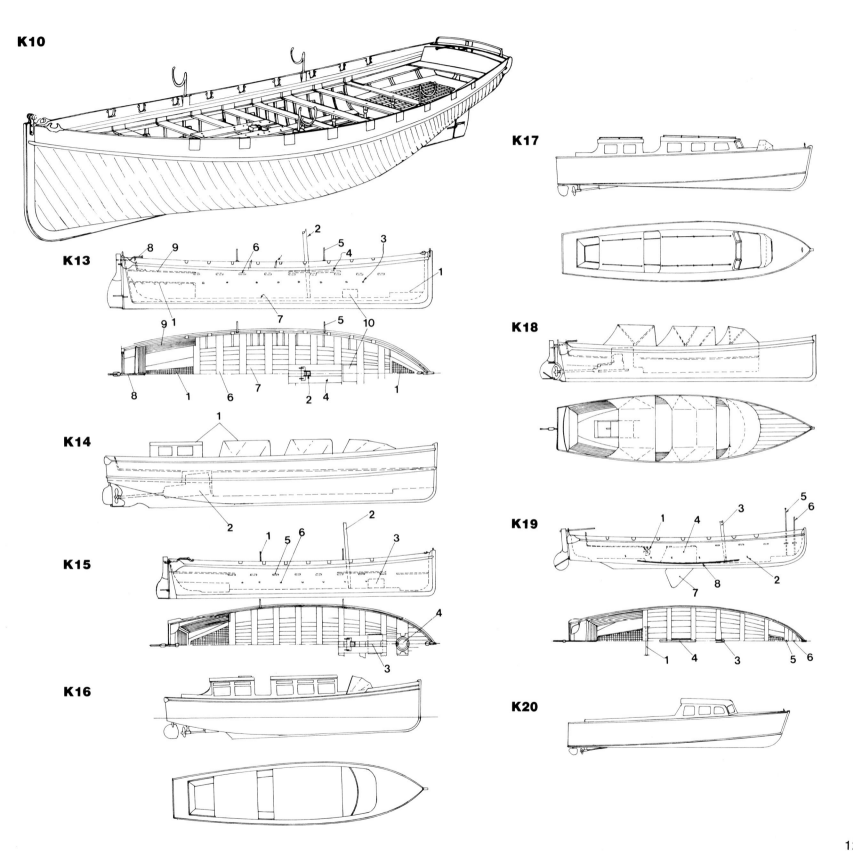

K Ship's boats

K21

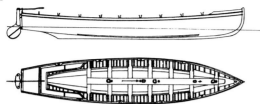

K25

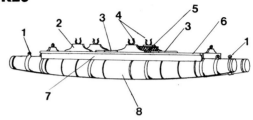

K22

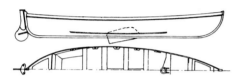

K23

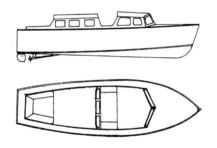

K26

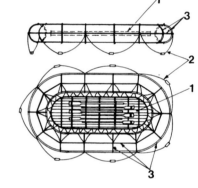

K27/1

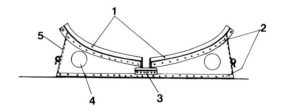

K24

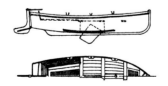

K27/2

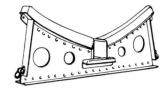

K27/3

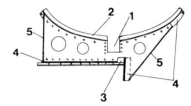

K27/4

K28

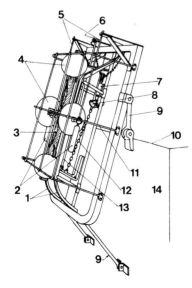

K21	**30ft GIG**	
K22	**27ft WHALER**	
K23	**25ft FAST MOTOR BOAT**	
K24	**16ft SAILING DINGHY (Hood's 16ft motor dinghy was of similar design but with an auxiliary petrol engine)**	

K25   BALSA RAFT

1   Lifting eyes
2   Elm chocks
3   Elm thwarts
4   Rowlocks
5   Paint locker
6   Elm rubber
7   Frame of pine and elm
8   Casks constructed of Canadian yellow pine strakes with solid elm ends and steel bands

K26   CARLEY FLOAT (small type, but larger type of similar design)

1   Floor (wood grating) with six paddles lashed to it
2   Man ropes
3   Rope lashings to which 1 and 2 are secured

K27/1   TYPICAL BOAT CRUTCH (midships of 42ft launch)

1   Teak lining
2   Tee bar
3   Angle bar supporting teak liner
4   Lightening hole
5   Edge of plate flanged

K27/2   TYPICAL BOAT CRUTCH (after end of 42ft launch)

K27/3   BOAT CRUTCH AT EDGE OF SHELTER DECK (35ft motor boat)

1   Clearance for keel
2   Teak lining
3   Cut out to allow drainage along deck edge
4   Tee bar
5   Edge of plate flanged

K27/4   NESTED BOAT STOWAGE (note: arrangement of griping band is similar for single and triple boat stowage)

1   Griping band
2   Portable crutch mounted on thwart
3   Shackle on crutch for attachment of griping band

K28   NIGHT LIFEBUOY

1   Runners
2   Calcium light tubes
3   Wood cross
4   Copper floats
5   Extractor rods
6   Buoy release knob
7   Catch spring box
8   Buoy release latch
9   Stays
10   Edge of shelter deck
11   Guard frame
12   Holding chain
13   Guide rod
14   Ship's side

L Aircraft arrangements

L1 and L4

AIRCRAFT CRANE (fitted on quarterdeck 1931 to 1932. Note: the hatched area shown on the profile was plated on both sides L4 1/150 scale)

1. Luff control
2. Training control
3. Hoist barrel
4. Hoist rope guide rollers
5. Training motor
6. Training gearbox (worm drive from motor)
7. Luff motor
8. Luff barrel
9. Hoist motor
10. Gear drive to hoist barrel
11. Gear drive to luff barrel
12. Control platform
13. Training pinion
14. Curb wheel (bolted to deck)
15. Luff ropes
16. Hoist rope
17. Working position
18. Maximum elevation
19. Hoist control

L2 PLAN OF AIRCRAFT ARRANGEMENTS ON QUARTERDECK (1931 to 1932. 1/150 scale)

1. Guest warp boom
2. Cross stern boom
3. Mushroom top vent added
4. Mushroom top vents removed
5. Mushroom top vent fitted with portable top (flanged and bolted base)

6. Mushroom top vent with portable top added
7. Spurnwater (removed 1932)
8. FIVH catapult, folded
9. Hatches with flush covers
10. Platform on catapult structure
11. Catapult operating platform
12. Deckplate to take fairlead for lifting rudder (broken line as built; solid line as modified during 1929-31 refit)
13. Eye plate removed
14. Jettisonable aviation fuel tank (removed 1932)
15. Awning stanchions
16. Aircraft crane
17. Stern hawsepipe for stream anchor, fitted with portable cover
18. Eye plates for anchor strops
19. Chequered plate removed during 1929-31 refit
20. Eye plate, port and starboard
21. Scuppers, port and starbord
22. Hinge
23. Centre bearing

L3 PROFILE OF FIVH CATAPULT (fitted during 1929-31 refit. 1/150 scale)

1. Launching cradle
2. Hinge
3. Ram position for launching aircraft
4. Ram and launching gear
5. Centre bearing
6. Roller path ring
7. Rollers
8. Operating platform

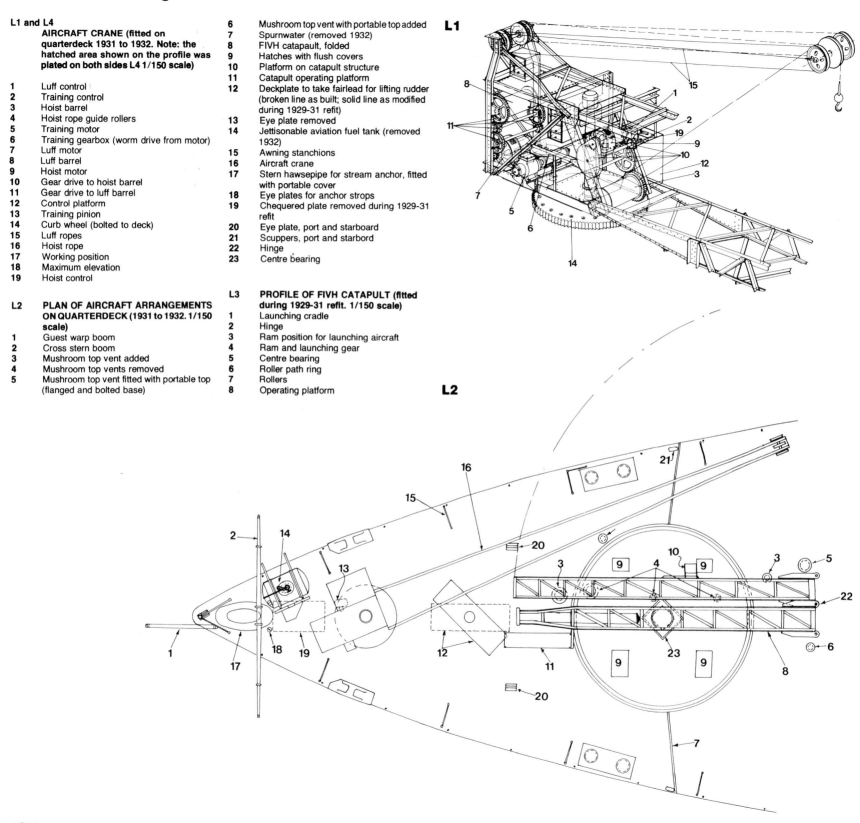

L3

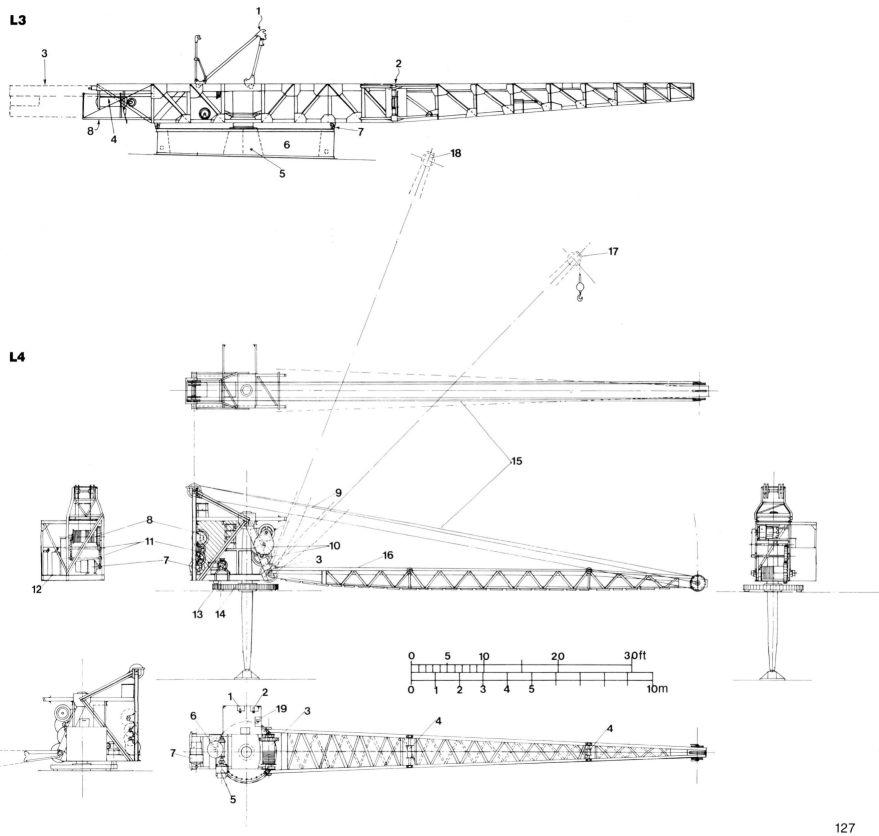

L4